THE MAKING OF
CLASSICAL EDINBURGH

'The city is both natural object and a thing to be cultivated;
individual and group; something lived and something dreamed;
it is the human invention *par excellence.*'

C. LEVI-STRAUSS

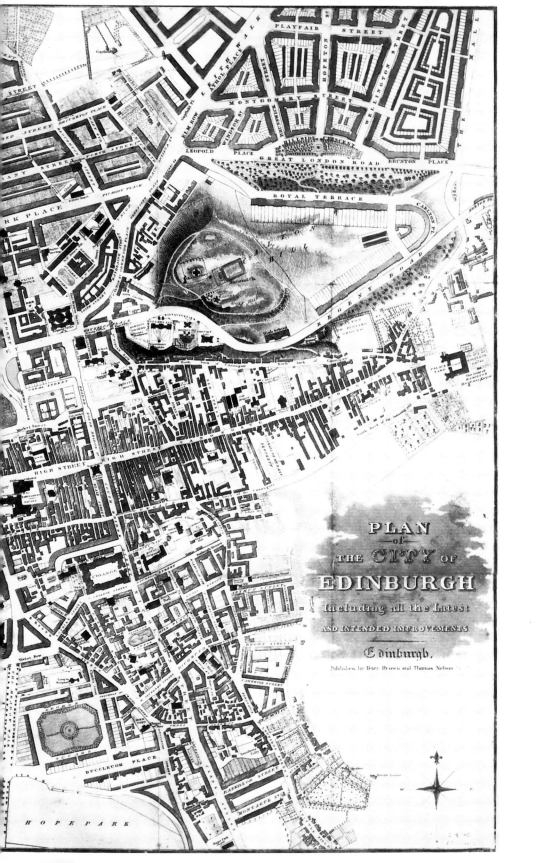

PLAN
—of—
THE CITY of
EDINBURGH
Including all the Latest
AND INTENDED IMPROVEMENTS
Edinburgh.
Published by Peter Brown and Thomas Nelson

© A.J.Youngson 1966
EDINBURGH UNIVERSITY PRESS
22 George Square, Edinburgh

First published 1966
Reprinted 1967, 1968, 1970, 1975
ISBN 0 85224 007 4

First paperback edition 1988

Printed in Great Britain by
Butler and Tanner Ltd, Frome
Somerset

British Library Cataloguing
in Publication Data
Youngson, A.J.
The making of classical Edinburgh.
1. Edinburgh. Architecture, 1750-1840
I. Title
720'.9413'4

ISBN 0 85224 576 9

Frontispiece, overleaf. *James Craig, a portrait by David Allan in the National Portrait Gallery, Scotland. Craig is seen with a variant of his plan for the New Town. His* Physicians' Hall *is shown in the other drawing.*

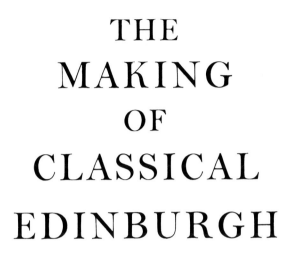

THE
MAKING
OF
CLASSICAL
EDINBURGH

1750–1840

A. J. YOUNGSON

EDINBURGH *at the University Press*

TO ELSPETH
WHO KNOWS EDINBURGH
BETTER THAN I DO

Preface

Europe is full of beautiful cities. Edinburgh is one of the most beautiful of all. It owes its singular character to the late and sudden flowering of Scottish culture, when, as Balfour put it, a country 'which had done nothing up to the eighteenth century, after the eighteenth century began seemed almost to do everything'. Edinburgh is the visible expression of this history. With the Enlightenment a new town arose, suitable to the enlarged ideas of the age, separated from the old town of Mary Queen of Scots, Mary of Guise, John Knox and the Covenanters only by a little valley. New Town and old town lie side by side, and the life of the city is the life of both.

This book is no more than an attempt to explain how a small, crowded, almost mediaeval town, the capital of a comparatively poor country, expanded in a short space of time, without foreign advice or foreign assistance, so as to become one of the enduringly beautiful cities of western Europe. It makes no pretence of being a guide to Edinburgh, nor of recalling the characters – and they were many – who made its streets a curious and often a distinguished scene, nor of assessing the work of the several eminent architects who contributed to the making of classical Edinburgh.

The book could never have been written without the help which I have received from several institutions and many persons. First and foremost, the Edinburgh Town Council made its archives freely available, and on them I have principally depended. The Heriot Trust likewise gave me access to its large collection of records, and the Royal College of Physicians, the Moray Trust and the Walker Trust were similarly helpful. To the Earl of Moray I am indebted for permission to see the muniments at Darnaway Castle, and to the Uni-

ix

versity of Edinburgh for a research grant which enabled me to visit the towns of Nancy and Richelieu.

In the matter of Scots legal terminology I received valuable help from my friend Mr Peter Millar, and Mr Eric Stevenson very kindly tempered some of my rasher architectural judgments. The typescript was read either in whole or in part by Professor S. E. Rasmussen, Professor D. B. Horn, Professor Denys Hay, Professor Asa Briggs and Dr Christopher Smout, and to each of them I am greatly obliged for valuable criticisms and suggestions. Sir John Summerson helped me to locate drawings in the Soane Museum, and his comments on the work of Adam and Craig were of much value. Dr J. C. Corson corrected some of my mistakes about the University buildings and guided me to the Playfair drawings. Dr D. C. Simpson very kindly allowed me to see and to quote from letters in his possession. Finally, Miss Armet, City Archivist in the Town Clerk's Department, Town Council of Edinburgh, constantly kept me on the right lines as regards sources, read the whole typescript, and throughout my work supplemented in innumerable ways my very imperfect knowledge of Edinburgh past and present. To all these persons, and to others who helped me with advice and encouragement, I wish to record my thanks.

A. J. Youngson Edinburgh 1966

The University Press is most grateful to Dr D. C. Simpson for permission to reproduce some of his collection of maps of Edinburgh, both from originals and from his published collection; *Edinburgh Displayed* (Lammerburn Press Ltd., 1962). The figures concerned are 14, 15, 23, 26, 28, 40, 64 and the map facing p 1.
A. J. Y.

Preface to the 1988 Reprinted Edition

Over twenty years have been added to the history of Edinburgh since this book was first published. Why continue to dwell upon the ever-receding past of this ancient city? Edinburgh is not as famous in the history of architecture and town-planning as Venice, Florence, Rome, Paris or London – possibly not as famous as several other European cities, although perhaps it ought to be. It possesses some very fine public buildings, but in this respect it is not unique. The general standard of the domestic architecture in the New Town is high, but it is not incomparable. What, then, makes Edinburgh so singular among cities? The answer is twofold. First, in the visual conjunction of Old Town and New Town anyone walking along Princes Street today is presented with one of the most eye-catching views in Europe, and must experience at the same time a wonderful sense of space and, if he or she has any imagination at all, of the passage of time. Secondly, the New Town even now retains its late eighteenth and early nineteenth century public buildings, terraces, crescents, squares, palace-fronts, churches and gardens almost as they were planned. They were all designed over one hundred and fifty years ago, and the *tout ensemble* is without parallel in scale, uniformity of general style, and state of preservation. Even during the last twenty years the march of progress has been resisted fairly successfully, due in no small part to the fore-sight and energy of Sir Robert Matthew and to the work of the Edinburgh New Town Conservation Committee which, with Government support, he helped to set up late in 1970. There are 12,000 separate properties in the New Town, most of them residences, mostly owner-occupied and almost all listed. Thus the New Town continues to be lived in, as was intended. It has not been commercialised or allowed to crumble away. But, with the rest of Edinburgh, it changes nevertheless. The stream of vehicles has become a torrent; the skyline is not what it was; and two or three of the photographs in this book are already mere remembrances of things demolished.

One of the reviewers of the first edition commented that I seemed to be surprised that in so poor a country so large a project as the New Town had ever been undertaken, let alone completed. I was surprised. But what surprises me most, more now than twenty-five years ago, is that those who worked to build the New Town and to make it as modern as the most modern, as comfortable and elegant as the most comfortable and elegant of all the cities of Europe, understood so well what they were about. They aimed for the top; and they knew how to get there. In two respects circumstances favoured them. The Scots system of feuing land, explained on p.xiv but its importance understated in the text, meant that the landowner could 'sell' land for development and yet retain full control, *sine die*, over what was to be built there. Thus Scots landowners could plan large areas in a unified way without having to pay for the development themselves; and this made coherent planning easier. Secondly, in both architecture and town-planning there were excellent and generally accepted ways to design in the later eighteenth century. As regards town-planning, there was newly-found agreement, on both sides of the Channel, that a properly planned city should have straight streets, wide avenues and well-proportioned squares set, ideally, in a park-like landscape. The idea of a whole street as a single composition was likewise novel, but acceptable, and it suited well with Palladian ideas of harmony, symmetry and proportion, which dominated British architecture. Almost every architect used and adapted to a domestic scale the forms of Greece and Rome; almost everyone wanted columns, balustrades, and careful detailing. Thus for several reasons the prospects for building a new town in Scotland and doing it well were good in the decades after 1760.

What ensured success, however, was the active support, and where necessary the intervention, by those Scotsmen who were men of means and who, having familiarised themselves with what was best in contemporary planning and architecture, were also men whose 'delicacy of taste' commanded respect. Their role is not given the importance it deserves in the following chapters. Yet it was crucial. Craig's plan, for example, as first submitted, was almost certainly modified after consultations which took place with, among others, Lord Kames (who wrote a book on aesthetics), and Sir James Clerk (the principal if not the sole designer of Penicuik House, of which the 'chaste splendours' were almost purely Palladian). Help with the proposed 'New Town between Edinburgh and Leith' was sought from James Clerk of Craighall, a lawyer, and Gilbert Innes of Stow, a banker, and it was they who had the vision and good sense to recommend that close attention be paid to the views of William Stark. When the proposal was put forward to build south of Princes Street, at the east end, and thus destroy 'the beauty and elegance of the general design' of the New Town, the opposition was led by Lord Cockburn and Sir William Forbes – once again, a lawyer and a banker.[1] Not much is known about the activities of these and other 'men of taste' but their influence was certainly very great. To name a few of them is in a way misleading, for the ideas of what constituted good architecture and good planning were at that time reasonably well understood and endorsed by all educated sections of society. It was the general pressure of educated opinion that prevented many mistakes, and supported genuine improvement.

The New Town may thus be seen as a product, not of several separate minds, but of the times in which it was conceived, that is to say, of the Enlightenment. Those who planned it, like those for whom it was planned, were 'citizens of the world, looking out upon a universe seemingly brand new because so freshly flooded with light',[2] a universe in which everything seemed far more intelligible than before, and in which everything could be improved by reason. Moreover, many reasonable men had recently made or were making the Grand Tour and had discovered in Italy the truth as well as the beauty of the ideal landscapes of Poussin and Claude. It is therefore not surprising that William Stark's plea that town-planners should follow the example of these great masters and also combine architecture with trees and distant prospects in their compositions did not fall on deaf ears. In the

[1] Yet another attempt to obscure the view of the Old Town from Princes Street has had to be fought off since this book was written. Enterprise contrary to the public interest never ceases.

[2] Carl Becker, *The Heavenly City of the Eighteenth Century Philosophers*, (New Haven 1957), p.34.

paintings of Claude we see temples belonging to a Golden Age, 'grazing flocks, unruffled waters, and a calm, luminous sky, images of perfect harmony between man and nature';[1] and it seems not absurd to suggest that the New Town is, as it were, an ideal landscape of this kind made tangible and habitable, in which are combined the intellectual order of classical architecture and formal planning with romantic views of trees and green slopes and distant hills. As I have elsewhere suggested, images of a Golden Age may well have been in the minds of Craig and of those who worked with him when they kept open the views south of Princes Street and north of Queen Street. There is the same sort of vision where the Queen Street gardens have been retained, where the Calton Hill remains a lofty grassy open space, where Lord Moray's pleasure grounds still slope, steeply wooded, to the banks of the Water of Leith; the vision of an earthly paradise, of a city and a community 'animated to correspond with the general harmony of nature'.[2]

Some such explanation of the general form of the New Town seems not unlikely, for the ideal landscapes of the seventeenth-century Italian painters were well known, and the idea of integrating urban architecture with landscape had been put forward by several writers before 1760. But it would be a mistake to imagine, as this book may seem to suggest, that the squares and public gardens of the New Town were from the start furnished with well-tended lawns and handsome trees, so that in all respects the earthly paradise sprang straight from the drawing board to leafy reality. Such is far from being the case. The surrounding countryside may have looked well enough. But almost all eighteenth-century squares had the appearance, to begin with, of being waste land rather than small parks, and the squares of the New Town were no exception. They were neither properly paved nor properly planted. For many years they had more than their fair share of rubbish, washing hung out to dry, dogs, cats, cows, and occasionally pigs. The public gardens were the same. Beautification, like sanitation, came later. Only after 1800 – London had led the way several decades earlier – was the drive begun to clean up these open spaces, plant trees, and create the 'artful wildness' which would appropriately complement

[1] Kenneth Clark, *Landscape into Art* (London 1949), p.65.
[2] Colin Maclaurin, *Newton's Philosophical Discoveries* (Edinburgh 1755), p.95.

the columns, domes, and classical proportions of the rising city.

For technical reasons the text of the first edition cannot be altered, and it is therefore inconvenient to put forward a large number of additions and amendments. Besides relatively minor mistakes and a few misprints, noted at the foot of the page, I have to correct the date of Craig's birth. I originally found evidence to suggest that he was born in 1740, but also grounds to suppose that he might have been born in the 1730s. If born in 1740 he was only 26 when he submitted his plan, and this seemed rather young. The records contained no evidence of his birth in the 1730s, and I did not search for a later date, thinking it improbable. I should have remembered that Nelson became a Captain at 21, and William Pitt Prime Minister at 24. It is now estab-lished that Craig was born in 1744. As regards St Andrew's Church, the prize for a design was indeed awarded to 'Mr Kay, Architect', but I was probably wrong in suggesting that Kay had much to do with the design that was actually adopted. That design seems to have been largely or entirely the work of Captain Andrew Frazer, who was an engineer officer in the army.

A. J. Youngson, Edinburgh 1988

Errata

page 315, *between* ·lines 19 and 20 *add:*
 Walter Robert Ballantyne, Justice of the Peace.
page x, plate 77,
 for Greyfriar's *read* Greyfriars'.
page 59, last line,
 for unsavourary *read* unsavoury.
page 92, line 23,
 for Queensferry Road *read* Queensferry Street.
page 157, line 22,
 for 1717 *read* 1777.
page 187, line 1,
 for Castle Street *read* Castlehill.
page 256, caption,
 for Greyfriar's *read* Greyfriars'.
page 307, line 43,
 for Sir James Summerson *read* Sir John Summerson.
page 312, lines 29–30,
 for the Duke of Queensferry *read* the Duke of Queensberry.

Contents

I
The 'Proposals' of 1752 1

II
Economic Background and Local Government 20

III
Public Building before 1784 52

IV
The New Town: Craig's Plan 70

V
Extensions Southward 111

VI
Public Works, 1800-30 133

VII
Private Development after 1800 204

VIII
Social Life 235

IX
After 1830 257

Appendix 287

Notes 295

Index 315

List of Plates

These photographs were taken specially for this book by Mr Edwin Smith

1. 'A continued and very magnificent street' – the High Street, looking NW from the Tron Kirk. p 2.
2. A close in the Old Town. p 3.
3. Milne's Court, Lawnmarket. Its several floors provided accommodation for the gamut of Edinburgh society, and typified the social integration of the 18th c town. p 14.
4. Milne's Court from the back court. p 15.
5. Milne's Court, the main entrance. p 32.
6. A stone's throw from South Bridge and the Tron, the 'south back' of the High Street retains local scale and vernacular flavour. p 33.
7. Parliament Square. The coat of arms above the old Exchequer Court doorway. p 48.
8. Edinburgh, looking w from the Crags to the Castle. p 49.
9. Front of Royal Exchange, High Street. p 58.
10. The scale of the engineering problem which faced the 18th c planners, in linking the Old Town (L) to the site of the New Town, is seen in this picture of the North Bridge spanning the valley. p 59.
11. North Bridge, looking s from Wellington statue. p 64.
12. Register House. *between* pp 64/65.
13. Detail of the dome, Register House. p 65.
14. George Square. p 69.
15. Edinburgh in the 1820's. This relief map shows the Old Town running from the Castle to the Crags, with the New Town to the left. p 76.
16. 'The principal reason for Craig's success is the excellent use of the site.' The picture shows the Castle, the Gardens retained as open space, and Princes Street. p 76.
17. Thistle Court, reputedly the first house built in the New Town. p 80.
18. No. 26 St Andrew's Square, N side, attributed to Sir William Chambers. p 81.
19. Town house for Sir Laurence Dundas, now the Royal Bank of Scotland; architect, Sir William Chambers. p 84.
20. Interior of St Andrew's Church, George Street. p 85.
21. Houses in Castle Street built in the 1790's. Sir Walter Scott lived here from 1802-26. p 92.

List of Plates

22. Charlotte Square, N side. The raised pavement, with mounting blocks, permitted easy access to carriages. p 93.
23. Drawing-room, No. 6 Charlotte Square (Courtesy, Lord Bute). p 96.
24. No. 6 Charlotte Square. p 97.
25. St James' Square, central doorway E side. p 98.
26. Balconies, E Register Street. The textured stone gives life to the plain façades of such Edinburgh tenements. p 110.
27. Buccleuch Place. p 111.
28. One of the six columns of Craigleith stone that support the portico of the University. p 128.
29. The Quadrangle, the University. p 129.
30. Doorway in Elder Street. p 132.
31. Staircase and vestibule, the Signet Library. p 133.
32. Parliament Square. Reid's concept is a close copy of Adam's University. p 134.
33. The interior, the Signet Library. p 135.
34. The Governor's house, Calton Jail, with the romantic ironwork of Waverley Station. p 138.
35. Steps up Calton Hill, with Nelson Monument in background. p 139.
36. Waterloo Place, cutting through Calton burial-ground. p 144.
37. The Regent Arch, Waterloo Place. p 145.
38. Waterloo Place, from Register House. p 148.
39. Calton Hill, from Calton burial-ground. The mausoleum is in memory of Professor Dugald Stewart. Behind, to the left, is Craig's Old Observatory, with Playfair's City Observatory behind, again. p 149.
40. Regent Terrace on the slopes of Calton Hill. p 150.
41. Hillside Crescent. Note the Greek key decoration of the railings to tie in with the Doric columns. p 151.
42. The High School. p 156.
43. The hall, the High School. Note the verve of the early cast-iron capitals. p 157.
44. The gateway to High School. p 158.
45. Craig's Observatory, Calton Hill. p 159.
46. National Monument, Calton Hill. p 159.
47. Side elevation, Royal Scottish Academy. p 168.
48. Rear front, Royal Scottish Academy. *between* pp 168/169.
49. The Mound, with New College in middle distance. p 169.
50. George IV Bridge. The upper level road system was not all gain. Here the steeple of mediaeval Magdalen Chapel is dwarfed by the new level of buildings. p 186.
51. King's Bridge, with the barracks of the Castle in the background. p 187.
52. St George's Church, Charlotte Square, as designed by Reid. p 190.
53. Fan vaulting of the nave, St John's Church. p 191.
54. The cavernous doorway to St Stephen's Church. p 192.

55. The Upper Library, the University. p 193.
56. Detail of the Upper Library. p 197.
57. View across Dean Valley to Eton Terrace. p 204.
58. Doorway in Duke Street. p 205.
59. Heriot Row. p 208.
60. Drawing-room in Heriot Row. p 209.
61. Nelson Street, from No. 20 Nelson Street. p 212.
62. Drawing-room, 20 Nelson Street (Courtesy, Professor and Mrs D. Talbot Rice). p 213.
63. Houses in Ann Street. p 214.
64. Ann Street. p 215.
65. Well-disciplined, domestic, Georgian architecture in Malta Terrace. p 218.
66. St Bernard's Crescent. p 219.
67. Lord Moray's Pleasure Grounds: a path above the Water of Leith. p 220.
68. Lord Moray's Pleasure Grounds: a path in Doune Terrace Gardens, with Randolph Cliff. p 221.
69. SE section of Moray Place. p 224.
70. Moray Place. p 225.
71. Ainslie Place. p 230.
72. Saxe-Coburg Place. p 231.
73. 37 St Andrew's Square. p 234.
74. Doorways in Broughton Street. p 235.
75. The High Street with Tron Kirk. p 244.
76. Interior, Assembly Rooms, George Street. p 252.
77. A Hanoverian tombstone in Greyfriar's Churchyard, with the old Edinburgh rising behind. p 256.
78. Gothic revival in York Road, Newhaven. p 257.
79. Dean Bridge. p 272.
80. The lesson of Edinburgh's great planning experiment survived into such early Council housing schemes as this, on the banks of the Water of Leith. p 273.
81. Physicians' Hall, Queen Street. p 280.
82. Playfair's National Gallery of Scotland, the Mound, with the same architect's New College behind. p 281.

List of Figures

[1]   Old Fishmarket Close. J. W. Ewbank *Picturesque Views of Edinburgh* (Edinburgh, 1825). p 5.

[2]   High Street, about 1750. *Symbolae Scoticae*, Edinburgh University Library. p 9.

[3]   George Drummond, Lord Provost of Edinburgh. Engraving by Mackenzie in *Collections as to Edinburgh*, v. 3, Edinburgh Public Library. p 16.

[4]   Watercolour of Edinburgh, looking N E from Castlehill, about 1750. SS EUL. pp 18/19.

[5]   Parliament Square, about 1750. Hugo Arnot *The History of Edinburgh* (Edinburgh, 1779). p 25.

[6]   Watercolour of Tay Bridge, Perth, possibly by Paul Sandby. SS EUL. p 28.

[7]   North Bridge, about 1800. SS EUL. p 51.

[8]   Verses by John Home, 1753. EUL La. III 584. p 54.

[9]   John Adam. The Exchange. *Contract for the Exchange* (Edinburgh, 1753). pp 56/57

[10] North Bridge from N W. T. H. Shepherd *Modern Athens* (London, 1829). p 61.

[11] View, about 1780, looking E from the drained North Loch. Engraving by W. H. Lizars. pp 62/63.

[12] North Bridge and Register House, about 1850. Photograph by courtesy of E. R. Yerbury & Son, Edinburgh. p 64.

[13] North Bridge and Register House, about 1780. Arnot. p 67.

[14] Map of Central Edinburgh, about 1780. J. Ainslie. *facing* p 68.

[15] James Craig. 'Plan of the new streets and squares intended for the City of Edinburgh, 1767'. pp 72/73.

[16] Nancy. Héré de Corny's plan. P. Patte *Monumens erigés à la gloire de Louis XV*. p 75.

[17a/b] Nancy. Place Stanislas during construction and in a recent photograph. p 76.

[18] Richelieu. Plan of the town. Tassin. p 78.

[19] Charlotte Square, N E corner. SS EUL. p 80.

[20] Sir William Chambers. Townhouse for Sir Laurence Dundas. Shepherd. p 83.

[21] David Kay. St Andrew's Church, George Street. Shepherd. p 85.

[22] James Craig. Physicians' Hall, George Street. Original drawing of street frontage reproduced by courtesy of the Royal College of Physicians, Edinburgh. pp 88/89.

[23] Shakespeare Square, from the plan of Edinburgh by R. Kirkwood, 1819. p 94.

[24] Medallion of Robert Adam, by J. Tassie. National Portrait Gallery, Scotland. p 96.

[25] James Craig. Plan for St James's Square, Edinburgh, 1773. Courtesy of the Heriot Trust. *facing* p 99.

[26] Plan of St James's Square. Kirkwood, 1819. p 99.

[27] Marble Relief from fireplace, drawing room, 6 Charlotte Square. Edwin Smith. p 100.

[28] Craig's New Town completed. Kirkwood, 1819. pp 106/107 and 108/109.

[29] Robert Adam. Design for Cowgate arch, South Bridge, 1786. Courtesy of the Soane Museum. p 113.

[30] Robert Adam. Designs for South Bridge, 1786. Courtesy of the Soane Museum. pp 114/115.

[31] Robert Adam. Impression of South Bridge and the Cowgate, 1786. Courtesy of the Soane Museum. pp 116/117.

[32] James Craig. Octagon and Crescent, South Bridge. *Plan for improving the City of Edinburgh* 1786. Courtesy of Edinburgh Town Council. p 118.

[33] James Craig. Elevation of the proposed Octagon, South Bridge. Courtesy of Edinburgh Town Council. pp 120/121.

[34] Early 19th c view of the Mound, by Kay. p 123.

[35] Robert Adam. The University; a watercolour drawing after Adams' design. EUL. pp 126/127.

[36] The Quadrangle, Old College. Playfair Collection, EUL. p 129.

[37/38] Robert Adam. Plan and elevation of University development, about 1786. Courtesy of the Soane Museum. pp 130/131.

[39] Sketch of South Bridge, looking N. SS EUL. p 132.

[40] Plan of Central Edinburgh, about 1827. Brown and Wood. pp 136/137.

[41] Robert Adam. The Bridewell, with the new gaol in background. Shepherd. p 138.

[42a/b] Waterloo Place. Two engravings showing the Waterloo Place Scheme under construction. p 141.

[43] Waterloo Bridge. One of the designs. Courtesy of the Edinburgh Town Council. p 143.

[44] Waterloo Place from E end of Princes Street. Ewbank. p 146.

[45] Waterloo Place and Calton Hill, by Leonard Rosoman, A.R.A. Courtesy of the artist. p 146.

[46] Calton Hill, in use as a public walk. SS EUL. p 153.

[47]   William Playfair. Original drawing of elevation for Leopold Place,
       E U L. pp 154/155.
[48]   A vision of the Calton Hill complex completed. Lizars. E U L. p 161.
[49]   The Bank of Scotland prior to alteration in 1868. s s E U L. p 163.
[50]   William Playfair. The Royal Institution in the 1920's.
       s s E U L. p 165.
[51]   Plan of proposed 'improvements', the Mound, 1830. Courtesy of
       Edinburgh Town Council. p 169.
[52]   Trotter of Dreghorn's plan for improving the Mound, 1834.
       Courtesy of Edinburgh Town Council. pp 170/171.
[53]   Elevation and plan of proposed Arcade on the Mound, 1834.
       Courtesy of Edinburgh Town Council. pp 172/173.
[54]   Terminus of Union Canal. Ewbank. p 179.
[55]   The Cowgate and George iv Bridge. A photograph, about 1860,
       reproduced by courtesy of E. R. Yerbury & Son. p 183.
[56]   Robert Adam. Design for St George's Church, Charlotte Square.
       Scots Magazine, 1814. p 190.
[57]   William Playfair. The University; drawing of acanthus leaves as a
       detail for a Corinthian capital. E U L. p 195.
[58/59] Adam & Playfair. The University, Museum front. Adam's
       original design and Playfair's modified version of it. E U L. p 196.
[60]   William Playfair. A drawing in the National Portrait Gallery,
       Scotland. *facing* p 196.
[61]   William Playfair. The University Library, original design. E U L.
       pp 198/199.
[62]   William Playfair. The University. Plan and elevation of
       Venetian window and corinthian columns in
       Museum front. E U L. p 201.
[63]   The University. Adam's East Front, as built. Shepherd. p 202.
[64]   Plan of the Earl of Moray's property. Kirkwood, 1819. p 203.
[65]   Reid and Sibbald. Plan for the area N of Queen Street.
       Courtesy, the Heriot Trust. p 207.
[66]   Robert Reid. Elevation for Heriot Row, 1803. Courtesy, the
       Heriot Trust. pp 210/211.
[67]   Royal Circus from India Place. Shepherd. p 213.
[68]   Stockbridge in the 1790's. s s E U L. p 214.
[69]   Mr Gillespie Graham and Mr Thomas Hamilton, from Crombie
       New Athenians (Edinburgh, 1847). p 219.
[70]   George Street, about 1840. s s E U L. p 227.
[71]   Robert Adam. Design for one of a pair of houses in St. Andrew's
       Square. Courtesy of the Royal College of Physicians,
       Edinburgh. p 234.
[72]   Old Assembly Rooms, West Bow. James Grant *Old and New
       Edinburgh* (N D). p 251.

[73] The Assembly Rooms, George Street. Shepherd. p 253.
[74] Leith Harbour from the Pier. Shepherd. p 259.
[75] Rennie's proposals for extension of Leith Docks. Grant. p 261.
[76] View of Leith Walk. Ewbank. p 264.
[77] View from the Pleasance. Shepherd. p 267.
[78] Terminus, Haymarket Station. p 278.
[79] William Playfair. Original drawing for Donaldson's Hospital. E U L. pp 282/283.
[80] William Playfair. Original drawing of the National Gallery and Royal Scottish Academy. E U L. pp 284/285.

Glossary of Legal Terms

Feu. The feudal system of land rights is described in Bell's *Principles of the Law of Scotland* as follows:

'The property of land in Scotland is held either directly and immediately under the Crown as paramount superior of all feudal subjects; or indirectly, either as vassal to some one who holds his land immediately from the Crown, or as sub-Vassal in a still more subordinate degree.' Sub-feuing may go on *ad infinitum.* The grantor of each feudal right is called the superior and the grantee the vassal or feuar. The superior, in granting the feu, imposes conditions in regard to the buildings which the feuar proposes to erect on the land feued, and states other terms of tenure, one of these being the payment of an annual feu-duty which normally remains a constant amount. These conditions and terms, unless waived by the superior, continue for all time and, so long as they are fulfilled, the feuar enjoys exclusive possession of the lands feued to him, with all the rights and obligations usually pertaining to ownership of property. When a feuar sells his land and any buildings which he may have erected thereon or which he may have acquired at the time of his purchase, the proceeds belong entirely to him, and the purchaser acquires the rights and is bound under the obligations (including the payment of feu-duty to the superior), contained in the title to the land.

Action of Declarator is one whereby a pursuer seeks to have a right, for example, of property or status, which is in question, judicially declared.

Decree-arbitral is the award granted by an arbiter upon the matter submitted to him.

Roup is a public sale, by auction, usually of heritable property. The conditions of the sale are set out in Articles of Roup which, on conclusion of the sale, also form the contract between the seller and purchaser.

Tack, or lease is a contract whereby the use of land or other immoveable subject is given by the landlord to the lessee in exchange for a yearly rent (or tack).

Writer to the Signet was originally, in the fifteenth century, a Clerk in the Office of the Secretary of State who was the Keeper of the King's Seal or Signet. When the Court of Session was instituted in 1532, Writers to the Signet became Members of the College of Justice and by 1600 a Society had been formed of those few Writers who received Commissions from the Royal Secretary and who combined Government Service with private clerical and legal practice. By the eighteenth century the Writers to the Signet had become the principal and most numerous body of solicitors in Scotland.

Faculty of Advocates was instituted in 1532 by the same Act as established the Court of Session. The Advocate, whose status is equivalent to that of the Barrister in England, is entitled to plead in every Court in Scotland, civil, ecclesiastical and criminal, and also before the House of Lords, the Judicial Committee of the Privy Council, and Parliamentary Committees. The Faculty is presided over by the Dean of the Faculty who is the leader of the Scottish Bar, excepting the Lord Advocate.

List of Abbreviations

NSA, New Statistical Account of Scotland.
OSA, Old Statistical Account of Scotland.
OEC, Book of the Old Edinburgh Club.
TCM, Town Council Minutes.

Overleaf. *Map of Edinburgh in the 18th century, before the expansion of the city beyond the confines of the Old Town. The Castle (at left) and Holyrood (at right) terminate the High Street and Canongate. The North Loch – site of Princes Street Gardens – bars northward expansion to 'Barefoot's Parks', where Craig was to plan his New Town. Salisbury Crags (lower right) and the Meadows, formerly a shallow lake (centre foreground) define the eastern and southern limits.*

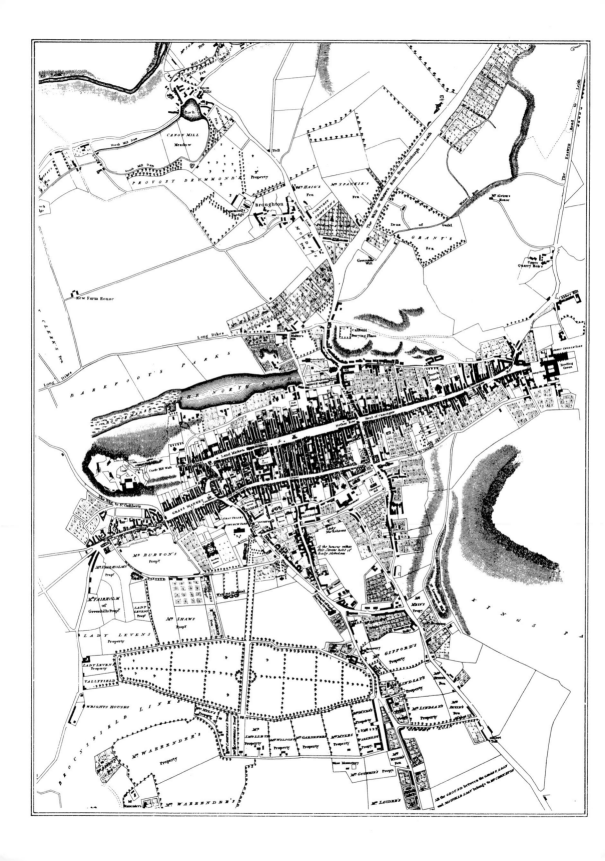

I

The 'Proposals' of 1752

When the two regiments of dragoons, intended to help in the defence of Edinburgh, retreated towards Leith in the face of the rebel army on 15 September 1745, they rode eastwards, very near the line of what is now George Street, and were watched by many Edinburgh citizens looking from the Old Town across the North Loch to the long dykes, as the crest of high ground in the open country lying between Edinburgh and the sea was then called.

In those days Edinburgh was a very small town, spilling out from the narrow confines of the old Flodden Wall,[1] but still restricted almost entirely to the narrow ridge which runs at a tangent from the base of Arthur's Seat to the stupendous rock of the Castle. The site provided a marvellous defensive position. It lay, moreover, near one of the greatest estuaries of the North Sea, facing towards Scandinavia and the Low Countries; and it was scenically striking. But it was an inconvenient place for many people to live, and it had become, in the course of the centuries, cramped and overcrowded:

The ground upon which [Edinburgh] is built is perhaps as singular, and in many respects inconvenient, as can well be figured. The Palace of Holyroodhouse, the eastmost boundary of the city, stands on a plain within two miles of the river Forth, from which it rises by a gradual ascent of ninety-four feet from the high water-mark. From Holyrood-house there begins the narrow point, or, if we may be allowed the expression, the tail of a hill, which gradually, extending itself in breadth, rises in a steep and straight ridge, from which its shelving sides decline; the ridge terminating in an abrupt precipice, the site of the castle, at the distance of a mile in length, and one hundred and eighty feet in heighth from Holyrood-house.

The ridge of this hill forms a continued and very magnificent street. From its sides, lanes and alleys, which are there called *wynds and closes*, extend like slanting ribs; so that, upon the whole, it bears a striking resemblance to a turtle, of which the castle is the head, the high street the ridge of the back, the *wynds and closes* the shelving sides, and the palace of Holyroodhouse the tail.

The declivity of the hill upon the south is terminated by a level strip, on which the street called the *Cowgate* is built; thence the ground rises precipitately to the south, and terminates in a plain.

Upon the north, the descent from the high-street is steeper, and more profound. It is bounded by an inconsiderable morass, which formerly being overflowed, formed a lake called the *North-loch*, from the north-side of which a bank rises, and spreads itself into a level field, constituting the area of the extended royalty.[2]

The securing of this extended royalty,[3] through which the lang dykes ran, was the grand object of the early proposals for the enlargement and adornment of Edinburgh. These proposals were comparatively modest in scope as far as new building went. There was no mention, to begin with, of expanding widely to the north, or to the south, east or west, and therefore no specific plan to turn Edinburgh into what it has since become, a city built not upon one but upon several hills, like Rome, San Francisco, or Valparaiso. Not until, in the nineteenth century, Waterloo Bridge, King George IV Bridge and King's Bridge had been added to the North Bridge and the bridge over the Cowgate could the words of a later historian of the city have been written: 'Spreading over many swelling hills and deep ravines, that in some instances are spanned by enormous bridges of stone, [Edinburgh] exhibits a striking peculiarity and boldness in its features that render it totally unlike any other city in the world . . .'[4]

1. 'A continued and very magnificent street' – the High Street, looking N W from the Tron Kirk.

The proposals that led to the transformation of Edinburgh from an old walled city to a curious co-partnery of old city and new town

have a fairly precise origin. In 1752 there was published in Edinburgh a pamphlet entitled *Proposals for carrying on certain Public Works in the City of Edinburgh.* This pamphlet opens with an Advertisement to the Reader, stating that on 8 July 1752 the Convention of Royal Burghs had resolved to build a Merchants' Exchange, a place for storing national records, and a building containing a Borough-room,[5] as well as to carry out other improvements in the City of Edinburgh. In order to gain support for this scheme, the Convention had further agreed to issue a pamphlet 'explaining and recommending the design', and to give it a wide circulation throughout Scotland. This pamphlet was the above-mentioned *Proposals.* It was apparently written by Sir Gilbert Elliott but certainly owed much to George Drummond, in the years 1750-51 Lord Provost of Edinburgh for the third time.

The *Proposals* are of extraordinary interest because of the light that they shed on the circumstances, ways of thought, intentions and ambitions of the originators of the enlarged town. The document, of considerable length, runs to some 7,500 words. It hardly repays quotation in full, but the bulk of the text is given in the following pages.

According to the Advertisement, the opportunity of which the Convention sought to take advantage was a fortuitous one:

> The narrow limits of the royalty of EDINBURGH, and the want
> of certain public buildings, and other useful and ornamental
> accommodations in the city, have been long regretted. An
> opportunity of remedying these inconveniencies was often
> wished for, and Providence has now furnished a very fair one.
> In *September* last the side-wall of a building of six stories
> high, in which several reputable families lived, gave way all
> of a sudden . . . This melancholy accident occasioned a general
> survey to be made of the condition of the old houses; and such
> as were insufficient were pulled down; so that several of the
> principal parts of the town were laid in ruins. – Nor was this
> favourable opportunity let slip.

And having vouchsafed his readers this disquieting glimpse of the ruinous character of some parts of the old city, the author proceeds:

2. A close in the Old Town.

Proposals for carrying on certain public works in
the city of EDINBURGH

Among the several causes to which the prosperity of a nation may be ascribed, the situation, conveniency, and beauty of its capital, are surely not the least considerable. A capital where these circumstances happen fortunately to concur, should naturally become the centre of trade and commerce, of learning and the arts, of politeness, and of refinement of every kind. No sooner will the advantages which these necessarily produce, be felt and experienced in the chief city, than they will diffuse themselves through the nation, and universally promote the same spirit of industry and improvement.

Of this general assertion the city of LONDON affords the most striking example. Upon the most superficial view, we cannot fail to remark its healthful, unconfined situation, upon a large plain, gently shelving towards the *Thames*; its neighbourhood to that river; its proper distance from the sea; and, by consequence, the great facility with which it is supplied with all the necessaries, and even luxuries of life. No less obvious are the neatness and accommodation of its private houses; the beauty and conveniency of its numerous streets and open squares, of its buildings and bridges, its large parks and extensive walks. When to these advantages we add its trade and navigation; the business of the exchange, of the two houses of parliament, and of the courts of justice; the magnificence of the court; the pleasures of the theatre, and other public entertainments: in a word, when we survey this mighty concourse of people, whom business, ambition, curiosity, or the love of pleasure, has assembled within so narrow a compass, we need no longer be astonished at that spirit of industry and improvement, which, taking its rise in the city of LONDON, has at length spread over the greatest part of SOUTH BRITAIN, animating every art and profession, and inspiring the whole people with the greatest ardour and emulation.

To illustrate this further, we need only contrast the delightful prospect which LONDON affords, with that of any other city, which is destitute of all, or even of any considerable number of

4

these advantages. Sorry we are, that no one occurs to us more apposite to this purpose, than EDINBURGH, the metropolis of SCOTLAND when a separate kingdom, and still the chief city of NORTH BRITAIN. The healthfulness of its situation, and its neighbourhood to the *Forth*, must no doubt be admitted as very favourable circumstances. But how greatly are these overbalanced by other disadvantages almost without number? Placed upon a ridge of a hill, it admits but of one good street, running from east to west; and even this is tolerably accessible only from one quarter. The narrow lanes leading to the north and south, by reason of their steepness, narrowness, and dirtiness, can only be considered as so many unavoidable nuisances. Confined by the small compass of the walls, and the narrow limits of the royalty, which scarcely extends beyond the walls, the houses stand more crowded than in any other town in *Europe*, and are built to a

[1] *'Ruinous character of the old city.' Old Fishmarket Close in the early 19th* C. *Ewbank*

5

height that is almost incredible. Hence necessarily follows a great want of free air, light, cleanliness, and every other comfortable accommodation. Hence also many families, sometimes no less than ten or a dozen, are obliged to live overhead of each other in the same building; where, to all the other inconveniences, is added that of a common stair, which is no other in effect that an upright street, constantly dark and dirty. It is owing to the same narrowness of situation, that the principal street is incumbered with the herb-market, the fruit-market, and several others; that the shambles are placed upon the side of the *North-loch*, rendering what was originally an ornament of the town, a most insufferable nusance. No less observable is the great deficiency of public buildings. If the parliament-house, the churches, and a few hospitals, be excepted, what other have we to boast of? There is no exchange for our merchants; no safe repository for our public and private records; no place of meeting for our magistrates and town-council; none for the convention of our boroughs, which is intrusted with the inspection of trade. To these and such other reasons it must be imputed, that so few people of rank reside in this city; that it is rarely visited by strangers; and that so many local prejudices, and narrow notions, inconsistent with polished manners and growing wealth, are still so obstinately retained. To such reasons alone it must be imputed, that EDINBURGH, which ought to have set the first example of industry and improvement, is the last of our trading cities that has shook off the unaccountable supineness which has so long and so fatally depressed the spirit of this nation.

Mr. FLETCHER of *Salton,* a very spirited and manly author, in his second discourse on the affairs of SCOTLAND, written so long ago as the year 1698, has the same observation. 'As the happy situation of LONDON (says he) has been the principal cause of the glory and riches of ENGLAND; so the bad situation of EDINBURGH, has been one great occasion of the poverty and uncleanliness in which the greater part of the people of SCOTLAND live'.

To enlarge and improve this city, to adorn it with public buildings, which may be a national benefit, and thereby to remove, at least in some degree, the inconveniencies to which it has hitherto been liable, is the sole object of these proposals. Before we enter upon a more particular explanation of them, it will be proper to mention the motives which have induced us at this time to offer them to the consideration of the public.

At no period surely did there ever appear a more general, or a better directed zeal for the improvement and prosperity of this country. Persons of every rank and denomination seem at length to be actuated by a truly public and national spirit. Private men who adventure to propose schemes for the public good, are no longer ridiculed as vain projectors; nor are the more extensive undertakings of societies and companies condemned without examination, as the engines merely of the factious and designing. Had we therefore this general spirit of our countrymen for our sole encouragement, we might rest assured that our proposals would meet with no unfavourable reception. But when we consider the rapid progress which our trade and manufactures have actually made within these few years, and attentively compare the present state of this country as to these particulars, with what it was in former times, we are persuaded, that an attempt to enlarge and beautify this metropolis, will now at length be deemed necessary. To trace the gradual advancement or decay of our trade and manufactures, through the several revolutions which this kingdom has experienced, would far exceed the bounds we have prescribed to ourselves: A very few observations will sufficiently answer our present purpose . . . before the Union of the crowns in the person of James VI the arts of peace were but little known or cultivated. Before that period, even those kingdoms which have since ingrossed the trade of the world, had made but very inconsiderable advances . . . amidst the distractions which constantly prevailed in this country, we had neither leisure nor inclination to improve those arts, which are generally the offspring of quiet times, and a well-ordered state . . .

Few persons of any rank, in those days, frequented our towns. The manners of our peers, of our barons, and chiefs of families, were not formed to brook that equality which prevails in cities. The solitary grandeur of a country-life, at their own seats, and

7

amidst their own vassals, suited better with the stateliness and pride of those petty sovereigns. EDINBURGH, though perhaps it might be styled the capital, yet in reality possessed none of those advantages by which a capital is usually distinguished. Though strengthened by the castle at one end, and a lake on each side, yet was it too near ENGLAND to be thought perfectly secure . . .

. . . The union of the two kingdoms [in 1707], an event equally beneficial to both nations, is the great aera from which we may justly date the revival of that spirit and activity which the union of the crowns had·well nigh suppressed . . . In some parts of the country, indeed, both trade and manufactures were, from about that time, very remarkably increased; yet in EDINBURGH and the neighbourhood of it, there was still a total stagnation. But since the year 1746, when the rebellion was suppressed, a most surprising revolution has happened in the affairs of this country . . . Husbandry, manufactures, general commerce, and the increase of useful people, are become the objects of universal attention . . .

. . . The meanness of EDINBURGH has been too long an obstruction to our improvement, and a reproach to SCOTLAND. The increase of our people, the extension of our commerce, and the honour of the nation, are all concerned in the success of this project. As we have such powerful motives prompting us to undertake it; so chance has furnished us with the fairest opportunity of carrying it into execution. Several of the principal parts of the town are now lying in ruins. Many of the old houses are decayed; several have been already pulled down, and probably more will soon be in the same condition. If this opportunity be neglected, all hopes of remedying the inconveniencies of this city are at an end.

The magistrates and town-council, the college of justice, and several persons of rank who happened to be in the neighbourhood of this place, [therefore propose

(1) To build an exchange 'upon the ruins on the north side of the high street'.

(2) 'To erect upon the ruins in the parliament-close' a building for law courts, the town council, 'several registers', the advocates library, etc.]

8

(3) To obtain an act of parliament for extending the royalty; to enlarge and beautify the town, by opening new streets to the north and south, removing the markets and shambles, and turning the *North-Loch* into a canal, with walks and terrasses on each side.

(4) That the expense of these public works should be detrayed by a national contribution.

The extending the royalty, and enlargement of the town, make no doubt the most important article. So necessary and so considerable an improvement of the capital cannot fail to have the greatest

[2] High Street, about 1750; left, the Luckenbooths, and, right, tenements soon afterwards demolished to clear a site for the Exchange.
EUL

influence on the general prosperity of the nation. It is a vulgar mistake, that the greatest part of our principal families chuse to reside at LONDON. This indeed is true with regard to a few of our members of parliament, and some particular families who were settled there before the union. The rest go only occasionally; and if their stay be long, and their expense by consequence greater than this country can well bear, it must be entirely imputed to the present form and situation of EDINBURGH. Were these in any tolerable degree remedied, our people of rank would hardly prefer an obscure life at LONDON, to the splendour and influence with which they might reside at home. An uninterrupted country-life, is what they will never be brought to submit to. Attention to the forming an interest, the pleasures of retirement, or a taste for agriculture, may induce them possibly to pass some part of their time at their country-seats; more cannot reasonably be expected. It might indeed be otherwise in ancient times, when the feudal customs prevailed, with their large dependancies and extensive jurisdictions. The institution of our government is now different: our manners must be different also. A nation cannot at this day be considerable, unless it be opulent. Wealth is only to be obtained by trade and commerce, and these are only carried on to advantage in populous cities. There also we find the chief objects of pleasure and ambition, and there consequently all those will flock whose circumstances can afford it. But can we expect, that persons of fortune in SCOTLAND will exchange the handsome seats they generally possess in the country, for the scanty lodging, and paltry accommodations they must put up with in EDINBURGH? It is not choice, but necessity, which obliges them to go so frequently to LONDON. Let us improve and enlarge this city, and possibly the superior pleasures of LONDON, which is at a distance, will be compensated, at least in some measure, by the moderate pleasures of EDINBURGH, which is at home.

It has been objected, That this project may occasion the centre of the town to be deserted. But of this there can be no hazard. People of fortune, and of a certain rank, will probably chuse to build upon the fine fields which lie to the north and south of the town: but men of professions and business of every kind, will still incline to live in the neighbourhood of the exchange, of the courts of justice, and other places of public resort; and the number of this last class of men will increase in a much greater proportion, than that of the former. *Turin, Berlin*, and many other cities, shew the truth of this observation. In these cities, what is called the *new town*, consists of spacious streets and large buildings, which are thinly inhabited, and that too by strangers chiefly, and persons of considerable rank; while the *old town*, though not near so commodious, is more crouded than before these late additions were made. The national advantages which a populous capital must necessarily produce, are obvious. A great concourse of people brought within a small compass, occasions a much greater consumption than the same number would do dispersed over a wide country. As the consumption is greater so it is quicker and more discernible. Hence follows a more rapid circulation of money and other commodities, the great spring which gives motion to general industry and improvement. The examples set by the capital, the nation will soon follow. The certain consequence is, general wealth and prosperity: the number of useful people will increase; the rents of land rise; the public revenue improve; and, in the room of sloth and poverty, will succeed industry and opulence . . .

Such being the nature and end of these proposals, we can have little doubt but they will meet with general encouragement. Whoever is warmed with a sincere concern for the prosperity of his country, will chearfully contribute to so national an undertaking. Extensive projects, which little minds are apt to condemn as impracticable, serve only to excite generous spirits to act with greater industry and vigour. Peace is now generally established; the rage of faction in this country is greatly abated: there is a concurrence of almost every circumstance, which can prompt us to undertake, or enable us to execute great designs. Such of our young men of rank and fortune as are not sunk in low pleasures, must find employment of some kind or other. If the great objects of war and faction no longer present themselves, may they not find a more humane, and not less interesting exercise of their active powers, in promoting and cultivating the general arts of peace? In the reign of Queen *Elizabeth*, ENGLAND was but a forming state, as SCOTLAND is now. It was then that the spirit of the ENGLISH began to exert itself. Ships were fitted out, nay fleets were equipped, by private gentlemen. In the same manner public buildings were erected, colonies were settled, and new discoveries made. In a lesser degree, the same disposition begins to discover itself in this country. Building bridges, repairing high-roads, establishing manufactures, forming commercial companies, and opening new veins of trade, are employments which have already thrown a lustre upon some of the first names of this country. The little detail of an established commerce, may ingross the attention of the merchant: but it is in prosecution of greater objects, that the leading men of a country ought to exert their power and influence. And what greater object can be presented to their view, than that of enlarging, beautifying, and improving the capital of their native country? What can redound more to their honour? What prove more beneficial to SCOTLAND, and by consequence to UNITED BRITAIN?'

This call to action is remarkable for its combination of economic motives and interests with others of a vaguer, often a more patriotic kind, born of an ancestry at least as old and much more illustrious. A larger and more handsome town will help business, occasion a greater consumption and a much more rapid circulation of money – 'the great spring which gives motion to general industry and improvement'. But the arts of peace, public entertainment, magnificence, the love of pleasure should also be promoted; partly, no doubt, because they too have a commercial significance, partly because prestige requires a competition with London, Turin, Berlin. It is indeed a curious amalgam. Full of history, it is an economic tract; commercially minded, yet it has a view to the 'prosecution of greater objects'; lofty in tone, it never loses sight of the shopkeeper's and tradesman's advantage; idealistic and utilitarian; noble and incurably middle-class; a bourgeois dream in a partly feudal society, and therefore itself shot through with feudal elements and romantic longings.

Some of the ideas put forward in this pamphlet, and others of a similar nature, had been entertained long before 1752. In 1688 the then Lord Provost, after visiting London, reported to the Town

Council that he had secured from the King, 'whenever the good Town shall think it convenient', permission 'to enlarge the bounds thereof by buying in ground without or purchasing closes and tenements within the town or for building bridges or arches for accomplishing any such designs'.[6] But James's flight in the same year put an end, for the time being, to these ideas. Over thirty years later, in 1723, an Act of Parliament allowed the use of money for

> narrowing the noxious lake on the north side of the said City,
> commonly called the North Loch, into a canal of running water,
> and making a communication street or way to the fields and
> grounds belonging to the said City, on the north side thereof,
> and for purchasing such houses and grounds as shall be by the
> said magistrates and Council, with the approbation of the
> Overseers, judged proper and necessary to be bought and
> purchased for making the said street or communication way. . . .

By this same Act the magistrates and Council were also enabled to purchase the property and superiority of the Calton from Lord Balmerino. For obtaining this Act of Parliament George Drummond on 24 June 1723 was paid expenses of £1,420 sterling, and given £500 as a compliment from the city. A few years afterwards, the Earl of Mar, an exile on the Continent for his share in the rising of 1715, drew up a paper in similar terms, outlining and recommending several of the developments which were later to take place:

> All ways of improving Edinburgh should be thought on: as in
> particular, making a large bridge of three arches, over the
> ground betwixt the North Loch and the Physic Gardens, from
> the High Street at Liberton's Wynd to the Multersey Hill,
> where many fine streets might be built, as the inhabitants in-
> creased. The access to them would be easy on all hands, and the
> situation would be agreeable and convenient, having a noble
> prospect of all the fine ground towards the sea, the Firth of
> Forth, and coast of Fife. One long street in a straight line,
> where the Long Gate is now; on one side of it would be a fine
> opportunity for gardens down to the North Loch, and one, on
> the other side, towards Broughton . . .
>
> Another bridge might also be made on the other side of
> the Town, and almost as useful and commodious as that on the

13

north . . . Betwixt the south end of the Pleasance and the Potter-row, and from thence to Bristo Street, and by the back of the wall at Heriot's Hospital, are fine situations for houses and gardens. There would be fine avenues to the town, and outlets for airing and walking by these bridges; and Edinburgh, from being a bad and incommodious situation, would become a very beneficial and convenient one; and to make it still more so, a branch of that river, called the Water of Leith, might, it is thought, be brought from somewhere about Coltbridge, to fill and run through the North Loch, which would be of great advantage to the convenience, beauty, cleanliness, and healthiness of the town.[7]

Here we have not only the North Bridge and the siting, more or less, of George Street, but also the South Bridge, residential development in the neighbourhood of George Square, and a forerunner of Craig's abortive proposal in his plan of 1767 to introduce some sort of canal or water-way in place of the stagnant North Loch.

When Mar wrote, in 1728, some improvements had already taken place in or around the Old Town, and others were completed before the *Proposals* of 1752. Milne's Square was built between 1684 and 1688, designed by Robert Mylne, master mason to Charles II, James II, William and Mary, and Queen Anne. Milne's Court, at the top of the Lawnmarket, was built some time between 1690 and 1700. It is the earliest of the post-Revolution housing schemes. James's Court, eight storeys in height, was erected in the 1720s; Argyle Square, 'after the fashion of London, every house being designed for only one family',[8] was completed about 1742. Brown Square and Adam Square, both in the same district, were being planned or actually built in the 1750s.[9] Some of these schemes were to the south of the Cowgate and therefore beyond the royalty; others, such as Milne's Court and James's Court, were within the walls, and were made possible only by the razing of buildings previously occupying the sites. These schemes were all planned to give the wealthier citizen a little more living space, a little more light and air, a little escape from the congested, narrow closes and the lofty, crowded, often dilapidated tenements with their dark and dirty common stairs. But within the walls the city was now so choked with

3. Milne's Court, Lawnmarket.

14

houses that there was no room to build; beyond the walls access was difficult. In these circumstances, the issue of the extension of the royalty was bound once more to be raised.

What is astonishing about the *Proposals* of 1752 is that they outlined a scheme which, in the course of the following eighty years, was actually carried out. The connection in history between splendid aims and grand intentions on the one hand and the subsequent pattern of events on the other is usually complicated, tenuous, difficult to understand. But in this case what was hoped for and intended was also what was done. Bridges were built and highroads repaired; the city was enlarged and improved and adorned with public buildings; people of rank came to live in it and it was constantly visited by strangers; Edinburgh indeed became a capital 'of learning and the arts, of politeness, and of refinement of every kind'. Seldom has the promised land glimpsed by one generation been so swiftly and accurately reproduced and entered into by another.

That the dream became reality was due to all the circumstances of the time, but also to one man above others. George Drummond was perhaps the most influential citizen of Edinburgh in the eighteenth century. Born in Perthshire in 1687, he came to Edinburgh while still in his 'teens, was appointed one of the Commissioners of Customs in 1715, and in 1716 was elected to the Town Council, which at that time had thirty-three members. A staunch Protestant and an ardent Whig, Drummond was soon recognised as a leading opponent of the Jacobites. He fought at Sheriffmuir, afterwards entered into a political correspondence with Joseph Addison, one of the Secretaries of State, and was for some fifty years an agent of the Government, in effect if not in name, and one of its principal supports in Edinburgh. In 1725 he became Lord Provost and engaged himself in the public appeal for funds to start an Infirmary; a house was rented for this purpose in 1729 and fitted up with a few beds. Then in 1738 the new infirmary building was begun, in what is now Infirmary Street, under Royal Charter. Again Drummond was one of the chief promoters – 'Forwarding the building of the Royal Infirmary is my only amusement . . . I am distinguished, and called the father of it, with which, Alas, I have too much pride and vanity not to be pleased.'[10] He raised volunteers for the defence of the city

4. Milne's Court from the back court.

15

*[3] George Drummond,
Lord Provost of Edinburgh.*
E P L

in 1745, but the then Lord Provost, timorous, irresolute, possibly a Jacobite at heart, allowed resistance to disintegrate, and Drummond, a marked man, joined Cope's army, was present at the battle of Prestonpans, and afterwards accompanied Cope to Berwick. In 1746, when Edinburgh needed a new Lord Provost, Drummond was the obvious choice, and was elected. He was Lord Provost again in 1750-52, 1754-56, 1758-60 and 1762-64.

Able, genial, resourceful, deferential, persuasive and astute, Drummond had an exceptionally good head for finance and an unusual capacity for getting his own way without hurting other people's feelings. But what really distinguished him above his contemporaries was the grandeur of his purpose and the selflessness of his aim. Perhaps he could afford to be selfless in his later public life, having married for the third time, advantageously, in 1739, and again, even more advantageously, in 1755. But his character and his course were

16

determined before 1739. Moreover, contemporaries did not take a cynical view of him: 'The chief magistrate is devoted to the service of the city, and its glory is his greatest aim. Disinterested are his views; his noble plans proclaim his merit, and his memory shall be dear to posterity.'[11]

Having done so much to establish the Royal Infirmary, it was natural that Drummond should enter wholeheartedly into the 1752 scheme for city improvements. There is no doubt that the *Proposals* owed a great deal to Drummond in their formulation as well as in their accomplishment, and that he had nursed some such ideas for many years. His contemporary, Thomas Somerville, wrote:

> I happened one day . . . to be standing at a window [in the old town] looking out to the opposite side of the North Loch, then called Barefoot's Parks, in which there was not a single house to be seen. 'Look at these fields', said Provost Drummond; 'you, Mr. Somerville, are a young man, and may probably live, though I will not, to see all these fields covered with houses, forming a splendid and magnificent city. To the accomplishment of this, nothing more is necessary than draining the North Loch, and providing a proper access from the old town. I have never lost sight of this object since the year 1725, when I was first elected Provost.'[12]

The conversation which Somerville here records seems to have taken place in 1763. Somerville tells us that he was in Drummond's company 'at Dr Jardine's, in the uppermost storey of his house in the north corner of the exchange'. This building was the first result, in stone and mortar, of the *Proposals* of eleven years before.

[4] *Watercolour sketch, about 1750, looking* NE *from Castlehill across North Loch to Bearford's Parks, site of the New Town.*

EUL

II

Economic Background and Local Government

It is hardly too much to say that until the middle of the eighteenth
century Scotland was a small country on the fringe of civilised Europe,
poor, little known and of little account. Distinguished Scots there had
been – George Buchanan, John Knox, Sir Robert Moray, Napier of
Merchiston – but the list is not long, and few people abroad looked to
Scotland for moral, intellectual or artistic leadership. Had Scotland
continued in this condition, she would not have built a splendid new
town; the dream would have remained a dream, for want of patrons,
architects, builders – and money.

But by mid-century the tide of Scotland's intellectual and economic
life was at last beginning to flow. The first great achievements
were in the fields of history and philosophy. By 1760 the reputation
of David Hume was European. Adam Smith's *Theory of Moral Senti-
ments* became well known in France during the 1760s, and four trans-
lations of *The Wealth of Nations* into French were made before 1800.
William Robertson, Principal of Edinburgh University from 1762-93,
enjoyed an international reputation in the last quarter of the century
as one of the two or three greatest historians of his day. In other
spheres too Scotsmen now began to acquire fame. Robert Adam became joint architect to the Crown in 1761, and during the 'sixties he
built Harewood House and Lansdowne House and remodelled the
interior of Syon House; well before 1770 he was, along with Sir
Robert Taylor and Sir William Chambers, the best known architect
in Britain. In 1774 James Watt arrived in Birmingham to join his
genius with the financial resources, the business acumen and the technical strength of Boulton; twenty years later Watt's steam engine
was beginning to be recognised as one of the greatest inventions of

the century. And in Watt's footsteps came the great race of Scots engineers – John Rennie, who began business in London in 1791, and who designed both Waterloo Bridge and Southwark Bridge across the Thames; Thomas Telford, who helped as a young mason to build Somerset House and who later founded the Institute of Civil Engineers after a lifetime of road, canal, bridge and harbour building, not all of it in Britain. In the same tradition were William Murdoch, Robert Stevenson, James Nasmyth, inventor of the steam hammer, and others. In skills more delicate than those of the engineer, Scotsmen were also prominent. The two Hunters, John and William, natives of Lanarkshire, were far and away the greatest surgeons in Britain from rather before 1770 until their deaths in 1783 and 1793, completely transforming both the practice and the teaching of anatomy. In the world of art Sir Henry Raeburn, although he perhaps never disputed Sir Thomas Lawrence's claims to be considered the greatest portrait painter of the day, was at least a rival, and the only rival, to the successor of Gainsborough and Reynolds. Burns, whose *Poems, chiefly in the Scottish Dialect* appeared in 1786, did not make a great impression outside Scotland until well into the nineteenth century; but he came in time to be acknowledged one of the greatest lyric and satiric poets of any age. And the just appreciation of Burns was made easier by the work of, among others, Sir Walter Scott – 'the wizard of the North', whose poems, appearing in the early years of the nineteenth century, achieved an instant popularity. And if the poems were widely read, the novels which followed them were even more popular. Literature, indeed, did much to make Scotland well-known, admired, unified, self-conscious, romantic and triumphant as never before.

This great upsurge of intellectual and artistic activity was accompanied by material progress of a scarcely less remarkable kind. The Union of 1707 had been accomplished in the face of considerable opposition. This opposition was partly an outburst of emotional patriotism; Scotland had suffered much at English hands, and now her parlous economic condition after the abject failure of the Darien scheme in 1700 was laid at England's door. There can be little doubt, however, that for a country placed as Scotland was at the beginning of the eighteenth century, complete political and economic union with

England offered the quickest and most effective means of creating or recreating conditions in which reasonably rapid economic development could be achieved. Only in this way, in fact, could Scotland begin to catch up with her more prosperous neighbour south of the border, a country which many Scotsmen envied as well as hated.

In the event, the short-period economic consequences of the Union were not such as to please everyone. It would be unreasonable to expect anything else; general changes in the conditions of economic life are bound to harm some people even while benefiting the majority. The interests of Edinburgh, capital as well as largest city, suffered probably more than any. The Privy Council and the Parliament removed to London; and, in consequence, many of the nobility no longer had an interest in maintaining their houses in the Canongate, which seem in many instances actually to have become ruinous.[1] There was thus loss to Edinburgh not only of prestige but of business, and a kind of business upon which the city must have extensively depended. The decline of some small ports along the Firth of Forth may also have been accelerated. And of course some firms in some industries throughout Scotland may have been unable to withstand the competition which free trade with England now allowed. On the other hand, it is obvious that there were other interests in Scotland which benefited from the Union. Trade between Glasgow and England's West Indian and American colonies had been built up in the last two or three decades of the seventeenth century, although on a small scale; the Act of Union legitimised this trade, and it immediately and greatly expanded. 'In the very first year after the Union the Scots fitted out several ships, I think seven or eight, to the English plantations, freighted with their own produce, the return of which [was] in tobacco or sugars, Etc.'[2] Whereas the annual import of tobacco to the Clyde averaged less than a quarter of a million pounds in the 1680s, it was over four million pounds by 1724. Tobacco manufacture was a pre-Union employment in Glasgow, and several sugar refineries likewise existed in the city before 1707. The Union did these businesses no harm, others were soon added, and merchants concerned in them grew prosperous. The Union also encouraged emigration to India, America and the West Indies. Many Scotsmen never returned, but of those who did, a substantial number

brought home very considerable fortunes, 'picked up estates thro'
the Country, and lived in a higher style than the old Gentry'.[3] (We
shall meet some of these later, prosperous householders in the New
Town early in the nineteenth century.) For agriculture also the
situation turned more favourable. England now offered a growing
market for the sale of cattle, and cattle-raising was an industry for
which Scotland had peculiar natural advantages.

Thus commerce, industry and agriculture all benefited from the
Union, even if some branches of commerce and industry suffered; and
the new opportunities were improved upon in subsequent decades.
Agriculture was of course the chief occupation of the people and the
principal source of such wealth as the country possessed. Considerable
progress was made in this basic industry before the middle of the
century. The new ideas just coming into vogue in Norfolk about
1700 – notably the planting of potatoes, clover and artificial grasses –
were mostly introduced into Scotland between 1705 and 1725.
Afforestation, or at least the planting of wind-breaks – so necessary
in many parts of Scotland – was also begun, and the processes of the
consolidation of properties and fencing, legislated for in the second
half of the seventeenth century, were carried further. In all this work
the advice and help of Englishmen, both farmers and stewards, was
important. Manufacturing industry also made progress. Many industries – many actual firms – survived the Union, and the industries
grew larger; sugar-refining, soap-boiling, rope-making, paper-
making, shipbuilding all fall into this category. The woollen manufacture perhaps did less well. Here one would expect English competition to have been particularly severe. Against that, transport
costs were high in the eighteenth century, and it has never proved
easy even for very efficient foreign manufacturers to undersell home
producers in the coarser grades of textiles. At all events, the history
of Scots wool making at the beginning of the eighteenth century is
obscure. Even less is known about the early eighteenth-century iron
industry, except that men and capital were drawn from England
after 1710. The state of the linen industry about the time of the
Union is also obscure, although it seems likely that it benefited from
the freeing of trade with England and the colonies. This industry
seems to have been very widely dispersed in the first two decades of

the eighteenth century, and was probably the major manufacturing industry in Scotland.

And what of Edinburgh, whose state the Union degraded and whose trade it took away? The judgment of Chambers has often been repeated:

> From the Union up to the middle of the century, the existence of
> the city seems to have been a perfect blank. No improvements
> of any sort, marked this period. On the contrary, an air of gloom
> and depression pervaded the city, such as distinguished its history
> at no former period . . . In short, this may be called, no less
> appropriately than emphatically, the *Dark Age* of Edinburgh.[4]

This is a picturesque, not to say a startling version of the ill-effects of Union. It does not accord with the facts. The north and east sides of Parliament Square, destroyed by fire in 1700, were rebuilt 'in a very handsome style'[5] between 1700 and 1715, and James's Court (after Milne's Court the second comparatively spacious building scheme carried out in the Old Town) was built about 1727. Also in this supposedly moribund city there was founded, in 1729, the Infirmary, which by royal charter became the Royal Infirmary in 1736; in 1733 the Orphan Hospital was begun, and in 1738 George Watson's Hospital, or school, began to be built. The Royal Bank, its foundation connected with the Treaty of Union, was set up in 1727, and Coutts's Bank, one of the most important private banks in Edinburgh in the eighteenth century, was in existence in the 1740s. The Friendly Insurance Office began work in Edinburgh in 1727, and in 1733 the Sun-Life Office established an Edinburgh branch. Not least significant, the Musical Society of Edinburgh, 'whose weekly concerts form one of the most elegant entertainments of that metropolis, was first instituted in the year 1728'.[6] The first daily newspaper destined to a long life was begun in 1705, the second in 1720, and the *Scots Magazine* was founded in 1739. In other words, once Edinburgh had had time to get over the initial effects of the Union and also, probably, the effects of the South Sea mania and its collapse in 1720, the evidence is that the city shared in the definite if gradual progress which the country was making before 1745.

The Jacobite Rebellion of 1745-46 threatened to overturn the peaceful circumstances in which this quite leisurely economic develop-

ment was going forward. But the rebellion failed, and its failure is one of the turning points of Scottish history. After the defeat of Prince Charles at Culloden, nothing could ever be the same in Scotland again. The 'long-disputed question of "the succession" was finally determined by the events of 1745',[7] and after that there was politically both far less to hope for and far less to fear in Scotland. Adherents of 'the King across the water' could no longer think of the restoration of the Stuarts as a practical possibility, and plotting

[5] *Parliament Square, about 1750. '170 years had breathed over it a grave grey hue.'* Arnot

25

and planning for that restoration virtually came to an end. Conversely, landed 'improvers', traders, capitalists of all kinds needed no longer to make any pessimistic allowance in their plans for the possibility of a political revolution on the grand scale. The long crusade for the Stuarts was at an end. Disaffection, open or secret, ceased to be an important factor in public life. And as a result, men – particularly those of wealth and importance – could concentrate their attention and energies as never before on economic activities and ambitions.

At no period surely did there ever appear a more general, or a better directed zeal for the improvement and prosperity of this country. Persons of every rank and denomination seem at length to be actuated by a truly public and national spirit . . . The great spring, however, which has set the whole in motion, is that spirit, liberality, and application, with which our nobility and landed gentlemen have of late engaged in every useful project . . . Animated by their example, persons of every rank and profession have caught the same spirit.[8]

What could be done depended to a very large extent on the state of communications. 'Good roads constitute one of the most important of all public improvements', remarked one observer. 'Without an easy communication among the various parts of a country, many of the most important improvements, particularly in agriculture, could not be effected at all.'[9] This line of thought was a popular one, and, as a result, a vast transport improvement was effected between the battle of Culloden and that of Waterloo – an improvement so vital and so extensive that only the drama of the much publicised Railway Age has been able to obscure it.

Travel in Scotland in the middle of the eighteenth century was slow, inconvenient, uncertain and hazardous. The roads, with a few exceptions, were bad to atrocious. The following description of all but the main roads of Forfarshire in 1813 could be generally applied to Scots roads in the eighteenth century:

. . . many of these roads are merely formed, by digging a ditch on each side of them, and throwing the spongy clay, here called mortar, upon the top of the road. Of course they are almost impassable, except in dry weather, or during hard frost. During

wet weather, horses sink to their bellies, and carts to their
axles; and it is with difficulty an animal can make his way
through them without any load. Where these roads are too
narrow, and are smothered with trees, they are often impassable,
even where they have been metalled, or laid with stones and
gravel. There are also a great many roads which still continue
in their antient state, and are mere tracts, over which horses,
and sometimes carts, find their way in dry weather.[10]

Conditions during autumn, winter and spring were much worse than
in the summer. In the 1760s the roads in Lanarkshire and around
Glasgow were commercially unusable for the carriage of grain until
they dried out in summer time: 'When our seed-time is over, and our
roads are become hard, then the great meal-trade of our farmers
commonly begins.'[11] It is significant that in most parts of the
country farm carts were not introduced until the eighteenth century.
Dependence on horse transport, each animal carrying only a small
weight, naturally required farmers to keep a great number of horses,
and these consumed the produce of the farms. The state of these
roads, bad and commonly impassable, was due to the casual use of
statute labour. Work was done, at infrequent intervals, by people
destitute of special skill, without competent supervision, reluctant
to work, and commonly resolved to do as little as possible. Gradually
from about the beginning of the last quarter of the century, this
statute labour began to be commuted into a money payment. Turnpikes also played a part, and by the 1790s were in operation in
several counties. At last the main roads began to improve.

Prior to 1800 or thereabouts this improvement was concentrated
on longer distance travel, and involved the building of a remarkable
number of important bridges in east central Scotland. The most
notable of these was also one of the first; the bridge built across the
Tay at Perth. This was one of the busiest river crossings in Scotland.
It is really astonishing that after the destruction of the old bridge by
a great flood in 1621, the crossing of the river had to be effected,
for no less than a hundred and fifty years, by means of a ferry. The
ferry-boats, 'which were always attended with considerable inconvenience and expense; and frequently with great danger',[12] numbered
about thirty by the middle of the century, some of them being em-

ployed occasionally as lighters on the river. Not until 1765 were plans begun for a new bridge, under the patronage of the Earl of Kinnoul. A subscription was opened; the Earl 'pledged a considerable part of his private fortune, to carry on the work'.[13] The Government supplied £4,000, and £700 per annum for fourteen years, all from the annexed estates, and a total of over £21,000 was shortly promised. The plans were prepared by Smeaton for a great bridge of ten arches with a total length of just over 900 feet; and the bridge was built between 1766 and 1771, at a cost of over £26,000. This was the greatest work of its kind in Scotland in the eighteenth century, and it went a long way to providing easy and safe communication between the northern and southern parts of the country. North of Perth, communications remained obviously inadequate for a few years longer, but numerous bridges, some of them quite large, were built across the Dee, the North Esk and the Isla in the last three decades of the century.

All this was most important work, making transport and communication easier, faster, cheaper. Travel by coach, at least along the main roads, became general throughout the lowlands. Instead of there being two stagecoach services in the whole of Scotland, slow and infrequent, as in 1760, there were over one hundred daily services by 1830, and they ran much faster; the time for the journey from Edinburgh to Glasgow, for example, was cut from a day and a half to 6 hours by 1799 and to $4\frac{1}{2}$ hours by 1830. From Perth five coaches set out each 'lawful' day to Edinburgh, Glasgow, Aberdeen, Inverness and Dunkeld; from Arbroath there were two daily services, one to Dundee and one to Montrose; in addition, there was a weekly service to Forfar. These achievements had been foreshadowed in the last decade of the eighteenth century. What was reserved for the nineteenth century was the improvement of the side, parish or country roads. Between 1800 and 1850 great numbers of these were straightened, widened, and metalled in a crude sort of way; innumerable fords with their ridin' stones and wadin' stones were replaced by stone bridges, while a large number of old bridges were replaced or widened. Countryside was joined to village and village to town as never before. The improvement of parish roads was one of the greatest changes made in early nineteenth-century Scotland.

The name of Telford is inseparably linked with civil engineering work in Scotland in this period. Telford's *First Highland Survey* was carried out in 1801. Its principal results were the resurrection of the proposal to build the Caledonian Canal and the proposal to improve a number of harbours for the fishing trade, the most important being Peterhead. The Second Report, submitted in 1803, was more concerned with internal communications between Lowlands and Highlands. The Government, which after 1745 had been anxious to 'pacify' the Highlands and was now concerned to stop their depopulation, accepted most of these proposals, and work went on from almost the date of the First Survey until Telford's death in 1834. Bridges were built, roads improved, and a score of harbours also benefited from Telford's attention. £20,000 was spent at Peterhead, £70,000 at Dundee between 1814 and 1825, where a new floating dock and a graving dock were built, and at Aberdeen between 1810 and 1814 work was carried out which completed that done by Smeaton in the previous century. Not connected with Telford's work were the very extensive improvements carried out at Leith. In 1799 the City of Edinburgh obtained powers to reconstruct the harbour at Leith according to plans previously prepared by Rennie. Two wet docks were built between 1801 and 1817 at a cost of about £175,000, in addition to three graving docks, warehouses and a drawbridge. In 1825 a further £240,000 was borrowed from the Government in order to extend the piers and breakwaters. Thus, with Government assistance, a completely rebuilt and greatly enlarged harbour, the most important on the east coast of Scotland, was created at Leith in the first three decades of the nineteenth century.

The work done did not stop the depopulation of the Highlands, and – except for the harbour-work – probably most of it was not of very great consequence for the economic development of Scotland as a whole. But canal building was highly beneficial. The Forth and Clyde Canal, completed in 1790, was intended to improve the food supply of Glasgow by cutting transport costs from the eastern counties by a half to two-thirds,[14] and also to facilitate the carriage of goods from Glasgow to the Forth estuary and so further east. It was eminently successful. The Monkland Canal, built between 1770 and 1790, was much more a coal canal. It too was successful, the output of the collieries of Old and New Monkland doubling, largely as a result of the cheap transport offered by the canal, between 1790 and 1810. The Union Canal, built for 'the conveyance of coals, of manure, of goods, and passengers',[15] linked Edinburgh to the Forth and Clyde Canal in 1822. In addition to these canals (and some others of lesser importance) a great deal of work was done on improving the navigation of the Clyde, 'the greatest artificial waterway in Scotland',[16] from the early 1770s to the setting up of the Clyde Trust in 1809 and on into the 1830s.

This heavy programme of capital works, the great bulk of it executed in the forty years between 1780 and 1820, radically altered the conditions of economic activity in Scotland and left scarcely any aspects of life quite untouched. Men and women could travel as never

before. Journeys once dangerous and taking several days were now
safe and could be completed in a few hours; young ladies and their
mamas could make expeditions on any day of the week which had
formerly been so troublesome and dangerous as to be almost entirely
reserved for the men. The transport of goods was likewise greatly
facilitated. Food for the growing towns was carried along the canals
and the roads direct to the towns; or to the ports for shipment along
the coast; or to and from the great markets where farmers sold to
merchants engaged in the wholesale trade – the cattle market on the
sands at Dumfries, for example, the market for oats at Barnhall of
Cambusnethan, which supplied the population of Glasgow, the great
grain market at Haddington, or, most important of all, the market
for cattle, sheep and oats at Dalkeith. Raw materials for industry
– coal, flax, raw cotton, stone, timber, leather, wool rags – also
moved down the roads and canals into the manufacturing centres,
and in return came manufactured goods, iron ware from Carron,
cotton cloth from Deanston, paper from Colinton and Penicuik,
books from Edinburgh and Perth, paint from Leith, steam-engines
from Glasgow and North Berwick, gunpowder – of all things – from
Roslin. Furthermore, the roads and canals now connected the harbours with all parts of the country, so that the trade of the ports was
much enlivened not only by their own improvement but also by
better landward connections.

Every kind of economic activity benefited from this great break-
through in the field of transport. Consider, for example, agriculture.
Agriculture was not only the most widely dispersed industry, it was
also the biggest throughout this period, both in terms of the employment which it gave and of the contribution which it made to the
country's income. Improved transport gave farmers new market
opportunities. But it also helped agriculture to develop better
methods. First, in a general way, it facilitated the spread of new
ideas. Generally speaking, agricultural improvements were introduced in Scotland not by tenants but by landowners, and any landowner, large or small, was likely to have travelled out of his own
district, to England or to the Continent, or at least as far as Edinburgh; and to have learned on his travels of new ideas in use elsewhere. (Barclay of Ury, we are told, 'acquired his ideas of Agri-

culture on the fertile plains of Norfolk'.[17] Robert Scott of Dunninauld, pioneer improver in the 1750s and Member of Parliament for the county of Forfar, 'in going up and coming down from London . . . was not inattentive to the system of agriculture followed in England. Finding it superior to any hitherto practised in Scotland, he tried to follow it . . .'[18]) The movement of ideas, like that of stage coaches, grew considerably faster between the early eighteenth and the early nineteenth century. Secondly, the roads and canals helped in the actual introduction of agricultural improvements. Lime, for example, became more freely available. In the mid-eighteenth century, proximity to a lime quarry was a considerable agricultural advantage. As roads improved, this ceased to be the case. Also the supply of lime was increased by the better supply of coal used in burning the lime. A further point is that better roads made it worth while to manufacture fertilisers in or near the seaports, using imported raw materials. A works of this kind, grinding bones and rape-cakes brought from Germany, existed at Cockenzie in the 1830s.

More efficient use of labour also was connected with the supply of coal. Fuel was scarce in late eighteenth and in early nineteenth century Scotland. Coal was dear and in most country places not available; 'burn-wood' was scarce; and the result was that many districts relied on peat. But getting a good supply of peat usually involved much hard physical work. The mosses used were often steep and usually far-distant.

> During the season, in which the poor people are employed in carrying [peat] out of the hills, they go to the moss, or so far in their way towards it in the evening; lie out in the open air all night, and load their horses in the morning. The great distance, badness of the roads, weakness of their horses, and scantiness of pasture, impose this cruel necessity. There is no cart road to the moss, peat and turf being carried by means of an awkward apparatus, on the backs of small, half-starved horses.[19]

This description, from the parish of Dornoch, is more unfavourable than most; but it was widely appreciated that 'the precious time consumed in digging, winning, and leading home peats, would be much better employed in improving the fields'[20] – if only fuel were more

5. Milne's Court, the main entrance.

32

readily available. Better transport partially solved this problem in the first two decades of the nineteenth century. Dornoch, for example, began to import coal from Newcastle about 1810. In many other areas coal began to be used by ordinary people for the first time, and although it remained dear in many inland areas in the 1830s – in Tweedsmuir it was almost a novelty in 1834 – an extensive diversion of agricultural man-power to the winning of peat was no longer necessary.

What of the rest of the improvements? One of the most important items was drainage. In parish after parish hundreds of acres of marshy land were recovered and put under the plough; in a few instances, even, the very peat mosses themselves were converted into agricultural land. All told, tens of thousands of acres were involved. 'The places which old people recollect of, fifty or sixty years ago, as dangerous for man or beast to tread on from their boggy nature, are now bearing luxuriant crops of corn.'[21] The result was that the yields commonly expected of every kind of crop rose steeply throughout Scotland.

The crops which farmers grew were changing, also. By the 1750s the growing of clover was becoming general in the more advanced parts of the country and the value of turnips and potatoes became fully appreciated a little later. The new availability of turnips, in turn, greatly encouraged the raising of cattle and sheep. The small Highland breed of cattle and the other nondescript varieties of the mid-eighteenth century gave way to the breeds developed in Aberdeenshire, Ayrshire and Galloway. A high proportion of the stock reared was sold, at such local markets as Crieff, Falkirk and Dumfries, to drovers for the English market. This trade was general throughout Scotland by 1800 but was especially important in the south-west and north-east where cattle rearing was increasingly recognised as 'the most lucrative part of the farming business'.[22] Sheep farming was developed on similar lines, with the additional encouragement of the rising demand for wool for the mills of Galashiels and Hawick. A switch-over to sheep farming was profitable principally in the upland districts and areas of poorer soil, and thus sheep farming spread particularly in hilly districts and in the Highlands. Here, it wrought great changes. The majority of landholders had no security

6. A stone's throw from South Bridge and the Tron, the 'south back' of the High Street retains local scale and vernacular flavour.

of tenure, and were miserably poor. As sheep farming spread north of Perthshire from about 1770, the evictions of the tenantry began, reaching large proportions after 1800.

As regards manufacturing industry, where development was very rapid, the making of linen was probably, until almost the very end of the eighteenth century, the principal occupation. The trade had its centre in Forfarshire, but was also important in Ayrshire, Lanarkshire and Perthshire. Yet most of this was comparatively new. The manufacture of *osnaburgs*, for which Arbroath was famous, was begun there only in the 1740s; from this, 'the rise and progress of the trade and manufactures of Arbroath are to be dated'.[23] Linen manufacture was begun in Aberdeen after 1746, the manufacture of sail-cloth only in 1795. Scores of bleachfields and flax spinning mills were established all over Scotland from the 1760s, and regional specialisation became a feature of the trade.

The other main textile industry of eighteenth-century Scotland was the manufacture of wool. It was in the 1770s that this industry seems to have begun to make real progress. In Galashiels, one of the greatest centres of the trade in the nineteenth century, output, small in the 1770s, seems to have rather more than doubled between then and 1790.[24] Spinning with water-power was introduced into the town in the 1790s, and no fewer than five new mills were erected between 1792 and 1804; further progress was made after the war. In the 1770s knitting frames were introduced into the hosiery trade. Their use was gradually established in southern Scotland, and in the early decades of the nineteenth century Hawick became recognised as the new centre of a much-expanded hosiery trade, followed by Dumfries, where the industry had been unimportant before about 1810. In the 1780s Kilmarnock emerged as the main centre for carpet weaving, and by 1825 carpets were being exported to London, Dublin and the United States. It was the cotton industry, however, which was the prodigious innovation of late eighteenth-century Scotland. It not only made an almost novel product; it grew faster than any industry had ever grown before, and it used revolutionary methods. These methods, even in the early 1780s, involved the use of machinery driven by water-power (steam-power came in after 1800) and the employment of large numbers of work people concentrated in factories. Such buildings had previously been unknown. The first cotton spinning mill in Scotland was built by English enterprise in 1779. Eight years later there were nineteen such mills in Scotland, and by 1812 there were 120. Between 1796 and 1833 cotton spinning capacity multiplied over sixfold.

The rise of the cotton industry was from an early date part and parcel of the growth of Glasgow. Before 1800 Glasgow was one town among several engaged in the cotton industry – there were mills in Perth, Aberdeen, Ayr and Stirling besides a fair number on the banks of fast flowing streams in country districts. But by 1830 the supremacy of Glasgow was established; some nine-tenths of the cotton spinning capacity of Scotland was located in the town. This did not kill the industry in other districts, however, for high quality work was, to begin with, beyond the reach of the factories; there was still room, in the first decade or two of the nineteenth century, for the small establishment and even for the individual spinning in his garret or cottage. Also, and for considerably longer, there was room for the handloom weaver. Although weaving by power was coming in towards the end of the war, there were still almost 50,000 handlooms for cotton in the Lowlands as late as 1838,[25] many of them, especially in Ayrshire, Lanarkshire and Renfrewshire, engaged in the highly skilled trade of flowered muslin.

The cotton industry was thus established as the greatest industry in Scotland by the early nineteenth century. The relative position of the iron industry is difficult to determine, but it is certain that output in Scotland was extremely small and that the industry remained comparatively unimportant until the Carron Ironworks was built in 1759. But Carron, which obtained equipment and skilled labour from England, was novel both in the scale of its conception and in its reliance on native ore supplies. Its success was at first doubtful, but its opportunity came with the demand for munitions in 1775, when war with America broke out, and it was shortly exporting the most modern types of gun to Russia, Denmark and Spain.

The success of this plant firmly established iron making in Scotland. Output, almost certainly less than 2,000 tons per annum before 1786, rose to some 28,000 tons by 1828. This iron found a variety of uses. As already mentioned, Carron made and exported cannon; the company also made stoves, grates, kettles and agricultural implements. But most companies sold their pig-iron to small foundries scattered all over the country. These small foundries made machine parts, wheels, axles, boilers and pipes, spades and ploughs, all for local sale. Thus, although the manufacture of pig-iron was concentrated in comparatively few places, its working up into finished articles gave employment in many towns and villages as well as to those employed in road, canal and sea transport.

Nor is this the end of the matter. Modern iron making and iron working needs coal. Coal had been mined in Scotland for centuries, and the coal trade was important before 1650. There are no reliable figures before 1854, but it is certain that output rose sharply from about 1760. According to Robert Bald, writing in 1812, output had increased three or fourfold in the preceding fifty years, and his very rough estimates appear to put it, for 1812, in the neighbourhood of three-quarters of a million tons.[26] The reasons which Bald gives for this increase are interesting. They are: the rise in the standard of living leading to an increase in domestic consumption for heating; the growth of industry and the use of steam-engines; and the burning of lime, principally for agricultural purposes. The largest industrial use was in the manufacture of iron. Labour for the mines seems to have been scarce,[27] but throughout the period an increasing number of villages came to depend mainly on the mines to give employment to men (and women) as hewers, bearers, gin-men, overseers, cinder-burners and – a numerically important occupation in many districts – carters.

These changes which were made in transport, agriculture and industry caused a great increase in the volume of production of goods and services in the seventy years between 1760 and 1830. How great that increase was we do not know; it was certainly greater than had been achieved in any preceding period of the same length. Against this must be set the fact that population also rose. In 1760 the population of Scotland was probably slightly over 1·3m[28]; by 1830 it was almost 2·35m, an increase of 80 per cent. It seems beyond question, however, that output must have increased much more. Whether these two sets of changes produced a higher standard of living for the majority of the population is an open question, but it seems likely that they did. Factory employment was relatively well-paid, for men, women, and to a lesser extent for children. Between 1760 and 1830 factory wages, in real terms, probably rose slightly; and what matters far more, a larger proportion of the working population was earning these higher wages in each successive decade. As regards skilled men outside the factories – ploughmen, masons, carpenters – their money wages seem to have rather more than doubled between about 1760 and 1790, and then to have reached a level about 50 per cent to 60 per cent higher than the 1790 level by 1830. These money increases should have kept the recipients definitely ahead of the rise in prices before the war, and they indicate some further betterment of their living standards between 1790 and 1830. The real wages of unskilled workers seem also to have risen, although not by very much. These men and women – the great bulk of the working population – had to spend most of their money on food. We know that labourers' money wages approximately doubled between about 1760 and 1790, and then rose by about a third between 1790 and 1830. Did these increases enable the ordinary worker to maintain his standard of living in the face of rising and latterly of falling prices? It is here that accurate knowledge of the behaviour of food prices would be very valuable. A common statement in the 1790s was that prices had doubled in the preceding forty to fifty years. But the evidence is that whereas meat prices doubled, the prices of wheat, barley and oats rose by only some 30 per cent. This seems to suggest at least a slight rise in the living standards of ordinary people. During the war they experienced great changes of fortune, and if there was a discernable trend it was probably downwards. After the war the fall in prices was very uneven, so that by 1830 grain prices were little or no higher than in 1790, whereas meat prices were considerably higher. This would suggest that by 1830 the living standards of the poor were probably a little above what they had been about 1790.[29]

These tentative conclusions are supported by a few other considerations. First, reduced transport costs lowered the final price of innumerable articles, some of them items of common consumption. The most striking instance is coal, which was very dear in many country areas in the eighteenth century.[30] The price of tiles, timber and other building materials must also have been reduced in this way. Secondly, technical progress rapidly reduced the cost of manufacture in many trades. Cotton is the outstanding example:

In 1786 the yarn known in the trade as No. 100 sold at £1:18/- a pound. Seven years afterwards the price had fallen to 15/1. In 1800 the price was 9/5, and in 1832 2/11. The cost price of a piece of calico was £1:3:10½ in 1814. In 1822 the same could be made for 8/11, and in 1832 for 5/10¾.[31]

No wonder that cotton gowns became increasingly 'attainable by women in humble circumstances'![32] And this new capacity to purchase articles on the borderline between necessities and luxuries was not limited to cotton: cheaper kettles, glassware, stoves, tea and crockery all contributed to raise the standard of living of ordinary people. Lastly, there is the testimony of observers, who were almost unanimously of the view that the basic standard of living rose in this period. The districts experiencing least improvement seem to have been either those most remote from the main currents of economic life or those where these currents flowed most turbulently. At sleepy Speymouth, for example, 'Scarcely any change has taken place among the small farmers, farm-servants, day-labourers, etc., since 1792, as to their mode of living – with the exception of a greater consumption of tea'[33]; and at bustling Blantyre no more could be said than that 'the comfort and intelligence of the people keep pace with their numbers'.[34] But even in and around places such as these skilled workmen, petty tradesmen and the tenants of moderate-sized farms lived in better houses, ate better, dressed better. And in the country generally the situation seems on balance to have improved. In Glasgow, working people periodically faced typhus and unemployment; but they were 'better lodged, clothed, and fed, than formerly; and since the formation of the Water Companies, they are more cleanly in their houses, and healthy in their persons'.[35] There were better houses in Dornoch too, 'having chimneys',[36] and in such diverse places as Moulin, Dalkeith and Aberlady. Gas-lighting was introduced into many Scottish towns between 1815 and 1830, and pavements for those on foot became commoner. Everywhere, throughout the period, dress was improving; tea, snuff and tobacco were coming a little more into use – 'their dress more gay and expensive; their living more plentiful . . . there is an imitation of superiors creeping into the country.'[37] The only serious drawback which observers constantly mentioned was drunkenness. A taste for whisky developed and became widespread in Scotland in the eighteenth century. Inept fiscal arrangements, which made illicit distilling a minor but important industry,[38] were altered in 1823, and legitimate distilleries took over some of the work of the illicit stills. But this did not reduce the amount of drinking, which seems, if anything, to have increased. It was a common calculation in the towns that there was a whisky shop to every twelve, fifteen or eighteen families. Whisky – 'emphatically the curse of North Britain' – was an important contributory cause of some of the worst misery among the poor in early nineteenth-century Scotland. The temptation to drink was omnipresent:

> There are 32 shops for the sale of spirits in this parish, which is just thirty too many, and the effect is as pernicious as possible. It is just so many persons scattered over the parish with their families and relations, whose living depends on the success with which they can prevail upon their neighbours to drink. One man is paid for teaching sobriety, but thirty-two have an interest in defeating his efforts, and human nature is on their side.[39]

Of course people remained very poor, in spite of improvement. The staple diet consisted of meal, milk and potatoes, with the addition of fish for those who lived on or near the coast. Of every parish it could have been said, as it was of Banff, that there existed 'a considerable number of persons, who, if not in absolutely destitute, are in very straitened circumstances'.[40] And those actually destitute created a problem attracting much attention, their numbers increasing in the period. In villages and country places the decline of spinning and other cottage industries meant that there was no longer employment suitable for old people; in larger towns people congregated looking for work, and unemployment was sometimes rife. Assessments for the support of the poor became more and more common, although there was widespread reluctance to admit their necessity. But in spite of these considerations there is no doubt that the writers of both the Old and the New Statistical Account were definitely of the view that the standard of living of the people was rising.

This rise was certainly less than the increase of national wealth. For when we turn from the lives of ordinary folk to those of the comfortably off and the wealthy, we find a picture of indisputable improvement. Both the so-called middle-class and the rich grew in numbers, and their comforts increased. The power to save and to invest, the power to spend and to live well – these were the hallmarks of progress. Industrialists grew more- numerous, new techniques became available in many industries and were taken up, profits were often high. Landlords improved their properties out of all recognition and drew incomes from them on a scale hitherto unimagined. Rents frequently rose five, six or even sevenfold between 1770 and 1830; and this is separate from the fact that during the war, when food prices rose very high, land was frequently sold at five or six times its valuation of only fifteen or twenty years before. Merchants shared in the general increase of activity, helped by cheaper and swifter transport and an improving competitive position abroad. In spite of recurrent crises; in spite of the war; in spite of depopulation in some areas and the pressure of immigrants into others; in spite of the weight of poverty which continued in every county and even increased in several – in spite of all this, Scotland in these years enjoyed a tremendous and sustained rise of national prosperity.

This economic miracle – for such, after centuries of near stagnation, it surely was – was bound up with one other great and significant change in the conditions of Scottish life: a rapid growth of towns and of the proportion of the population living in them.

In 1801 the number of people living in the six largest towns in Scotland was 228,427. This number was a little over one-seventh of the total population.[41] Glasgow, having overtaken Edinburgh in size during the last few decades of the eighteenth century, was the largest town, with a population of 77,000. Edinburgh had 67,000. Other towns were very small, not one of them with a population of over 10,000. By 1831 the situation had substantially altered. Those living in the largest six towns now formed not one-seventh but one-fifth of the population.[42] Glasgow had left the capital far behind, and its population was now over 200,000 compared to Edinburgh's 136,000. No other town grew as fast as Glasgow in these decades, but a few grew faster than Edinburgh: Aberdeen, Hawick, Kilmarnock. Most of the smaller towns, however, occupied much the same position in 1831 as in 1801; growing only a little faster than the population of Scotland as a whole, they remained small. Their importance thus declined relatively to that of the largest towns,[43] and the modern pattern began to emerge; dominance by a few cities.

Men and women moved into these towns usually in search of employment ('A perpetual influx of the unemployed from the north press into Edinburgh and its vicinity')[44] or in response to the lure of higher wages. Many rural districts were losing population about 1790, due to enclosure and the demolition of cottar houses: 'The village of Gosford is entirely destroyed, and that of Balncrief falling into decay'[45]; of Longniddry it was remarked forty years later that there had been 'a considerable number of cot-houses, not a vestige of which now remains and the place where they stood is under crop and very productive.'[46] The clearances in the Highlands, of course, were on a larger scale, a source of distress and misery and causing a flow of population towards the towns. On the side of the towns, industrial employment was often the attraction. In the 1790s Culross was losing population because of 'the flourishing state of manufactures, especially of late, in Dunfermline and Glasgow, and the numerous buildings and public works carrying on in Edinburgh, by which all the surplus hands have been drained off'.[47] In Glasgow, in 1841, out of 122,000 people in occupations employing at least 300 people each, more than 20,000 were in the cotton trade. In the next ten years cotton provided enough additional employment to support the whole of the increase in the population of Glasgow. The growth of Kilmarnock in the same period can be explained largely in terms of the carpet manufacture. Hawick grew chiefly because of the development of fine woollens. But the explanation is too simple if it is confined to manufacturing in the narrow sense, or to the growth of factory enterprises. Aberdeen, for example, grew in this period because it was a notable seaport, a channel for goods to and from the thriving mercantile, agricultural and – to a lesser extent – industrial north-east of Scotland. But the best example of a town whose growth did not depend on manufacturing industry is Edinburgh. Edinburgh was a consumption-oriented town if ever there was one. What were the principal occupations in Edinburgh in 1841?[48] Aside from domestic service, that grand employer of female labour throughout the nineteenth century, they were, in descending order of importance – boot and shoemaker; common labourer; dressmaker; tailor; clerk, legal and commercial; laundry worker; blacksmith; porter etc.; cabinet maker and upholsterer – and so on down a long list of handicrafts and service trades. In some kinds of business Edinburgh excelled: in coach-making, for example (coaches were exported to Russia and the Baltic), in printing, book-binding and publishing. But these were not factory industries. Nor, in any case, was manufacture of any kind the chief business of the town. It is not clear that it had a chief business – although the 913 writers and attorneys distinctly suggest one, along with their clerks.[49] But although it was a city of law it was still more a city of infinite variety; a city of professional service, of craft service, of menial service; a city of handsome homes, fine public buildings, wealth and enjoyment.

This character it acquired through the ambitions and exertions of many men. The growth of wealth in Scotland after the middle of the eighteenth century was of course a prerequisite. Profits made in industry and trade, rents drawn from mining and agriculture in an increasingly prosperous countryside – these certainly formed the financial basis of private development in Edinburgh; and through the banks they also helped to finance the schemes of the Town Council. But what the Town Council could do, and what private citizens would agree to do, depended very much on the organisation and status of the Town Council, on its relations with the Government in London, and on the distribution of power throughout society: in a word, on the state of politics. And in the political no less than in the economic sphere great changes took place.

A series of Acts designed to break up the clan system and weaken if not destroy the power of the chiefs was passed immediately after 1746. Prominent among these were the Disarming Act, the Act for 'restraining the use of the Highland dress', the Act which annexed forfeited Jacobite estates to the Crown, and the Heritable Jurisdictions Act. These measures not only diminished the power of the Highland chiefs – men like the Duke of Gordon and the Duke of Argyll; they correspondingly and greatly increased the power of the principal law officers of Scotland, and especially of the Lord Advocate, on whose advice the majority of legal and political appointments in Scotland were made. This office, now of cardinal importance, was held by several able and influential men in the second half of the eighteenth century, including Robert Dundas (Lord Arniston the elder), his son, also Robert Dundas, and his grandson, yet another Robert Dundas, who was, in Cockburn's words, 'Lord Advocate in the most alarming times, and at a period when extravagant and arbitrary powers were ascribed to that office'.[50]

But it was Henry Dundas, second son of Lord Arniston the elder, who became the supreme political authority in Scotland. Henry Dundas was born and educated in Edinburgh. At the age of twenty-four, when he had been only three years at the bar, he became Solicitor General for Scotland; eight years later, in 1774, he was elected to Parliament for Midlothian; and from that time onward he devoted himself to politics and lived principally in London. When the Coalition Ministry was dissolved in 1783 and Pitt formed a new government, Dundas became Treasurer of the Navy, and soon afterwards was given the office of Keeper of the Scottish Signet for life, and the patronage of all places in Scotland.[51] Surrounded thenceforth by political wire-pullers and expectant placemen, it was Dundas's genius to enjoy political omnipotence and yet to retain his hold upon the affections of the majority of people in Scotland. His talents were outstanding. He possessed, said Lord Kames, quickness of mind, oratorical gifts, a comprehensive understanding; and to these he added moderation of opinion, and exceptional powers of administration. Especially in Scotland, his position was impregnable; for he was at once well connected, energetic and prudent; and his manner, frank, gentlemanlike and friendly, made him acceptable and even popular in quarters where his political opinions were not shared.

In his time, from his appointment to be Lord Advocate in 1776 to his fall from power, as Lord Melville, in 1806 – and indeed for the following quarter of a century also – there were two issues which dominated the political life of Scotland: parliamentary reform; and burgh reform. The second of these was of direct importance to the development of Edinburgh.

Inevitably, Dundas was an interested party in both issues. His chief source of power, says Omond,

> was the hold which he had over the representation of Scotland.
> He was the great election agent for Government in Scotland.
> Peers and members of the House of Commons were alike his
> nominees. It was he who prepared the list of representative
> peers, which, in accordance with the custom of those days, was
> sent down from London and meekly accepted by the nobles who
> met in Holyrood at each general election. As for the House of
> Commons, a consideration of the small number of persons who
> had the franchise explains the ease with which the elections were
> controlled. At the general election of 1790, when the power of
> Dundas was at its height, the number of county voters in
> Scotland was two thousand six hundred and twenty four . . .
> The general election created little excitement. In Midlothian,
> which returned the Lord Advocate, Robert Dundas [Henry
> Dundas's half-brother], and in twenty other counties, there was
> no contest . . . The total number of burgh electors in Scotland
> was twelve hundred and eighty-nine. The largest constituencies
> were those of Edinburgh, Glasgow, and Selkirk, which had each
> thirty-three voters; but the average constituency numbered about
> nineteen. Edinburgh alone had a member for itself. The other
> royal burghs of Scotland were arranged in fourteen groups or
> districts, and each district returned one member to Parliament.
> The electors were the town councillors of the various burghs.
> They appointed delegates. The delegates met at the head
> burgh of the district, and chose the member. In 1790 there were
> contested elections in seven of the fourteen districts. For
> Edinburgh Henry Dundas was himself returned without
> opposition . . . The county franchise was, by such means,
> controlled by a few persons, most of whom supported the
> Ministry.[52]

The town councillors, who alone had the right of voting for the burgh members, were self-elected.

This was the system, allied to a similar system within the burghs, to which so many people objected both while Dundas was in power and increasingly for a quarter of a century after his departure from office. There was an attempt at burgh reform in 1782, and in 1787 a scheme was submitted to Parliament. But the Tory leaders, including Pitt and Dundas, opposed it; and even very moderate proposals could not be agreed because some men thought they went too far and others that they did not go nearly far enough. In any case, it soon became evident that the essential step towards the cure of all political grievances was a measure reforming the representation of the people. But after 1790 any movement towards either burgh or national electoral reform had to make headway against the general alarm inspired by the principles and practice of the French Revolution. This 'was, or was made, the all in all. Everything, not this or that thing, but literally everything, was soaked in this one event.'[53] Fear bred repression. A series of State Trials for sedition, seditious practices or the circulating of seditious writings took place in 1793 and 1794, many of them conducted by the judges – including the notorious Lord Braxfield – with scant regard for the correctness of legal procedure. From then until the end of the war the reform movement made only very gradual progress.

The fall of Lord Melville in 1806 was the first notable encouragement which the Whigs in Edinburgh received. From that date their influence gradually increased, until at last, in 1830, the Whig Party came to power. Francis Jeffrey was appointed Lord Advocate, and Henry Cockburn became Solicitor General for Scotland. The country was face to face with the question of Parliamentary Reform. On 1 March 1831 Lord John Russell explained the Government's plans for Scotland. There were to be fifty Scots members in the House of Commons instead of forty-five. The corporations of the burghs were to lose their exclusive right to send members to Parliament, and, instead, every ten pound householder was to have a vote. Similar arrangements were proposed for the counties. By these means, it was reckoned, the number of parliamentary voters in Scotland would be increased from about three thousand to about sixty thousand.

Petitions in favour of the bill 'whitened the benches of the House of Commons like a snowstorm'. But the Government was defeated in April and a general election began. The contest took place in the midst of uproar and confusion.

At Jedburgh, Sir Walter Scott, then in failing health, went to vote for the Tory candidate. He was groaned and cursed at on his way to the polling place. A woman spat at him from a window; and as he drove home cries of 'Burke him!' were heard from an excited crowd. Other disgraceful scenes took place in various parts of the country. The polling for Lanarkshire took place in a church. A furious mob filled the gallery, from which stones and mud were thrown at the member for the county. He was returned; but when the poll was over an escort of soldiers was needed to conduct him through the angry crowd which surrounded the building.[54]

In Edinburgh, the very heart of Scots Toryism, where the sole electors were the thirty members of the Town Council, there was a contested election for the first time in forty years. Jeffrey, the Whig candidate, was not elected by the councillors in spite of overwhelming popular support; in the resultant riot the Lord Provost was very nearly flung over the North Bridge,[55] and fighting between rioters and troops continued well into a bright moonlight night.

This was the last Edinburgh election under the old system. The third Reform Bill finally passed the House of Lords in June 1832, and the corresponding measure for Scotland in July. There was tremendous rejoicing. When, two years later, Lord Grey visited Scotland,

> his reception was like a royal progress. At Floors, where he was the guest of the Duke of Roxburghe, a fete was held in his honour. He spent the Sunday night before he entered Edinburgh at Oxenfoord, the seat of Sir John Dalrymple . . . and left the parish church of Cranston after service between two rows of persons assembled from all parts of the country, who uncovered as he passed. On the following day, Monday the 15th of September, when he entered Edinburgh, the streets and house-tops were more crowded than they had been since the day when George the Fourth came to Holyrood.[56]

The triumph of the Whigs was of immense importance for every town in Scotland and not least for Edinburgh because it now became possible to deal with the question of burgh reform. The system which required reform was very ancient. The basic Act affecting the

City of Edinburgh had been passed in 1469. Its most important provisions were that the retiring members of the Council should choose their successors and that the retiring Council and the new Council together should choose the office-bearers for the coming year. The ancient rights of the citizens to vote for the city rulers were thus taken away, and an entail of municipal rule and influence was put in their place. Similar arrangements came into force in the other royal burghs. In 1583 another Act was passed which settled the membership of the Edinburgh Town Council at twenty-five, consisting of seventeen merchants and eight craftsmen. Other modifications were made in 1658, 1673 and 1730. But none of these later provisions touched the principles established in 1469 and 1583. The town was governed by a strictly limited number of merchants and craftsmen; to be elected to the Town Council it was all but essential that a man belong either to the wealthy and exclusive Merchant Company or to one of the incorporated trades; the only people with a vote in the election of the new Town Council were the members of the existing Town Council. The principles of the closed shop and the self-perpetuation of power could hardly go further.

Nor was this all. A seat on the Town Council brought to its possessor money as well as power and prestige. Councillors were not embarrassed by any self-denying ordinances:

on the contrary, when any public work was to be undertaken
a preference was given to councillors as a matter of course:
and the same favour was extended in respect of public appointments. The deacons of trades were *ex officio* members of Council
and these offices were matters of keen contest, being in
fact worth a good deal of money. The deacon of the masons
claimed as a right to be employed as builder to the Corporation and to charge his own prices without check. The
other deacons expected like favours and thus things went comfortably round until interrupted by the advent of burgh
reform.[57]

The amount of feeling raised by helpless disapproval of the secret, arbitrary and sometimes corrupt proceedings of the Council (disapproval which was occasionally, no doubt, not unmixed with envy) is hard to imagine. A passage from Cockburn's *Memorials,* written

47

in the 1820s but not published until 1840, gives some idea of it. The Council he says,

> met in a low, dark, blackguard-looking room, entering from a covered passage which connected the south-west corner of the Parliament Square with the Lawnmarket. At its Lawnmarket end this covered passage opened out on the south side of 'The Heart of Midlothian' . . . The Council Chamber entered directly from this passage, and, if it had remained, would have been in the east end of the Writers' (Signet) Library. The chamber was a low-roofed room, very dark, and very dirty, with some small dens off it for clerks.
>
> Within this Pandemonium sat the town-council, omnipotent, corrupt, impenetrable. Nothing was beyond its grasp; no variety of opinion disturbed its unanimity, for the pleasure of Dundas was the sole rule for every one of them. Reporters, the fruit of free discussion, did not exist; and though they had existed, would not have dared to disclose the proceedings. Silent, powerful, submissive, mysterious, and irresponsible, they might have been sitting in Venice.[58]

Cockburn was a Whig, and his picture of Tory rule is no doubt a little highly coloured. Moreover, modifications of the system were gradually introduced. As town development came to require additional powers, these were not automatically vested in the Town Council. Private Acts of Parliament were obtained, sponsored by the Town Council, which established Commissioners for special purposes. The first local statute of this kind established Commissioners for the government of the so-called Southern districts, districts which lay outside the Royalty and which were therefore not within the jurisdiction of the Town Council. This was in 1771, and the Commissioners in question were, to some extent at least, popularly elected. In the following year another Act gave powers for lighting, cleansing and watching the districts of Canongate, Pleasance and Leith Wynd. In 1805 and 1812 Acts were passed which introduced a unified and potentially efficient police system throughout Edinburgh and the latter of these Acts also gave to the Commissioners appointed by the Act powers to regulate the lighting and cleansing of the town. But in the important series of Acts which constituted

7. Parliament Square. The coat of arms above the old Exchequer Court doorway.

48

Commissions to carry out public works, the Commissioners were nominated in the Acts, not elected, and established and powerful interests were always well represented. Thus the important Improvement Act of 1785 appointed as Commissioners Henry Dundas, the Lord Provost, the Lord Advocate, Sir William Forbes, Lord Braxfield, two town councillors, two merchants, a Writer to the Signet, and James Brown, the creator of George Square. Later Commissions were similarly constituted. It is hard to believe that these Commissions were not, in fact, instruments of patronage, although they also seem to have been a device to secure a limited sharing of power with 'outsiders'. This system continued until 1831.

The victory of reform in Scotland was a victory for the people. It was also a victory for the Whig lawyers in Edinburgh. They were the leaders of public opinion, and it was they whom the Tory Party and the Town Council had to fear. Men like Henry Cockburn, Henry Erskine and Francis Jeffrey could think, write and speak; training in law made them a tactical match for their opponents; the Law Courts gave them the opportunity to be heard in public; their social position set them above considerations of political intimidation and likewise above short-run considerations of personal advancement. They were not quite alone. There were active and influential men among the eighty or so members of the Royal College of Physicians, and among the bankers, of whom by far the most notable was Sir William Forbes of Pitsligo.[59] There was also the University. Of the handful of professors in the University – the 'Town's College', financed and largely administered by the Town Council, like almost everything else – two or three gave valuable support to the reform movement; notably Dugald Stewart, John Playfair and Andrew Dalzel. But their position was difficult, and their contribution correspondingly small.

There was thus no other group in Edinburgh than the Whig lawyers to act as a counter-balance to the Town Council. This was partly because no institutions of an independent character were allowed to exist except the church, which took no part in politics, and partly because the lawyers were the only large, highly-trained professional body. There were hundreds of lawyers in Edinburgh in the later eighteenth century, members of the Faculty of Advocates or Writers to the Signet, all working in or near the central law

8. Edinburgh, looking w from the Crags to the Castle.

courts of Scotland, which were, as they always had been, in Edinburgh. Their work was intimately connected with the affairs of the landed gentry and the nobility:

> At the end of the eighteenth century and for very many years
> to come, nearly all the landed proprietors in Scotland had their
> legal advisers in Edinburgh, Writers to the Signet for the most
> part, who made their wills and their complex family trusts,
> arranged the heritable bonds which were then almost the sole
> means of investment or of estate financing, and guided through
> the Courts the lengthy and involved lawsuits, without which, it
> almost seemed, no gentleman's estate would be complete.[60]

No professional group compared with them in numbers and influence through the whole of this critical period, and in both numbers and influence they continually increased.

It was thus under the old and largely unreformed Town Council that Edinburgh tackled the ambitious projects and the pressing problems of the late eighteenth and early nineteenth centuries. The lawyers were a restraining and stabilising influence, and they helped to give continuity to Edinburgh's development even after burgh reform. The Commissioners brought special knowledge and shared some of the responsibility. But broadly speaking it was oligarchic rule, the rule of tradesmen and a few merchants backed by men of taste, which started and carried out, or facilitated, the great developments.

All towns of any consequence undertook building programmes in these decades. In Glasgow, the first house in Buchanan Street was built in 1777, George Square and streets to the east were planned in 1782, and St Andrew's Square, Brunswick Street, Hutcheson Street and John Street were all laid out before 1790. In Aberdeen, Union Street, George Street and King Street were laid out and Union Bridge built in the early years of the nineteenth century. Perth, taking advantage of the new opportunities provided by Smeaton's bridge, opened George Street in 1772, Charlotte Street, going west from the bridge and leading to much early nineteenth-century building, and on to the Dunkeld road, in 1783, while elegant Marshall Place, facing the South Inch, began to be built in 1801. Dundee obtained a Bill in 1825 for opening new streets, such as Union Street,

Reform Street and Panmure Street. Edinburgh, better prepared and more ambitious, to whom prosperity came no less definitely but perhaps less suddenly, formulated the greatest building plans ever conceived in Scotland, and built the New Town.

[7] *North Bridge and the back of the High Street, about 1800.* E.UL.

III

Public Buildings before 1784

In the *Proposals* of 1752, the building of a merchants' exchange was given pride of place, and its accomplishment was facilitated by the ruinous condition of some of the houses in the High Street to which the pamphlet refers. The High Street was the heart of the old city and it was much admired – not only by Scotsmen. Defoe thought it 'the largest, longest and finest Street for Buildings and Number of Inhabitants, not in Britain only, but in the World'.[1] Topham, who visited the city in 1774–75 was equally enthusiastic: 'You have seen the famous street at Lisle, la Rue royale, leading to the port of Tournay, which is said to be the finest in Europe; but which I can assure you is not to be compared either in length or breadth to the High Street at Edinburgh.'[2] The citizens basked in the visitors' praise, and joined in the chorus of approval: 'With regard to the High Street in general, it may be observed that its length and width, beauty and magnificence are, by travellers, said to be excelled by none in Europe, and it is really far from being equalled in London.'[3] Long, wide and populous, the High Street was not only a public thoroughfare from the Castle to the Canongate; it was also a theatre of civic life. There were houses *in* the High Street – about which Topham complained – as well as bordering it. These were the Luckenbooths,[4] houses of four storeys with shops below, of which the most famous in the eighteenth century was Creech's land. Here Alan Ramsay had had his shop, where in 1725 he had established the first circulating library in Scotland. In 1771 this shop passed into the hands of William Creech, publisher to Burns, Henry Mackenzie, Adam Smith, Dugald Stewart and many others; his breakfast-room, says Grant, 'was a permanent literary lounge, which was known by

52

the name of "Creech's Levee" '.[5] All around were the shops of mercers, clothiers, drapers. In Parliament Square, a few yards away, were the jewellers and the goldsmiths, close by the Law Courts. It was here that Smollett, staying with his sister in the Canongate in 1776, found 'all the people of business in Edinburgh, and even the genteel company . . . standing in crowds every day, from one to two in the afternoon',[6] along with the ubiquitous caddies, 'corduroyed men from Gilmerton bawling coals or yellow sand, and spending as much breath in a minute as would have served poor asthmatic Hugo Arnot for a month',[7] Newhaven fisherwives, herb women, the Town Guard with their antique Lochaber axes, and every other kind of citizen in great numbers. Trade, shopping, gossip, fashion and business had for centuries been the life of the High Street, circulating round the Luckenbooths, Parliament Square, and the old Mercat Cross which stood in the middle of the street.

Those who formulated the *Proposals* evidently felt that this was not good enough. Doing business in the street should be beneath the dignity of an Edinburgh merchant; besides, most towns had an exchange[8]; and so, 'when several tenements near the Cross became ruinous, it occurred to many that so lucky an opportunity for a well situate Exchange ought not to be lost'.[9] It was agreed that a work 'so much to the Honour of the Town and the Interest of the Inhabitants' should be started by the making of a plan by 'proper persons',[10] and as a result Drummond 'caused Mr. John Adam architect make out a plan'[11] for the Exchange. He also asked for plans for a large hall for the annual meetings of the Conventions of Royal Burghs, plans for Council Chambers, and a plan for a residence for the Lord Provost. Commissioners, including the father of James Boswell, the Duke of Argyll, Sir Alexander Dick of Prestonfield and at least one Edinburgh merchant, met late in 1752, and in 1753 began to negotiate for the purchase of land not only to free a site for the Exchange – on the north side of the High Street almost opposite St Giles – but also to prepare the way for a new road to the north and south, leaving the High Street near the Market Cross.

Money, however, was the limiting factor. It was recognised that the ordinary revenues of the city would not suffice for all these new buildings as well as for 'makeing ane easy and convenient access to

VERSES on laying the Foundation of the EXCHANGE of *Edinburgh*,

September 13. 1753.

THIS Day, fair Æra of *EDINA*'s Fame,
   The Muse exulting, joins the loud Acclaim
Of *Scotland*'s Glory; Hails the Patriot Band,
Auspicious Guardians of their native Land!
Dejected long pale *Caledonia* lay,
And wrapt in Darkness, scarce durst hope for Day:
Her Sons, despairing, saw her hapless Plight,
And fled, impatient of the painful Sight,
To Climes remote; unsheath'd the conq'ring Sword,
Or plan'd Dominion for a foreign Lord.
Let *Belgian* Annals tell who sav'd their State,
Let *Sweden* say, who made *Gustavus* great?
Whilst thus thro' *Europe*'s Fields the Wand'rers Roam,
Weak and forlorn, decay'd, the Hive at home;
The Rights of All, the Few, the Strong invade,
And barb'rous Chiefs with Iron Sceptre sway'd.
Now SCOTLAND's Youth, with better Omens born,
Salute the Dawning of a brighter Morn.
Already Commerce, and her sweeping Train
Of polish'd Arts, in CALEDONIA reign;
Her Seas, her Mines, exhaustless Treasures yield,
And CERES smiles on the once barren Field:
O'er her fierce Floods imperial Arches bend,
And *Roman* Ways her steepest Hills ascend:
When PHOEBUS lights the Land beneath the *Bear*,
He sees BEHEMOTH on the *Scottish* Spear;
And rolling back to where the Citron blooms,
Beholds his *Indians* cloth'd from *Scottish* Looms.
Last of the Arts, proud ARCHITECTURE comes,
To grace *EDINA* with majestic Domes.
BRITONS, this Day is laid a PRIMAL STONE;
Firm may it be! But trust not that alone!
On Public Virtue found; His Favour gain,
Without whose Aid *the Builders build in vain.*

the high street from the south and north – which in the view of extending the Royalty of the City is absolutely neccessary to be done'.[12] Accordingly, Drummond 'talked with some persons of quality Judges and others upon the subjects'[13] and returned with the extraordinary proposal that if *in addition* to what was already proposed the town undertook to build a library for the Faculty of Advocates, a room for the Lords of Session to robe in and a number of offices for clerks, then 'the whole undertaking would be so acceptable to the nation in general'[14] that enough money would undoubtedly be forthcoming! Subscriptions were accordingly called for, and before the end of 1752 almost £6,000 had been promised. The largest subscriber was the Crown, with £1,934, followed by the Royal Burghs with £1,500. The aristocracy was prominent, the Dukes of Argyll, Athol and Buccleuch subscribing £200 each. The Incorporation of Surgeons promised £105 and the Incorporation of Taylors £100. Also in the lists are the names of many gentlemen, of advocates, merchants, jewellers, goldsmiths, of some masons, wrights and painters, of one historian and two professors. Many came from far afield. There are one or two London addresses in the list, and several in 'Lithgow'. The Town of Elgin subscribed £10.

In 1753 an Act was obtained to facilitate the purchase at an agreed valuation[15] of the ground and houses necessary for building the Exchange. This measure was entitled, 'An Act for Erecting several Public Buildings in the City of Edinburgh; and to impower the Trustees therein to be mentioned to purchase Lands for that Purpose; and also for Widening and Enlarging the Streets of the said City, and certain Avenues leading thereto.' It made no mention of the aim of extending the Royalty.

In August 1753 it was decided to begin with the Exchange and to finish that work first. Thirty-three Commissioners were appointed. £5,000 was borrowed from the Bank of Scotland and the same amount from the Royal Bank. The loan was secured on the revenue from the ale duty, but in addition all the members of the ordinary Council became 'personally bound conjunctly and severally to each Bank' for three years, this obligation to be thereafter shouldered by their successors in office. In the same month the Commissioners accepted a plan for the Exchange submitted by John Adam. The

[8] *Verses by John Home, 1753. A broadsheet.* EUL

Overleaf [9] *John Adam. The Exchange, South front. From 'Contract for . . . the Exchange,' Edin. 1753.*

The SOUTH FRONT
To Serve as an Exchang

a New defign'd SQUARE

he City of Edinburgh

building was to enclose a court, 83 feet deep and 89 feet from east to west, with a piazza for the merchants along the whole of the north side. There was to be a large number of shops and houses, for sale, but the principal feature was a Custom House, valued at nearly £6,000, which formed the central part of the Exchange, and which was to be retained by the Magistrates and leased by them to the Government. The contract for building was given to a group of five undertakers – one mason, three wrights and an 'architect'. The foundation stone was laid in September 1753, the roof was on the building early in 1758, and work seems to have come to an end about 1760, although the building was never completed according to the original plans. The finance of the scheme was highly unsatisfactory, at least from the point of view of the undertakers. They had agreed to clear the site and build the Exchange for £19,708; subsequent adjustments seem to have reduced this figure to £14,830. They had also shouldered a debt of £11,749 in respect of the purchase of the areas involved.[16] They expected to recoup themselves by selling the new properties, and went ahead on the understanding that the Town Council would advance them £18,000, payable in instalments, of which £12,950 was due when the roof was completed. But all that the undertakers ever received from the town was £4,100, and they were compelled to borrow the rest of the money they needed at the legal rate of five per cent. Meanwhile, the town was using its credits with the banks to purchase the necessary land and properties for the scheme. In 1764 the undertakers declared that they could not complete their part of the bargain, and referred to their 'great sufferings by this undertaking'; the town, which seems to have been principally at fault in failing to supply the working capital which it had promised, blamed the undertakers for having been 'so ill qualified', and endeavoured to solve the financial problem by selling off at tempting prices the remainder of the new properties – shops, dwelling houses, and coffee houses. In this it was successful. By the beginning of 1765 all the properties had been disposed of, and after repaying the bank debt there was a surplus of over £200. But the unfortunate undertakers still owed £2,006 in 1766, and there is no proof that this money was ever fully recovered.

9. Front of Royal Exchange, High Street.

The Exchange – now the heart of the City Chambers – was never used for the most obvious of the many purposes for which it was intended; the Edinburgh merchants, that is to say, continued to deal and chaffer in the street. But it was a valuable property in the city, and the financial outcome was not so unfavourable as to deter the Magistrates from proceeding to more ambitious schemes. The first of these was the provision of what the 1753 Act called 'more commodious access to the High Street of the said City, from the fields on the North'. The idea of improving communications northward was an old one – it had appeared in the Earl of Mar's paper of 1728 – and there were two reasons for pressing it. First, extension of the Royalty to include lands on the other side of the North Loch would be of little value unless these lands could be made more accessible from the Old Town. The existing road, the Eastern Road, round the east side of the Calton Hill, was long and difficult, and in any case did not lead in the desired direction. If some way of traversing the North Loch could be created, the prospect of extending the city northward would be enormously improved. But this point was seldom mentioned, at least in public, because the rural landowners concerned were opposed to extensions of the Royalty. Some of the land – Allan's Parks, the property of Dean of Guild Allan[17] – had been bought by the city in 1758, but the proposed extension of the Royalty still encountered opposition in 1759. The second argument for the new 'avenue of communication' was that it would facilitate communications with Leith. Leith, alike not within the Royalty, was the port for Edinburgh, and the government of Leith had resided in the Town Council, as superiors of the port, since the Middle Ages. It was therefore perfectly natural that the magistrates should seek to improve communications between Leith and Edinburgh, and this could hardly be objected to even by those who objected to extensions of the Royalty. Drummond may have hoped to overcome this opposition by building the bridge first and securing the extension of the Royalty afterwards: if so, he was successful, although he died in 1766, the year before the passage of the necessary Extension Act.

Drainage of the North Loch – as put forward in the *Proposals* – began in 1759, about the time that the Exchange was nearing completion. It was in an unsavourary state: 'On the side of the Loch, the

10. The scale of the engineering problem which faced the 18th c planners, in linking the Old Town (L) to the site of the New Town, is seen in this picture of the North Bridge spanning the valley.

butchers have their slaughter-houses, and the tanners and skinners their pits.'[18] There was considerable debate as to whether to build a bridge or a 'mole', and if a bridge, upon what general plan. Then in July 1763, an advertisement inviting tenders for a bridge to be built across the North Loch was published in the following terms:

As it is greatly desired, for the public utility, that a road of communication be made betwixt the High-street of Edinburgh, and the adjacent grounds belonging to the city and the other neighbouring fields, as well as to the port of Leith, by building a stone bridge over the east end of the North Loch, at least forty feet wide betwixt the parapets of the said bridge, and upon an equal declivity of one foot in sixteen from the High-street, at the Cape and Feather-close, in a straight line to the opposite side leading to Multrees-hill . . . As the proposal for carrying on the above work was some time ago made to the Town-council, and they having cheerfully agreed to the same, this advertisement is publicly given to all who are willing to undertake the said work . . . And it is resolved that a sub-scription be forthwith opened, for a voluntary contribution, as well gratuitously as by way of loan, for carrying on the Bridge over the North-loch . . . and so soon as there shall be a sufficient sum subscribed, the subscribers shall be duly advertised to meet, in order to make choice of proper persons as Trustees, for carrying what is proposed into execution.

The Magistrates and Council of the City of Edinburgh, hereby intimate to all gentlemen, farmers, and others, that they are at full liberty to take and carry off the dung and fulgie of the North-loch, immediately, and that without payment or other gratuity therefor.[19]

A 'subscription' was opened, that is to say, members of the public were invited to give or to lend money for the scheme; stone from a quarry in Bearford's Parks was declared suitable; search was made for a foundation; and in October 1763, Drummond, acting as Grand-master of the Free-masons in the absence of the Earl of Elgin, laid the foundation stone, ten years and one month after the laying of the foundation stone of the Royal Exchange. The ceremony took place amid 'the repeated acclamation of the brethren, and of a most

numerous concourse of spectators' and was afterwards celebrated with 'social harmony and joy'.[20]

A plan for the bridge evidently existed in 1763, as the above-quoted 'Advertisement' refers to it. But further delay ensued, and the final preparatory steps were taken only after one of the baillies pressed the matter in a Town Council meeting late in 1764 on the ground that the need for a bridge had become "particularly obvious at this time, when there is such Complaint or rather outcry for the scarcity of houses'.[21] In January 1765 appeared a notice inviting 'all Architects and others' to submit plans, the successful designer to receive 'as a reward, thirty guineas, or a gold medal of that value'.[22] The Bridge Committee assisted by 'several other Noblemen and Gentlemen of knowledge and taste in architecture',[23] met to consider the plans, of which there were at least seven, and decided that those

[10] *North Bridge from* N W. *The fishmarket and fleshmarket were both located beneath the bridge.*
shepherd

61

submitted by David Henderson entitled him to the premium. They
nevertheless next asked for estimates relating either to Henderson's
plan or to one submitted by William Mylne, himself a member of the
Committee[24]; declared in May that Mr Henderson 'had failed in
finding Security to execute the Bridge agreeable to his estimates'[25];
and finally, in July, accepted William Mylne's plan with alterations
by John Adam, along with Mylne's estimate, 'the lowest given in'.
(Mylne, incidentally, may have been the author of the original 1763
plan.) What David Henderson thought of these manoeuvres is not
recorded – at least he appears to have received the thirty guineas.
But as things turned out, he was not done with the North Bridge yet.

The contract for building was signed in August 1765. The bridge
was to be 1,134 feet overall, almost 70 feet high, and 40 feet between
the parapets over the three arches. The work was to be completed
by November 1769, and the contract price was £10,140. To meet
this expense, the Lord Provost 'hoped' that at least £2,500 would

be available from 'Subscriptions for Public Purposes', and it was moreover agreed 'to appropriate the Bank Stock belonging to the City'[26] which would realise £6,000. Mylne was to be paid in successive moieties as the work progressed; and it was anticipated that the feuing of lots in the neighbourhood of the bridge would more than compensate the city for its expenditure. Work seems to have proceeded expeditiously. The first (northmost) arch was completed by 1 June 1768, and early in 1769 the bridge was open at least to pedestrians. But in August, 1769, part of the side-walls of the south abutment of the bridge collapsed, burying five people in the ruins.[27] This led to much additional expense and a long dispute between Mylne and the Town Council. Smeaton, John Adam and John Baxter were called upon to advise, and repairs were carried out by Mylne at an expense of at least £2,000. The work was now hopelessly behind schedule, and the Town Council was pressing for its completion. Mylne was advised in 1770 to advertise in the Edinburgh

[11] *View, about 1780, looking* E *from the drained North Loch, and showing Princes Street completed as far* W *as Frederick Street.*
Lizars

63

papers to the effect that 'masons may expect proper encouragement and a continuance of employment in Edinburgh',[28] and throughout 1771 the Town Council's clerk of works made a regular return of the 'Number of hands employed at the Bridge Likewise as many hands as can be Employed in Executing the same'. Most of these returns have been preserved, and the following picture emerges. (The figures are for the earliest available week in each available month.)

11. North Bridge, looking s from Wellington Statue.

Overleaf *12. Register House.*

NUMBERS WORKING ON NORTH BRIDGE, 1771

Date	5.3.71	9.4.71	14.5.71	18.6.71	5.7.71	7.8.71	4.9.71	2.10.71	6.11.71	3.12.71
Masons hewing	13	12	12	11	13	16	10	8	10	16
Masons walling	24	37	31	36	32	27	29	18	19	9
Labourers	51	59	60	86	80	72	38	40	37	40
Carters	17	18	18	24	24	24	24	10	6	6
Wrights	—	3	1	1	2	1	2	2	4	1
Total	105	129	122	158	151	140	103	78	76	72

The bridge was completed for use in 1772, with the addition of 'Ballusters' at a cost of £259 12s.

But doubts, disputes, inspections, minor modifications and the settlement of accounts continued Mylne, pressed for money, met his difficulties by borrowing £2,500 from the city between November 1771 and September 1772. In the end, however, he appears not to have suffered seriously, if at all. Most of the additional expense incurred through the failure of the original structure in 1769 seems to have been borne by the town. The town also shouldered large additional expenses in the way of surveying, overseeing, buying land and making roads. As late as 1784 money was being paid for further structural alterations – carried out, ironically enough, by the David Henderson whose plan had been accepted and then rejected nineteen years before. The final cost cannot have been less than £16,000.[29] Areas near the bridge, however, were sold for good prices – the Postmaster General for Scotland paid £650 for a site for a post office – and in the end the Town Council probably made rather than lost money.

While the affair of the North Bridge was thus being wound up, the third important public building project in Edinburgh was getting under way: the building of Register House. The Public Records of Scotland – such of them as survived – had been kept for generations in 'two laigh rooms under the Inner Session House' in a state of dilapidation and neglect; they were 'in a perishing condition for want of being rebound, the ratts, mice and other vermine having defaced the most valuable of them'.[30] The suggestion of a building to house the records was made at least as early as 1722, and the 1752 Act which led to the building of the Exchange gave Commissioners power to build a register house. But nothing came of these proposals. In 1765, however, representation by the Lords of Session and Barons of Exchequer were made to the Treasury, pointing out the need and emphasising the absence of 'any fund immediately liable to bear the expenses'[31] which building a repository would involve. The Government responded almost at once by making available £12,000 from the money obtained from the sale of the forfeited estates, and Trustees to administer the fund were appointed.[32]

Without delay the Trustees set about finding a site, and they

13. Detail of the dome, Register House.

settled on the north-west quarter of the garden of Heriot's Hospital as being the most convenient large open area within the city.[33] The Governors of Heriot's agreed to feu the necessary land, but objections were raised as to the inconvenience of the site (it was, after all, a considerable distance from the Law Courts, being on the extreme southern edge of the then city boundary, and on the far side of the Cowgate), and delay ensued. Not until 1769 did the Trustees make any fresh move. By this time the North Bridge was partly completed, and Craig's Plan for the New Town had been made and accepted. It was now natural for the Magistrates to suggest a site in the extended royalty, and the Trustees agreed to build on 'the area at the end of the New Bridge.' That part of the site owned by the city was given gratis to the Trustees, the Town Council believing that the scheme 'would turn out to the advantage of the City and would promote the feuing out of the grounds on the north of the Bridge'[34]; the rest of the site was purchased from three owners for £2,698.

At about this time Robert Adam and his brother James were appointed architects, and in 1772 an elevation of the building was in existence. On 27 June 1774, the foundation stone was laid. The building was to be of stone from Craigleith or Ravelston quarries, and drains were to be made leading to the 'great Canal' which appeared on Craig's Plan but never in reality. It was also arranged that

> when the work comes to go on, there shall be no building during the winter, that is after the last day of October, nor before the first of March, and that the building shall be carried on so leisurely from year to year as to allow the parts built successively to settle and consolidate, before the others are put above them.[35]

Robert Adam had undertaken, on behalf of himself and his brother, to

> visit the work once every year, if necessary, or once in two years, at the rate of $2\frac{1}{2}$ per cent on the money expended on the building, and Fifty Guineas as the expense of each journey to Edinburgh, without charging anything for the plan already drawn or their trouble in adjusting thereof.[36]

In the absence of the brothers the work was supervised by James

Salisbury, as Clerk of Works, appointed on Robert Adam's recommendation at a salary of £100 per annum. John Adam, who resided in Edinburgh, visited the work from time to time, and in August 1776 Robert Adam travelled from London. Construction had gone as far as the top of the pillars and cornice, and Adam advised that by the summer of 1777 the 'carcase' of the building should be completed and the whole roofed in. But funds were running low. Securing an additional £2,000 from the Exchequer in the spring of 1778 the Trustees were enabled, after a fashion, 'to put the copestone on the carcass of this noble edifice'. But at that point work stopped altogether. Desolate and uninhabited, Adam's masterpiece remained for six years 'the most magnificent pigeon house in Europe'.[37]

At last, in November 1784, the Government voted an additional £15,000, again from the moneys of the forfeited estates, and between

[13] North Bridge and RegisterHouse, about 1780. Despite faulty drawing, the grandeur of this early contribution to the expansion of the town is well conveyed.
ARNOT

67

1785 and 1788 the first part of the building, some two-thirds of the whole of Adam's original design, was completed, and occupation began. Not so elaborate, and not finished in so high a style as Adam's original design allowed for, the General Register House, with its fine dome decorated with large medallions, is nevertheless a splendid and ingenious building. Its total cost up to the start of the Napoleonic War – extensive additions were made after the war[38] – was £31,000. All of this sum was supplied by Government, except for £3,000 obtained by selling the feu-duties payable to the Trustees in respect of properties in near-by Leith Street and Gabriel's Road.

The building, or the prospect of the building of a new register house in the Extended Royalty no doubt encouraged the city to embark on new projects of its own. The next to be undertaken was a very obvious one, envisaged at least as early as 1752; the bridging of the Cowgate. The North Bridge, in full use from 1772, connected the Old Town with the lands to the north. What was now wanted was a similar connection to the south. The many wynds which led down from the High Street to the Cowgate were steep and narrow, and the ascent on the other side was no easier.[39] Moreover, every year more people, and more influential people, wished to make the passage between the Old Town and the lands to the south, for at this time these lands were being developed almost as rapidly as the area of the New Town itself. Argyle Square, later swept away to make room for Chambers Street, dated from the 1730s. Brown Square, near Bristo Port, was rising in the early 1760s, 'houses that were deemed fine mansions, and found favour with the upper classes, before a stone of the New Town was laid'.[40] About the same time Robert Adam, on ground now occupied principally by the University, built 'two very large and handsome houses, each with large bow-windows, which, being well recessed back and having the [old] College buildings on the south, formed what was called Adam Square'.[41] Most important of all, George Square, formed on a plan more than six times as spacious as Brown Square and in a 'superior style, both as to size and accommodation',[42] was also building in the 1760s. This was the first truly modern house-building project in Edinburgh, and the first true square. These areas, all south of the Cowgate, were the most aristocratic and the most fashionable parts of Edin-

68

burgh (they were not within the Royalty and therefore not within the jurisdiction of the Town Council) in the 1760s, the 1770s and 1780s. In Argyle Square lived Lord Cullen and Dr Hugh Blair; Lord President Dundas lived in Brown Square until his death in 1787; while in George Square lived the Duchess of Gordon, the Countess of Sutherland, Lord Melville, Viscount Duncan, Lord Braxfield, and many other almost equally distinguished persons, including Walter Scott, W.S., father of the famous novelist.[43] To make it easier to reach this new residential area from the Old Town was an obvious move; and the idea was put forward as early as 1775. Difficulties appeared, however, principally over finance – the outbreak of war with the American colonies in June may have caused the shelving of the project – and not until 1784 was the idea revived.

14. George Square. The rough courses of the house on L (about 1770) gives way to the bleak dressing of the later fronts.

IV

The New Town: Craig's Plan

The prospect of the extension of the Royalty[1] and the start made on the construction of the North Bridge in 1765 had prompted the magistrates to consider what regulations should be made about building in 'the fields to the north'. They realised, doubtless, that without some encouragement by them their new property might for long remain undeveloped. They probably also reckoned that unless they guided development in a suitable way, the vision of 1752 would not be realised – the vision, that is, of a town distinguished by 'the neatness and accommodation of its private houses; the beauty and conveniency of its numerous streets and open squares, of its buildings and bridges, its large parks and extensive walks'.

Accordingly, in March 1766 an advertisement appeared announcing that the ground to the north had been surveyed and that plans would shortly be called for; then, in April, came the following more lengthy notice:

> The Bridge of Communication between the High-street of Edinburgh and the grounds lying to the north of the City, being in great forwardness, and it being expected that the bridge will be completed before the time fixed upon by the contract between the Town-Council and the Undertaker, the Lord Provost, Magistrates and Council are desirous to give all encouragement to such persons as incline to build upon the grounds belonging to the Town upon the north, and propose to feu them with all expedition, according to a scheme to be hereafter made public, for preventing the inconveniences and disadvantages which arise from carrying on buildings, without regard to any order or regularity. This notice is therefore made inviting Architects and others

70

to give in Plans of a New Town marking out streets of a proper
breadth, and by-lanes, and the best situation for a reservoir,
and any other public buildings, which may be thought necessary;
they will be furnished in the Council-Chamber with a survey of
the grounds and their heights or risings upon a proper scale.

Directions about the submission of plans follow, and the advertisement closes with the following words: 'The person whose plan shall
be judged most proper, will receive as a reward of merit a gold
medal, with an impression of the arms of the city of Edinburgh, and
the freedom of the city in a silver box.'

On 21 May 1766, it was noted in the Town Council Minutes that
six plans had been received, and on 2 August that Plan No. 4 by
Mr James Craig had been adjudged the best by the Lord Provost
and Mr John Adam. What happened between this date and July 1767,
when Craig's plan was finally adopted, is not clear. We know only
that a committee of the Town Council 'considered several amendments proposed by Mr. Craig', that 'Mr. Craig by their direction
had made out a new plan', and that final acceptance came only 'after
many meetings and consulting with Lord Kaimes, Lord Alemour,
Commissioner Clerk and Mr. Adams and other persons'. What
Craig's amendments were, and how far and in what respects his new
plan differed from his original plan we do not know.[2] Nor do we
know, unfortunately, the names of any of the other competitors in
this momentous competition.[3]

Craig's plan has been fervently eulogised and contemptuously
derided. The New Town owes its superiority, says Arnot, partly to
situation, partly to 'the whole being built conform to a regular and
beautiful plan'.[4] But in the *Dictionary of National Biography* the same
plan is damned as 'utterly destitute of any inventive ingenuity or any
regard for the natural features of the ground'. The truth is that the
plan is entirely sensible, and almost painfully orthodox.

Planning new towns, or fundamentally re-modelling old ones, was
a familiar occupation in the eighteenth century. The most famous of
all English town plans was never put into execution: Wren's plan
for the rebuilding of London after the Great Fire in 1666. This
'plan', however, was more in the nature of an 'embellishment' connecting significant buildings by straight avenues in such a way that

*Overleaf [15] James Craig.
'Plan of the new streets and
squares intended for the City
of Edinburgh, 1767.'*

71

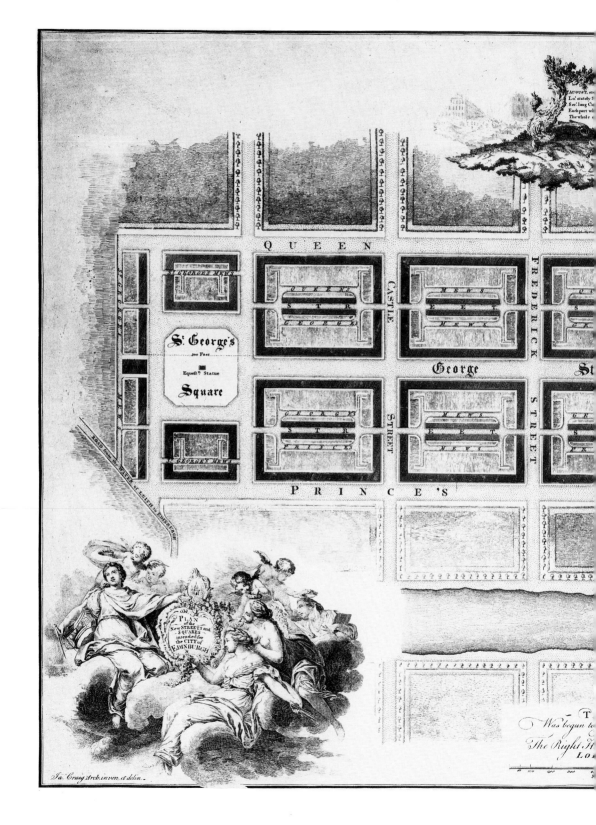

QUEEN

CASTLE

FREDERICK STREET

St GEORGE'S MEWS

St George's
300 Feet

Equestn Statue

Square

QUEEN STR
GEORGE'S

MEWS
MEWS

George St

St

GEORGES ST
PALACE

MEWS
FEET
MEWS

St GEORGE'S MEWS

PRINCE'S

PLAN
of the
New STREETS and
SQUARES
intended for
the CITY of
EDINBURGH

Ia. Craig Arch. inven. et delin.

Was begun to

The Right H.
LO

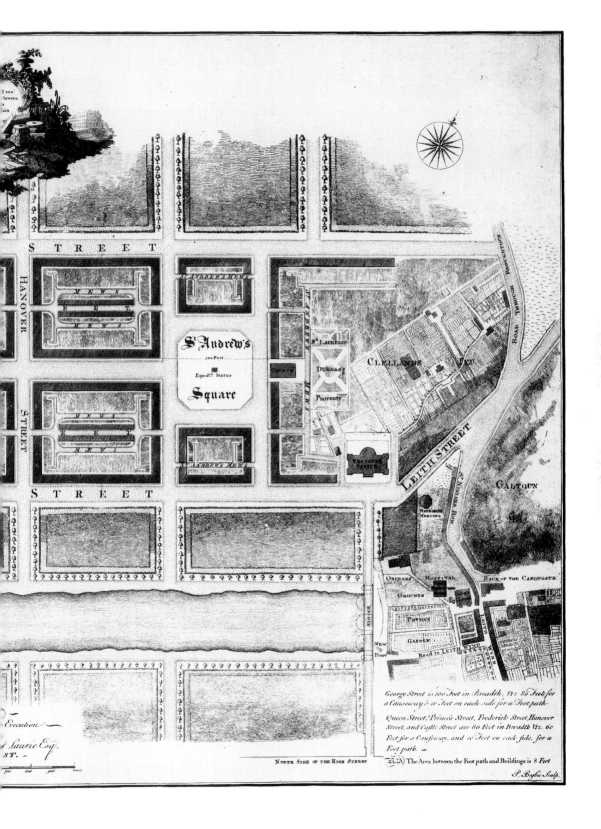

STREET

HANOVER

STREET

STREET

MEWS
E E T
MEWS

MEWS
E E T
MEWS

St.Andrew's
500 Feet
Equest.ᵈ Statue
Square

ST. ANDREW'S MEWS

ST. ANDREW'S MEWS

ST. ANDREW'S MEWS

CHURCH

St. LAURENCE

DUNDAS

PROPERTY

CLELLANDS FEU

ROAD THROUGH PROVISIONS

PROVISIONS

LEITH STREET

CALTOUN

METHODIST MEETING

NEW PENNING'S

ORPHANS HOSPITAL

BACK OF THE CANONGATE

GROUNDS

PHYSICK

GARDEN

Road to LEITH WYND

LEITH WYND

Kirk Brae

New Pons

I see
breeze,
_a_
ith
_of_

Execution
t Laurie Esq.
ST. —

700   500   900   1000

NORTH SIDE OF THE HIGH STREET

George Street is 100 Feet in Breadth; Viz: 80 Feet for
a Causeway & 10 Feet on each side for a Foot path

Queen Street, Prince's Street, Frederick Street, Hanover
Street, and Castle Street are 80 Feet in Breadth Viz: 60
Feet for a Causeway, and 10 Feet on each side, for a
Foot path. —

) The Area between the Foot path and Buildings is 8 Feet

P. Begbie Sculp.

the avenues terminated in impressive, monumental vistas. In any case, it had no influence on the subsequent development of London, which as a city grew in the eighteenth century by the building of a succession of formally disconnected residential squares. The very earliest of these was Covent Garden, building in the 1630s. It was followed by St James's Square and Berkeley Square, and then after 1700 by the development of the Grosvenor estate and the building of Hanover Square. These squares were related to one another in a largely accidental fashion, and they gave the town so casual a unity that it had to some extent the appearance and character not of a single city but of 'an agglomeration of villages'.[5]

Much the most important exercise in town planning in Britain before 1760 was the work done by John Wood in Bath. Wood was a surveyor turned architect, a disciple of Palladio, who worked out his designs for Bath between 1725 and 1750. Queen Square, the Circus and Royal Crescent, all planned by Wood although only the first was built by him, are joined to one another in an informal way, and their grouping is reminiscent of that of the seventeenth- and eighteenth-century London squares. There is, however, an important element of originality in Wood's work – his use of curving streets – circus and crescent – with all the houses joined together in what sometimes forms a single palace façade. This multiple house-building, the laying out of a whole street as a unit, was saved from dullness and wearisome uniformity by the elegant and varied detail of the architecture, coupled with the feeling of movement and variety given by the curve of the streets. The Circus was actually built by Wood's son between 1754 and 1764. It was the last major building scheme completed in Bath before Craig drew up his plan for Edinburgh.[6]

On the Continent, town planning had been far more extensively studied and practised. As early as the fifteenth century important works were published by Alberti[7] and Filarete,[8] and new editions of Vitruvius' *De Architectura Libri Decem* were popular in the seventeenth century both in France and in Italy. In the eighteenth century a new stimulus was given to the study of town planning by the ambition of Louis XV. Wishing to glorify the monarchy by beautifying Paris and getting rid of some of the slums, he authorised an architectural competition. The result was a partial development on the site of the Place de la Concorde, and, more important, the publication by Pierre Patte of his *Monumens érigés à la gloire de Louis XV*. In this important book Patte brought together the scattered and spatially limited proposals of the several competitors and assembled them on a master-plan, producing a scheme for the re-development of the city as a whole. The book was published in 1765, but many of the ideas contained in it were in circulation from the time of the holding of the competition in 1748.

The circular plaza and the square were much in evidence in these plans. Squares were a common feature of continental town planning by the eighteenth century – the Place Vendôme was built at the same time as St James's Square and Berkeley Square – but continental squares were quite different from London squares. In the latter, the houses were as a rule simple, anonymous brick buildings on a modest scale, and the centre of the square was a fenced-in garden with grass and trees. Continental squares, on the other hand, especially those built before 1750, were large open spaces, containing possibly a statue, and surrounded by imposing, palace-like façades. 'The Baroque *place* was entirely dramatic in conception, forming an effective vista with entrance, approach and climax.'⁹

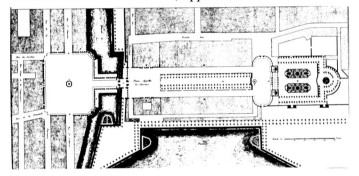

[16] *Nancy. Héré de Corny's plan for inter-related squares. Patte*

A movement away from this kind of square, towards something at once finer and more intimate, developed in Europe gradually in the eighteenth century, and this movement embraced the notion of planning an entire area by having two or even three squares in formal relation to one another. In the 'new town' of Nancy this innovation helped to produce one of the small masterpieces of eighteenth-century town planning. Nancy is a particularly interesting

Overleaf 15. Edinburgh in the 1820's. This cast-iron relief shows the Old Town running from the Castle to the Crags, with the New Town to the left.

[17a & b] Nancy. Place Stanislas during construction, and in a recent photograph.
The triumphal arch is in the foreground.

example of town design for several reasons. For one thing, it was built in the 1750s, and was thus the last 'new town' built in Europe before Craig drew up his plan. It was, moreover, the most successful design incorporating linked 'places' to that date, being a considerable improvement on the Place Royale at Reims. The lay-out, by Héré de Corny, was included in Patte's *Monumens érigés à la gloire de Louis XV*, and it is possible that Craig had seen this book before he made his own plan. It must be said, however, that if Craig did learn from Héré's design, he learned nothing except the bare idea of linked squares. The essence of the design at Nancy is the close juxtaposition of two open spaces, the Place Stanislas and what is in effect a large forecourt to the Palais du Gouvernement, joined by a triumphal arch and the wide and tree-lined Place de la Carrière. Such a description, however, gives no idea of the variety, ornateness and charm of Héré's town. The buildings in the Place Stanislas are of varying heights, the whole square is balustraded at the roof line and decorated with urns and figures, in each corner are intricate gilded screens of wrought ironwork, masterpieces of the metal-worker's art of the eighteenth century, and in two of the corners ornate monumental rococo fountains play in the shadow of the over-arching chestnut trees. It has been said with some truth that it is not the buildings but the spaces between the buildings which give the Place Stanislas its style and charm. As for the Place de la Carrière, it is unusually wide in relation to its length, and is not so much a street as a promenade, tree-lined and elegant in its proportions, with an air of privacy, dominated by the Arc de Triomphe at one end and the Palais du Gouvernement at the other. One feels that it was built, like the Place Stanislas, to set off to advantage the elegant clothes and the courtly manners of the eighteenth century.

Obviously, there is very little of this in Craig's New Town. If Craig was trying for the same effects as Héré he was doomed to disappointment. His grand plan is more mechanical and symmetrical than the Frenchman's. But the chief differences are in the buildings themselves. Here, of course, Craig had little if any responsibility; he was not, so far as we know, invited to design, or advise on the designing of, the houses. The final result may well have been a dis-appointment to him. St Andrew's Square, as it existed in the eighteenth

16. 'The principal reason for Craig's success is the excellent use of the site.' The picture shows the Castle, the Gardens retained as open space, and Princes Street.

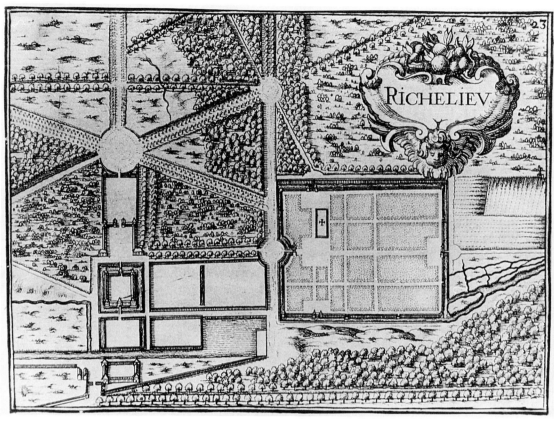

[18] Richelieu. Plan of the town, built in the 17th c, on a regular pattern of squares linked by parallel streets.

ᴛᴀssin

century, was more like a London residential square than like the Place Stanislas. Nor has George Street much in common with the Place de la Carrière. The houses in the latter may be undistinguished, but they are not so dull as the original houses in George Street. The spirit of the two towns is in fact quite different. And while it is possible that Craig adopted the idea of two linked squares after seeing Héré's design, it is equally likely that he obtained the idea from other plans or publications of the day.

It was a popular notion in the middle of the eighteenth century. For example, in John Gwynn's *London and Westminster Improved* much is made of the advantages of 'a range of squares',[10] of how London might be embellished with squares 'regularly built'.[11] A few circuses and at least one octagon are illustrated in four detailed and excellent maps. This book was published in the same year that Craig produced his plan, and a copy of it was in Craig's possession at the time of his death.

By comparison with contemporary Nancy, therefore, Craig's New Town is a poor affair – merely two squares joined by a straight central street flanked by two others. This is basically simple, recti-linear or grid-iron planning, and it is exceedingly old. The exact elements and essential relations of Craig's plan, indeed, are to be seen in the town of Richelieu, near Tours, built to the order of Cardinal Richelieu in 1633. Here again are two squares, joined centrally by a straight street, with a flanking street on each side. Richelieu is, of course, far smaller than the New Town of Edinburgh, and the proportions are different; the squares are not far separated from one another, the streets are narrow, the houses relatively high. But the general form is precisely the same. No one familiar with Edinburgh can walk through the streets of Richelieu without being struck by the similarity. Whether Craig knew anything about Richelieu we cannot tell. The rectilinear approach which is common to both these town plans is, of course, much older than Richelieu.

What makes Craig's New Town so pleasing, then, even today? It cannot be the originality of its design.[12] Craig was not only not original, he even failed to make use of several new ideas available to him – the circus, for example,[13] or the effect made by two sym-metrical buildings, taller than the rest, at the entrance to a square. The principal reason for Craig's success – in so far as a reason is to be found in Craig's share of the work – is the excellent use of the site. The two outer streets – Princes Street and Queen Street – have houses on one side only, and these look outwards across the street, in the one case over the low ground towards the Castle and High Street, in the other down the slope towards the Firth of Forth and the distant hills of Fife. This feeling of spaciousness combined with order is no doubt enhanced by the good proportions of the streets and buildings.

The idea of laying out a street with a prospect opposite houses built on only one side is to be found in Bath. Bath's Royal Crescent is a design of this sort, and it is conceivable that Craig may have got the idea from Wood's plan. More probably this merit of his design

79

[19] *Charlotte Square,* N E *corner, looking 'down the slope towards the Firth of Forth'.*
E U L

was derived from the site. Certainly Craig, and the Town Council who employed him, did not follow Wood – as in principle they might have done – in planning a single unified frontage to a set of houses. In this the Edinburgh planners may well have been influenced by economic considerations. The demand for houses near the centre of Bath in the 1750s was reasonably assured; in the New Town of Edinburgh it was not. To build sets of houses (architecturally unified or otherwise) would have been in these circumstances a fearful speculation. The magistrates did the next best thing: they passed a series of Acts and resolutions laying down the lines on which building was to proceed.

The first of these, dated July 1767, dealt with general matters. Pavements were to be ten feet wide, laid and kept at the expense of householders 'as is practised in the Old Town'; houses were to be built along a continuous line; no sign posts were to project from the walls, and the Council was to make a sewer 'in the middle of the street' – presumably George Street. This last item gave rise to some trouble. It was recognised that 'executing the common Shores [sewers] for the New Town in proper manner was of the utmost

17. *Thistle Court, reputedly the first house built in the New Town.*

80

consequence for the convenience and health of the inhabitants',[14] but also that no one in Edinburgh had sufficient knowledge of the job. Craig was accordingly paid thirty guineas to go to London 'and remain there so long as necessary for learning everything relative to these Shores'; and he was in London in December.[15]

Another Act relating to building in the New Town was passed early in 1768. It dealt chiefly with the proper marking out of areas and streets, but also contained two clauses of greater interest. The first laid down that steps should be taken to build a new reservoir on Castlehill, so that feuars in the New Town might be supplied with water as readily as those living in the Old Town. The other clause relates to house-building. But, far from limiting the freedom of the individual to design as he chose, this clause extended it; for 'as people's taste in building is so different, that it is not possible to lay down a fixed and determined rule of what dimensions each lot should be, every person should be allowed to take so many feet in front as they choose' – a direct invitation to freedom of planning and that sort of irregularity of elevation which was conspicuously absent in the New Town as finally built.

There is no record of any more detailed regulations being passed until 1781, by which date St Andrew's Square had been entirely built and building was going on as far west as Hanover Street. In February 1781, an Act was passed which, however, was 'disregarded and attempted to be evaded' in the next few years, builders 'pretending ignorance' of its main provisions. Accordingly, in 1782, a new Act was passed in stricter and more detailed terms, and the provisions of this Act were re-enacted in 1785. The principal clauses were as follows:

(1) When any application is given to the Council for a feu, the same to be remitted to a Committee, but the Committee to make no report thereupon, nor is the feu to be granted, until such time as a plan and elevation of the intended building, signed by the person applying, be given in to the Committee and approved by them.

(2) That no feus shall be granted in the principal streets of the extended royalty for houses above three storeys high, exclusive of garret and sunk storeys, and that the whole

18. No. 26 St Andrew's Square, N side, attributed to Sir William Chambers.

height of side-walls from floor of sunk storey shall not exceed 48 feet.

(3) That the Meus Lanes shall be solely appropriated for purposes of building Stables, Coach houses or other offices, and these shall in no case whatever be built on any of the other Streets of the extended Royalty.

(4) . . . That the houses in those two streets now to be called Rose Street and Thistle Street, shall not exceed two storeys, exclusive of the sunk and garret storeys, and that . . . the whole height of the side-walls from floor of sunk storey, shall not exceed 33 feet.

(5) That the casing of roofs shall run along the side-walls immediately above the windows of the upper-storey, and no storm or other windows to be allowed in the front of the roof, except sky-lights, and that the pitch of the roof shall not be more than one third of the breadth or span over the walls.

(6) That every person or persons acting contrary to all or any of these rules and regulations, shall be bound to pay . . . the sum of £30 of additional purchase money, besides being liable in damages, and repairing his or her transgression.

(7) That in all time coming every person who obtains a feu in the extended royalty shall be bound to build thereon, within one year from obtaining the feu, otherwise he shall not only forfeit the same, but also be liable in payment of £30 sterling . . .

(8) That no proposal for a feu be agreed to Unless it contains a reference to this Act . . .

This Act seems to have been fairly effective. It applied, however, to only that part of Craig's New Town – less than a half of it – which lay between Hanover Street and Charlotte Square. All the building east of Hanover Street, done between 1767 and 1785, had been subject only to the very general controls of July 1767.

The only other important action taken by the Town Council in the development of the New Town was the building of St Andrew's Church. This was first suggested by Sir James Hunter Blair, an ex

[20] *Sir William Chambers. Town house for Sir Laurence Dundas, now the Royal Bank of Scotland.*
shepherd

Lord Provost, in 1781. The absence of any church in the New Town was, he pointed out, an inconvenience to the great number of 'families of distinction' residing in the New Town; moreover, a church there would promote the feuing of the extended Royalty, and at the same time assist the Poor House, 'as it will add considerably to the Collection at the Church door'.[16] It was agreed that the Council was short of money for public works, but Sir James suggested that £3,000, for which 'a decent handsome Church even without a Steeple' might be built, could be borrowed from Heriot's Hospital against the security of the two penny duty (on ale), the debt to be paid back out of future seat rents. This arrangement was agreed to, and the money duly borrowed in 1781.

The difficulty was to find a site. In Craig's plan a large single building is shown on the east side of St Andrew's Square, looking straight up George Street; a corresponding building appears on the west side of Charlotte Square. These single buildings were to be churches. But when the Town Council decided in 1781 to build a church in the New Town – lo! the site in St Andrew Square was already occupied by the splendid mansion of Sir Laurence Dundas. It is fairly clear how this came about. Sir Laurence Dundas was a man of wealth and enterprise. The son of an Edinburgh baillie who went bankrupt, he rose from obscurity to be Commissary-General of the army in Flanders, 1748-59, and acquired a very large fortune. Some time before the first printing of Craig's plan in 1767, Sir Laurence had acquired a fairly large piece of ground, 360 feet by 175 feet, lying east of St Andrew's Square, in a line with George Street, and just outside the Royalty. On 4 September 1767, only one month and one day after the first feu in the extended royalty had been taken, Sir Laurence feued from the city for £450 'an Area in the East Square'. This description in the record of feus is noteworthy, for the location of all other feus is exactly specified. Evidently Sir Laurence was able to persuade the official concerned to suppress the fact that the land which he was buying, next to his own land, was the proposed site for a church. In a few years he had erected, across the middle of a lane and partly on his new feu, the finest house in the New Town, a three-storey building of splendid dignity and fine detail, built to the plans of Sir William Chambers.[17] His original property was left unbuilt on to form the garden of his house.

Edged out of its intended position by Sir Laurence, an inferior site for the church had now to be found. The Council decided that the best site was in George Street, opposite the Physicians' Hall – dessigned by Craig – on ground already feued to John Young, wright, in 1767. Accordingly, the Council received back the fore-part of this land – Young had already built to the rear 'a dwelling house, enclosed the same and erected shades [sheds] proper for my business'[18] – and in exchange the Council gave Young a corresponding piece of ground just to the west. The Council was obliged to agree to a number of building limitations laid down by Young, and also that there should be 'no burying in the Church or any part of the Area belonging to it'.[19] A prize of ten guineas was offered for the best design for the new church, and this prize was awarded in September 1781 to David Kay, architect, in respect of what was called Captain Fraser's Plan[20]; this was probably an instance of an amateur cooperating with a professional in architectural design – not an uncommon thing in the eighteenth century. The contract was signed

19. Town house for Sir Laurence Dundas, now the Royal Bank of Scotland; architect, Sir William Chambers.

84

[21] David Kay. St Andrew's Church, George Street, 1783-7. 'The interior (plate 20) is one of the small masterpieces of 18th c Edinburgh.'
shepherd

in the summer and the church completed in two years time. Later, in 1786-87, a spire was added. The total cost of the building, spire and all, was £5,183 6s. 11d.[21]

St Andrew's Church is an oval building, fronted by a portico with four columns and a triangular pediment, the whole surmounted by a slender tower and spire. The proportions are elegant without being remarkable, and the exterior is perhaps somewhat plain. Closely surrounded as it is now by other buildings, the originality of the general design is not easily seen and appreciated. It is the interior of the church, however, which is chiefly remarkable – nineteenth-century alterations have not altered its very individual character. Carried out in an entirely classical style, the simplicity of which harmonises with the smooth curves of the general design, the interior is one of the small masterpieces of eighteenth-century building in Edinburgh, a triumph of classical inspiration and a work of singular purity and taste. The plaster ceiling is decorated after the later manner of Robert Adam. It is most unfortunate that this beautiful church is not sited as originally intended, looking down George Street.

Long before the completion of St Andrew's Church, however, long before it was even begun, the most important of all disputes concerning the development of the New Town was under way. This concerned the right to build on the south side of Princes Street.

In 1769 John Home, coachbuilder, acquired ground on the south side of Princes Street, at the east end, next to the North Bridge. At various dates he added to this land, until by the summer of 1770 he owned a 162 foot frontage on Princes Street stretching back some 300 feet.[22] Some of this land he sub-feued, and, presumably with the intention of creating a street frontage to the east, he seems to have planned a street leading down the slope from Princes Street immediately west of the bridge. This street, extremely steep, subsequently came into existence, and was called St Ann's Street. In June 1770 Home, along with Young and Trotter, upholsterers, applied for further land to the west of the area already owned by them. The Council feued the ground, but stipulated that no building on it should rise above the level of Princes Street. Then, late in 1770, Home and his friends prepared to build.

At once an outcry arose. Several feuars in the New Town objected most strenuously, and after raising a summons of declarator and damages against the Council, they presented, on 5 October 1771, a Bill of Suspension and Interdict to prevent the progress of the building. The principal begetter of this Bill was Sir William Forbes, and the most notable name among the list of fourteen signatories was that of David Hume.[23] The Bill stated that the feuars had come to live in the New Town very largely because it was understood that:

> no buildings were to be erected to the south of Prince's-Street, by which means the proprietors of houses on that street in particular, would enjoy advantages which they considered as of the greatest value, viz. free air, and an agreeable prospect. While, on the other hand, the fine opening from the city upon that street gave at once an idea of the beauty and elegance of the general design. It was therefore matter of just surprise to the feuars, when they came to learn, that the Town-council, or

persons acting by their authority, had sold a large spot of
ground southward of Prince's-street, and to the west of the
bridge, for the acknowledged purpose of building houses,
making a coach-yard, wrights shops, and the like.

The fact that no chimney tops were to be within thirteen feet of the
level of Princes Street was not a concession, the feuars went on, but
the establishment of a deformity and a nuisance. And matters were
growing worse:

The magistrates and town council, however, or those by whom
they suffer themselves to be guided or influenced, made still a
further stretch; and, some time in the end of the year 1768 or
beginning of the year 1769, feued out to John Hume coach-
wright, a large spot of ground to the south of Prince's-street
aforesaid, with the liberty to build, or, at least, without re-
striction; and, in process of time, it was discovered, that Mr.
Hume had bargained with Messrs Young and Trotter, upholsterers, Mr. John Neil merchant, and John Reid and
Richard Thomson, masons in Bristo-street, who had projected
houses, ware-houses, and the like, opposite to, and on the
level of Prince's-street. This also was complained of as a most
gross violation of public faith, and a real injury to the town itself.

The feuars' case rested on the fact that in Craig's plan no building
was shown south of Princes Street, but, on the contrary, the whole
area was depicted as laid out in gardens sloping down to a canal.
The Town Council's case rested on the argument that Craig's plan
did not represent a contract to the details of which they were bound
to adhere, and on the fact that in the relevant Act of Council, dated
29 July 1767, clause six read, 'As it is not intended at present to feu
out the ground betwixt the South Street [Princes Street] and the
North Loch, the feuars upon that street should have an obligation in
their favour, that if houses were afterwards built there, they should
not be nearer to their houses than 96 feet.' The feuars replied that
they had never had an opportunity of reading this Act, and had
therefore been misled. The rights of the case cannot now be decided.
Possibly the feuars were deceived, deliberately or accidentally;
possibly they deceived themselves by failure to read the Act. In any
case, it was now up to the lawyers. The Court of Session rejected

Overleaf [22] *Craig. Physicians' Hall, George Street,
1776, original drawing of
street frontage. Demolished in
1844, the Hall was considered
'a chaste and elegant imitation
of ancient Grecian archi-
tecture'.*
RCPE

the Bill of Suspension, but the House of Lords, in April 1772, reversed the decision. Lord Mansfield delivered judgment in characteristically trenchant fashion:

> Let me earnestly recommend to this Corporation to call to their
> aid the same assistance they set out with – let them consult
> with their standing counsel what may be for their honour,
> what for their interest, neither of which they seem for some
> time to have understood. I give my opinion, therefore, my
> Lords, for continuing this injunction, not only on the plain and
> open principles of justice, but from regard to the public, and
> from regard to this misguided Corporation itself.

This decision, however, did not settle the matter, but merely obliged the Court of Session to decide the action of declarator. As before, the Court decided in favour of the Town Council. The feuars, who to the great good fortune of posterity were men of substance and determination, gave notice of an appeal to the House of Lords. By this time, however, the buildings in question were nearing completion, and a compromise was sought. The matter was submitted to arbitration, and on 19 March 1776 the arbitrator[24] pronounced a decree-arbitral. The houses under construction were to be completed; west of a line represented approximately by the present Waverley Steps only a few workshops, below the level of Princes Street, were to be allowed; apart from that, the land westward as far as Hanover Street was to be 'kept and preserved in perpetuity as pleasure ground'.

This ruling left the ground south of Princes Street and to the west of Hanover Street still free for feuing and building. Indeed, it was expressly declared that this was so, provided that houses built there should be not less than 96 feet from those on the north side. No attempt, however, seems at any time to have been made by the Town Council to exercise this right, and an Act of Parliament of 1816 prevented any such building in all time to come. Thus was saved, in spite of the Town Council, the most important asset and the true singularity of Edinburgh; the physical separation and the visible conjunction of the Old Town and the New.

The buildings which were erected on the south side of Princes Street near the North Bridge were for the most part of a mean character, those in St Ann's Street being described as follows in 1817:

> The whole were reared and finished in the meanest and most
> irregular manner, presenting to the view over the parapet wall
> of the North Bridge a range of dirty and deformed chimney tops
> and of heavy roofs, in which the most curious eye could scarcely
> discover any feature of the sublime or beautiful. They were
> occupied, too, exclusively by keepers of ale houses and small
> shops, or by chairmen, porters, and common mechanics; and,
> in particular, by a numerous and exalted colony of operative
> tailors, whose gay and glaring signboards were the first objects
> that struck the traveller as he crossed to the Old Town; and
> whose newly washed or dyed old clothes, of all odious colours
> and smells, were displayed from the upper stories of these
> tenements, none of which had either offices, or back court, or
> yard of any description.[25]

These remained, little altered, from 1776 until their demolition over
a hundred years later.

The feuars who fought and were victorious over the Town
Council were only fourteen in number; a small part of the rapidly
growing body of citizens of the New Town. Feuing had begun in
1767. On 3 August, within a week of the final approval of Craig's
plan, John Young, wright, feued the first three lots at a total purchase price of £450.[26] He was followed, before the end of the year,
by seventeen other feuars, including Sir Laurence Dundas. In the
following year, eleven feuars took ground from the town. Almost
all the earliest building was in St Andrew's Square – 'the novelty of
a Square in Edinburgh, and the overwhelming degree of elegance
which this one was expected to possess, made it more popular at
first, as a situation for building, than any other part of the plan'.[27]
Even in the earliest years, however, a few houses were built in
South St Andrew's Street, South St David's Street, and in Princes
Street. After the first burst of enthusiasm in 1767 and 1768, not
much feuing was done for a few years; the partial collapse of the
North Bridge in 1769 no doubt discouraged intending residents.

Activity revived in the late 1770s, falling away again in 1782 and
1783. Then in 1784, towards the end of the American War, sales
suddenly leapt upwards and continued at very high levels from 1785

to 1792. With the outbreak of the Napoleonic War, bringing extreme business and financial uncertainty, sales collapsed for a few years, but they rose again to old levels for the last few years of the century, with the start of feuing in York Place in 1798. None of this, it may be noted, shows any significant correlation with the price of consols.

It is also possible to trace, in a rough sort of way, the westward progress of building. St Andrew's Square was very largely feued before 1780, and St Andrew's Street and St David's Street at much the same time.[28] The first feu was taken in Hanover Street in 1784 and in Frederick Street in 1786. Hanover Street was almost completely built by 1790, and Frederick Street a few years afterwards; as the latter street neared completion, building began in Castle Street, in 1792. Princes Street and George Street were built up correspondingly, but building in Queen Street and in Rose Street moved westwards more slowly.

Charlotte Square was in large part a separate essay in planning and building. When Craig drew up his plan, the Town did not own all the ground between Calton Hill and what is now Queensferry Road. This imposed certain limitations on the plan. In the east, St Andrew's Square could not be set far enough east to centre it on the line of the North Bridge as well as on the line of George Street; while in the west the line of Queensferry Road obliged Craig to plan a rather inconvenient junction of Hope Street with Princes Street – an inconvenience which remains to the present day. Craig ignored the fact that the town did not own the ground lying between Castle Street and Charlotte Square; agreement regarding this ground was reached in 1785. He also ignored the fact that the north-western boundary of the town's property ran in an oblique line which cut across the outer sections of the north-west corner of the square which he proposed to build at that end of George Street. Nothing was said of this difficulty at the time. But by 1788 the matter was more urgent, and the Lord Provost of the day declared that the completion of Craig's plan was impracticable:

21. Houses in N Castle Street built in the 1790's. Sir Walter Scott lived here from 1802-26.

on account of want of ground, and a right of servitude belonging to the Earl of Moray over 90 feet in breadth of ground belonging to the Community, a square at the west end of George

Street in the extended Royalty, similar to St. Andrew Square
cannot be made, and the original plan thereof must of necessity
be altered.

The Lord Provost believed, however, that there would be 'ground
sufficient in that place for building a Circus or a Crescent'.[29] Fortunately, the Town Council did not give up. Negotiations were
entered into with the Earl of Moray, and these resulted in a verbal
agreement regarding the boundary line between the two properties.
This agreement presumably set back the boundary line by the
amount necessary to allow the north-west corner of the square to be
built, and the set-back was apparently sufficient to allow building to
go on unimpeded by the Earl's stipulation in 1792 that 'no houses
shall be built within 30 ells of the said new line of march from the
east to the west end thereof'.[30] Negotiations thus gave room for the
building of the square; although one of the limiting effects is still to
be seen in the bevelled corner at the junction of Charlotte Street and
Albyn Place.[31]

In August 1791 it was noted that the agreement with Moray
should be reduced to writing 'without loss of time, that Charlotte
Square may be feued out'.[32] Robert Adam was commissioned by the
Town Council to produce a unified scheme of frontages for the houses
in the square. This was something quite new in Edinburgh, where
a certain uniformity of design was the utmost that had so far been
attempted. The result seems to have been a strong tendency in the
direction of monotony and lack of distinction. The original houses
in Princes Street, for example, were very plain, with a very simple
fenestration. Some were of only two storeys, and many of them had
only a common stair, entered from the Mews Lane behind. Farington,
who visited the city in 1788, remarked that 'the spirit for improvement is fully exhibited in Edinburgh, but it is to be lamented that
in many instances it has not been under better regulation'[33]; he was
particularly unfavourably impressed by the smallness and poor
proportions of the buildings in George Street, a street 'so wide in
proportion to the height of the buildings, that in the declining line
of perspective they appear like Barracks'.[34]

Much depended on the style of private house-building, for there
were few public buildings in the New Town. St Andrew's Church

*22. Charlotte Square, N side.
The raised pavement, with
mounting blocks, permitted
easy access to carriages.*

93

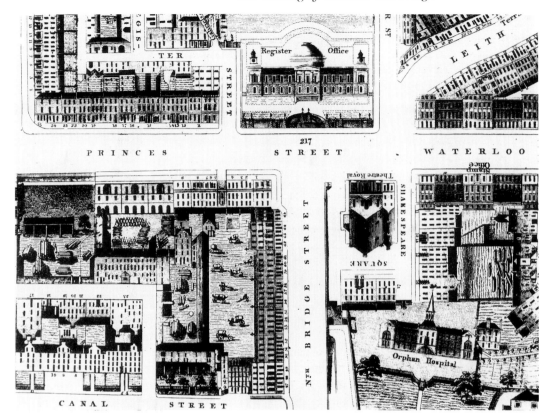

[23] Shakespeare Square. Detail from the remarkable Plan engraved by Kirkwood, 1819.

was in the wrong place, and St George's Church had not yet been built. The Register House was incomplete. Almost opposite the Register House was the Theatre Royal, built in 1768 – one of the first buildings in the New Town. Its appearance from the North Bridge excited the rage of Arnot, who declared that 'it produces the double effect of disgusting spectators by its own deformity, and obstructing the view of the Register Office, perhaps the handsomest building in the nation'.[35] Yet the appearance of the theatre, although modest, seems to have been not altogether unpleasing, and it probably did something for that 'grim little enclosure',[36] Shakespeare Square, which sealed off the east end of Princes Street with a few lodging houses, taverns, oyster shops and the theatre. (This tiny square was built almost entirely between 1772 and 1778.) Apart

94

from these the only public buildings were in George Street: the
Assembly Rooms, built by public subscription at a cost of over
£6,000 and opened in 1787; and the Physicians' Hall, the only
important building by Craig in Edinburgh, put up in 1776 and 1777.
This building was a disappointment to the Royal College of Physicians, who found that 'its internal arrangements were not so
convenient as might have been desired'.[37] The College was also
vexed at the expense; the contract with Craig – who built as well as
designed the building – was for £2,725, but by November 1779,
£3,850 had been paid, and Craig wanted another £105.[38] In connection with this account, he wrote a letter which is of some interest
as one of the few surviving from his hand, and almost the only one
which is not a colourless business communication: this letter con-
cludes:

> If the Committee does not pay me the account of Extraordinary
> work I presented to Dr. Grant the 2nd curt. amounting to £105
> beside the rise of wages which I was obliged to pay the masons
> and wrights etc. owing to their Combination, I shall repent the
> day I ever laid a stone of their building – The Royal College are
> all Gentlemen as individuals, how far they will behave genteely
> as a Society time must soon determine.[39]

The Physicians' Hall stood for over sixty years, and judging from
prints and from the architect's elevations,[40] it was reasonably well
proportioned. But it did not please everyone. Farington, in particular, complained that 'the capitals are a third too large for the
pillars'.[41]

If it was the wish of the Town Council to counter criticism of this
sort and to rise above poverty of invention and meanness of scale,
the selection of Robert Adam to design Charlotte Square was the
ideal move. Adam was the most famous architect of the day and he
was still at the height of his powers. He was, moreover, peculiarly
a master of the art of designing unified house frontages – the innovation made by Wood in Bath in the 1750s – and his flair for vigorous
and varied ornamentation was ideally calculated to offset the drab
and unambitious appearance of so many New Town houses. The
idea that he should be employed to design the frontages of 'the new
square' – for which a certain 'Nisbet plaisterer' had already drawn

something – was first suggested late in 1790, and early in 1791 a definite request seems to have come from the Lord Provost, who wanted elevations, according to John Paterson,[42] 'not much ornamented but with an elegant Simplicity Such as the north frount of the College to use the provests words'.

Adam made his design in 1791. The contract with the Town Council has disappeared, but a letter written by James Adam after Robert's death in 1792 asks for payment on account of a promise to his brother of 200 guineas for the elevations for Charlotte Square. This letter also states that the builders were to pay five guineas for each working drawing of an individual house. The Town Council ordered payment of 100 guineas.

*23. Drawing-room, No. 6
Charlotte Square
(courtesy, Lord Bute).*

Charlotte Square is a rectangle, each side 500 feet in length, with streets entering at each corner. The east side is divided by the end of

96

George Street, from which there is a view, across the garden which occupies the whole centre of the Square, with tall trees and, in springtime, thousands of blue and yellow crocuses, of the pillars and green dome of St George's Church. The frontages, monumental, yet elegant and human in their proportions, are completely unified in treatment, and the north side is a replica of the south. Every side is three storeys high, plus attics and basement, and the splendid north and south sides are centred on a pediment mounted on four Corinthian pillars. The appearance is enriched by restrained use of balustrades, festoons, and circular panels; while a prominent feature consists of recessed and arched doors and windows at street level. The north side is the best preserved: elsewhere, dormer windows have been opened into the attics, although this was expressly prohibited in the conditions of feuing. Yet in spite of the departures from Adam's design, Charlotte Square is a marvellous achievement. Spacious; elegant; symmetrical without needless duplication; full of variety yet harmonious and devoid of fussiness; it has been described with truth as 'one of the major achievements in European civic architecture of the period'.[43]

The first feu in the Square was taken in 1792 and the house on this site was built so rapidly that the premium of ten pounds promised to the first builder to roof a house in the Square was paid in September of the same year. But other buildings were slow to follow. The Napoleonic War had broken out and money was dear. Two feus were taken in 1796, one in 1797 and two in 1798. All of these were on the north side of the Square. As Adam had designed the north side to contain nine houses, this means that by 1800 only two-thirds, at most, of the north side was built, and nothing else. Thus Charlotte Square, although belonging in its original conception to Craig, Adam and the eighteenth century, is to a large degree the product of a later day.

24. No. 6 Charlotte Square.

Another square which deserves separate consideration is St James's Square, lying just to the east of the eastern boundary of Craig's New Town. The ground plan of this square was also designed by Craig; it is dated 1773. The square is now to be demolished, having become neglected and derelict. But it was attractive once, located on the crest of Multrees Hill, near a green slope where people gathered to watch the crowds returning from the races on Leith sands, and in 1773 the promoters of St James's Square saw for it a brilliant future, and they commended its advantages in terms which seem to make a mockery of its later dismal and dilapidated state:

> Plan for a new designed Square the property of
> Mr. Walter Ferguson, Writer in Edinburgh.
> Advantages of the situation of this Square.

1. It is dry, healthy, and commands pleasant and extensive views particularly above 20 miles of the Firth of Forth and great part of the Harbours and Grounds on both sides of it.
2. It is of easy access from the New Bridge by a Road 34 feet broad along the east side of the Reposition for the Records.
3. It is at the distance of a moderate walk of 8 minutes from the Parliament House, the high church, and the Exchange; of 9 minutes from the College of Physick Gardens, of 6 minutes from the Markets, and not 3 minutes from agreeable airings in the country.
4. Being without the Royalty, it is free from all the Taxes, Imposts and Burdens to which the inhabitants within the liberties of the City of Edinburgh are subject; and of the Land Tax:—
   N.B. There is plenty of Clay and sand on the Ground for making Bricks.

25. St James's Square, central doorway E side. This building, now demolished, had an almost Roman severity and grandeur typical of this phase of New Town development.

The square was built between 1775 and 1790. Robert Burns lived here for several months in 1787. The buildings round the square were designed, unlike those in St Andrew's Square, to provide a unified 'palace-front' appearance; but the elevations were undistinguished. If, however, these elevations were by Craig, they are interesting as an example of his capabilities as a domestic architect.

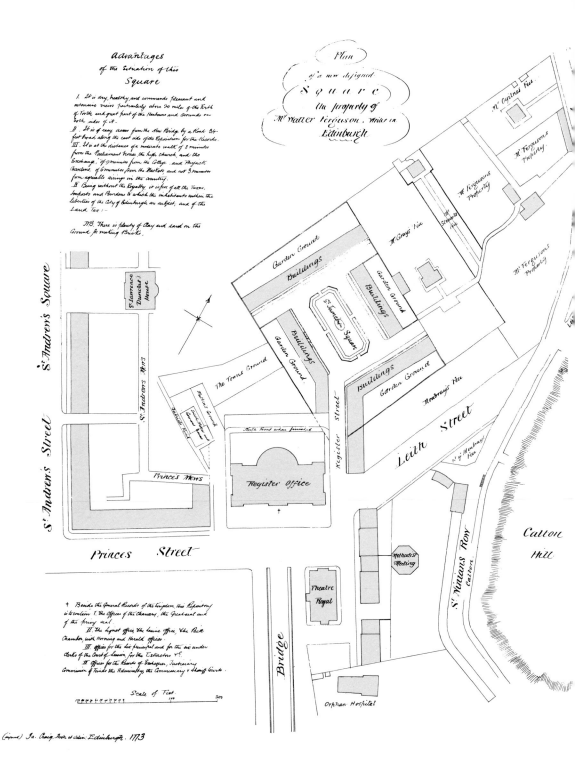

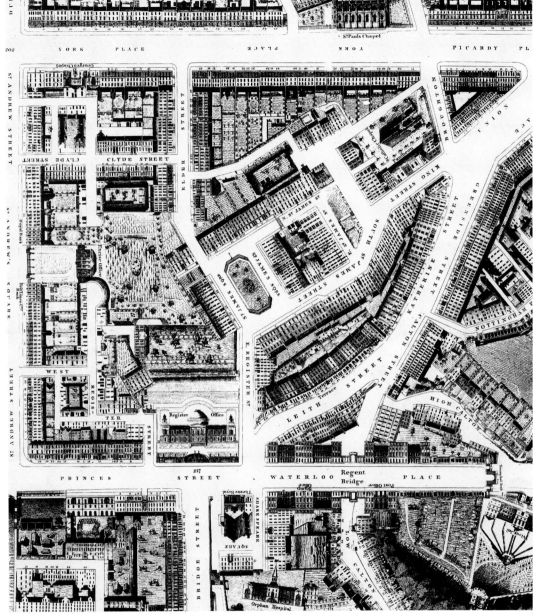

[25] facing, *Craig. Plan for St James's Square, 1773* (Heriot Trust) *and*
[26], above. *St James's Square completed.*
Kirkwood

Little is known about the actual builders who built the houses in Craig's New Town. They often took feus themselves, built a house, and sold; this happened in the case of eight lots out of twenty-four feued in 1767, three lots out of ten feued in 1768; the other lots were purchased by prospective residents. The figures for other years are similar, although occasionally the proportion of lots feued by builders rose as high as 60 per cent. During the building boom of 1784–92 there were some twenty-odd builders feuing in their own names and building; there may have been others who confined themselves to building to order. Most of these builders were no doubt working on a small scale with very limited capital; and each, as a rule, worked in the New Town for only a few years. But there were exceptions. William Pirnie, who built St Andrew's Church, was building in the New Town from 1772-86, although he took only four feus in this period. Robert Wright took his first feu in 1788, his sixth and last in 1803; this may have been the same Wright whose name appears in a partnership, Wright and McKean, masons, taking eight feus between 1792 and 1805. Others who feued and built on a considerable scale were Ed. Butterworth, who took nine feus between 1788 and 1794 and then, after long years when building

100

activity was at a low level, reappeared as a feuar in Charlotte Square in 1808; Alexander Reid, a member of the Town Council from 1789 to 1791, who took five feus between 1789 and 1797; and John Brough, builder, upholsterer and cabinet maker, who took fourteen feus between 1773 and 1784, and who was bankrupt in 1789. The greatest feuar of all, however, was John Young, who took the first five feus in the New Town in 1767, and then, between 1776 and 1795 feued no less than seventeen other lots. He was a member of the Town Council in 1790 and again in 1792 and 1793.

These men not only operated over long periods; there is also evidence that some of them were men of substance and consequence. Thus in 1781 John Young was highest bidder at the roup of an area in St Andrew's Square, offering £126 purchase price plus £4 12s. in feu-duty. Payment was not due until Whitsunday 1782, but Young, on being offered a discount of £8 8s. for sixteen months interest, 'instantly paid' the purchase price.[44] The behaviour, on another occasion, of James Tait, mason, also suggests the established man of business. Tait claimed in 1792 that he had 'within these few years feued from the Council and built agreeable to the regulations more ground than almost any other person whatever has done'.[45] In 1797 he wrote the following letter to the Town Council:

Sir, Hereby make you the following offer to feu from the Town of Edinburgh Lot 7 South side of Charlotte Square, and Lot 8 and 9 on the west, and sixty two feet six ins. fronting Charlotte Street, the purchase money to be for the whole £426: 17/5, eight twelfths payable at Whitsunday 1799 at which time the feu duty is to commence, the front next the Square to be built to Mr. Adams Elevation, the front near Charlotte Street to be built to an Elevation of my own, which shall be made out and given unto you when I shall begin to build that house, the whole three lots to be Redhall Stone in front, it is understood by us that I shall be free from the expense of making and putting up the Sphinx, Bulls head, Swag husks and Ribbon knots, you are also to allow me to make Lot 8 and 9 fifty feet deep as a house of less size so high Stories will not do to the present times, if you agree to my offer your answer in a day will oblige, and an Act of Council to be delivered in a week hence if convenient. I

am Sir, Your Obedt. Servant, Jas. Tait. P.S. It is understood
that I may be allowed the liberty of laying the Earth taken out
of the foundation in front to level up the Street and Square. J.T.[46]
To this peremptory communication, demanding an immediate reply
and at the same time shouldering onto the Town Council the cost of
the decorative details of Adam's design while altering the ground
plan, the Town Council returned a meek assent. Something must
have gone wrong, however, for this feuing is not to be found in the
Record of Feus.

The efforts of all these builders drove the New Town westwards
from St Andrew's Square to Charlotte Square between 1767 and 1792,
and one would think that the Town Council would have been well
satisfied with the progress of the scheme, and that the financial outcome could not have been other than satisfactory. Such, however,
does not seem to have been the case. In 1784 the Council declared
that 'abstracting from the great expense the city was put to in purchasing Grounds and building the Bridge, the purchase money
hitherto received [from feuing] has but barely answered the expence
laid out upon levelling and paving the Streets Common Sewers
etc.'.[47] And the Council's anxiety was evidently real enough to cause
a general review of the whole policy of urban development.

We do not know what sort of review of its financial position the
Town Council carried out in 1784, but it is clear that the city's
financial arrangements were by that date extremely complex. There
were two streams of revenue, and a third was just beginning. The
first, sometimes called the proper revenue, consisted of the import
on wines; shore dues at Leith; market dues at vegetable, corn and
cattle markets; feu duties and returns from landed property owned
by the city; all or a part of which was often referred to as the *Common
Good*.[48] This revenue was available for general purposes. The second
stream consisted of the twopenny duty on every pint of beer or ale
brewed, brought into or sold within the liberties of the city. This
ale duty, begun in 1653, was extended in 1723 so as to allow the
magistrates to increase the city's debt by not more than £25,000,
such additional borrowing to be principally for the carrying on of
public works. The yield of this tax, sometimes called the appropriated
revenue, fell from almost £8,000 in 1724 to little over £2,000 in

1776; this decrease, caused, according to Arnot, by increased consumption of tea and whisky leading 'to the propagation of idleness, vice and disease . . . among the poor',[49] was certainly an embarrassment to the city's finances. The third stream of revenue consisted of the income from assessments on house and shop properties of £10 or more yearly rental. These assessments were first levied by the Police Commissioners for the Southern Districts constituted in 1771, but the system extended rapidly from 1785.

This plan of finance was enormously complicated in the details of its operation, particularly with regard to the special levies or assessments. Some of these levies were calculated as so much per cent on the purchase price, others as so much per cent on four-fifths of the real rent, others as so much per cent of the actual yearly value. The City Guard was paid for on a per capita basis. Some citizens enjoyed partial exemption from rating, however levied, and these included almost the whole of the legal profession, the royal tradesmen, and the city ministers. Some Acts applied only to some localities, so that about 1800 it was reckoned that almost half the properties in the burgh enjoyed at least partial exemption. Moreover, the system of valuation employed by the Police Commissioners differed significantly from that of the thirty stent masters who fixed conjectural values and rentals for the Town Council, so that 'in one year a particular district was valued for police purposes at £61,945, and for municipal purposes the same district was valued at £37,899'.[50] Expenses of collection varied from 3 per cent to 4 per cent of the yield.

Not all of these complications and anomalies had appeared or developed fully by 1784, but the situation was already complicated and obscure. It is possible, however, to determine in a fairly precise fashion what had been spent on the whole New Town project north of the Bridge and – rather less precisely – what return had been received.

The initial outlay had been for land. The main purchase, that of Bearford's or Barefoots Parks, the area lying approximately between the North Loch and Rose Street, was bought as early as 1716 for £2,200. This expense, incurred fifty years before building began, can hardly be reckoned an outgoing in respect of the New Town. Six later purchases, however, must definitely be so reckoned. These were:

Allan's Parks, bought in 1758 for £1,050;

How Acres, bought in 1765 for £1,200;

Henderson's Feu, bought in 1763/4 for £480;

Whitecroft or Halkerston's Croft, bought in two parts in 1758 and 1765 for a total of £1,800;

Buchan's Feu, bought in 1769 for £500;

Dickson's Feu, bought in 1782 for £750.

Most of these properties paid an almost nominal feu duty or none at all. The total capital outlay for land after 1716 was therefore £5,780.

Secondly, the Council had the expense of levelling and causeying the streets, of providing drains, and of laying sewers at least along the main streets. These tasks the Council seems to have taken quite seriously – at least it spent a good deal of money on them. Thus in 1784, while the Council deliberated their future policy, there was an expenditure of £405 for levelling and causeying the streets in the extended Royalty, plus £70 for quarrying, shaping and carting the stones required. Also, £249 was spent on stones for sewers, £225 for laying the sewers, and there were miscellaneous items which added another £340. The total expenditure of £1,287 is higher than was usual at that time, the average figure for the years 1767 to 1783 being £880. There was thus a total expenditure on these items in this early period of just under £15,000 – to be exact, £14,910. This, too, was a capital expense.

To be set against these once-and-for-all outgoings were the receipts from the sale of land. In the first year of feuing these receipts were most encouraging, totalling £3,984. But this figure was not to be reached again until after 1784. In several years the figure was below £500. The average, 1767-83, was £940; a total receipt of £15,987.

Certain other items should be taken into consideration. One, on the debit side, is water supply. This was an expense, but until after 1783 an inconsiderable one, principally because it was a 'rule established' that feuars paid the cost of the water pipe in front of their respective buildings.[51] Sanitation also cost a little, but not much. There is a record of the appointment of an 'additional scaffinger for the Extended Royalty[52] in 1791', but we do not know whether this doubled the scavenging force in this part of the town or increased it by some smaller proportion. Probably it doubled it. Against this sort of expense must be set the fact that sanitation could be a source of profit. Thus in 1791 after advertising, the Council received a letter from 'Robert Brown writer in Edinburgh, whereby in name of himself and other farmers in the neighbourhood' [an interesting example of dual occupation, this] 'he made an offer of £100st. yearly, for a five years Tack of the whole dung of the new extended Royalty'.[53] Dung was an important source of city revenue in the eighteenth century. Cleaning the streets was certainly a very small net expense, if it was a net expense at all. Lastly, it may be proper to add to the expenditure the cost of building St Andrew's Church, on which well over £3,000 had been spent by 1784.

We thus know that the city spent almost £6,000 on land, over £3,000 on St Andrew's Church, and on streets, drains, sewers etc. almost £15,000; a total of approximately £24,000 for the years 1767-83. Against this there stands the figure for receipts from land sales, £16,000. The conclusion must be that not only were the Council not making a fortune over Craig's New Town, they were definitely losing money. And this is equally true from the income point of view: for whereas income from feus in the early 1780s was about £350 per annum, the interest charge on the deficit of £8,000, at 5 per cent, was about £400 per annum.

The remedy which the Council adopted in 1784 was the seemingly mild one of raising feu-duties by 50 per cent. This was not of itself going to bring in a great deal more money. But it has to be remembered that a feu-duty is a perpetual charge on property, and a rise in feu-duty is liable to slow down sales, operating in the same way as a rise in the rate of interest. The magistrates must have been well aware that in thus raising feu-duties they ran the risk of slowing down the rate at which the New Town was growing, and thus of postponing the day when land sales might match capital expenditure.

Fears of this sort would have been understandable in 1784. In fact, the situation was about to improve, at least to some extent. A period of exceptionally rapid economic development throughout Great Britain was just beginning, and the growth of the New Town was to keep pace with the growth of the economy. Sales of land in the later 1780s were to be consistently over £3,000 per annum, and

Overleaf [28] *Craig's New Town completed.* Kirkwood

105

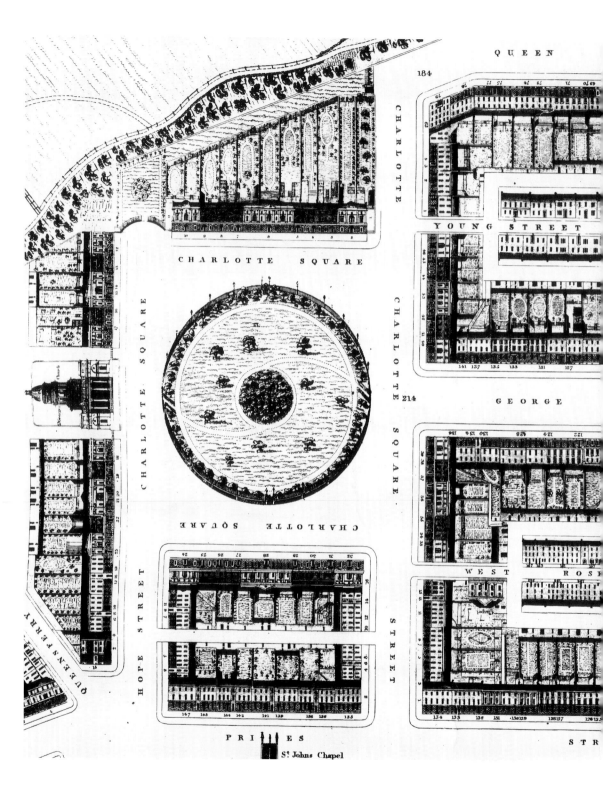

QUEEN

184

CHARLOTTE

CHARLOTTE SQUARE

YOUNG STREET

CHARLOTTE SQUARE

CHARLOTTE SQUARE

214

GEORGE

CHARLOTTE SQUARE

HOPE STREET

STREET

WEST ROS

QUEENSFERRY

PRI   ES

St Johns Chapel

STR

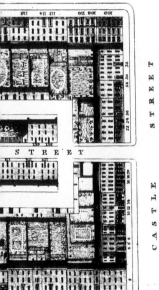
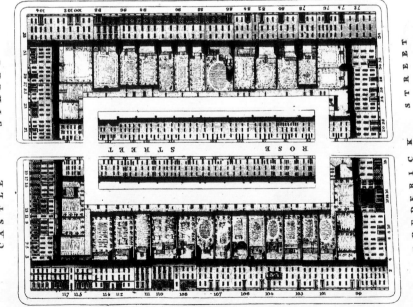

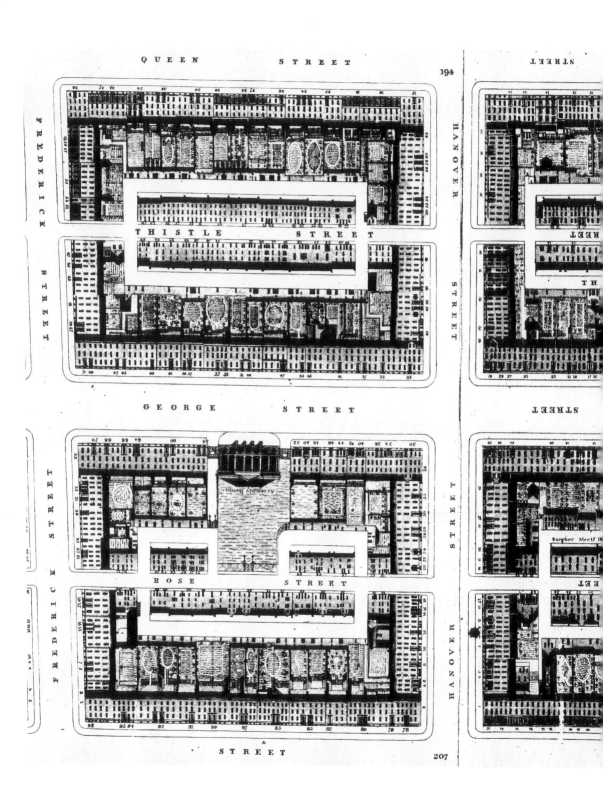

QUEEN STREET

STREET

FREDERICK STREET

HANOVER STREET

THISTLE STREET

GEORGE STREET

FREDERICK STREET

HANOVER STREET

ROSE STREET

STREET

Assembly Rooms

Burgher Meet H

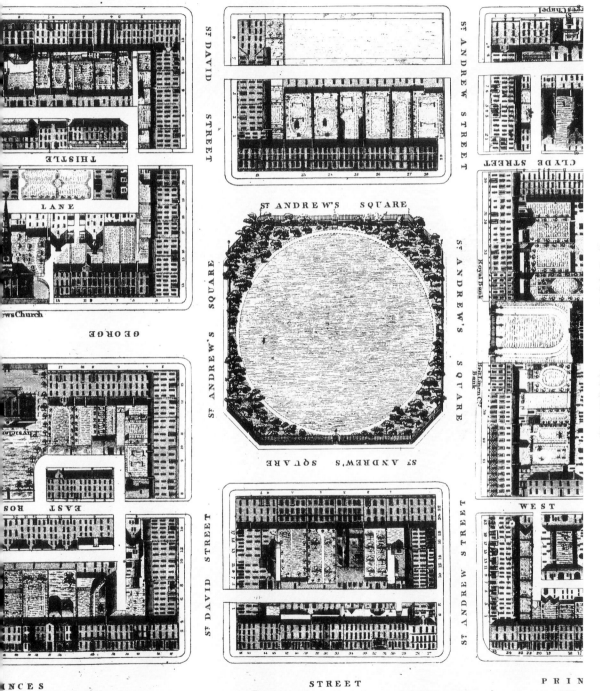

although from 1795 to 1797 they were disappointing, the average
from 1784 to 1797 was nevertheless over £2,500. In all, the Council
received £35,664. Expenditure, it is true, rose almost as fast,
amounting to £33,524. To this should be added some proportion
of the outlays on water supply, which totalled well over £4,000
between 1787 and 1792.[54] If the New Town is debited with half this
expenditure, then the deficit of £8,000 on capital account which
existed in 1783 remained almost unaltered in 1797. But the income
from feu-duties offered some consolation, for by 1797 this amounted
to £1,824 from the New Town – five times as much as in 1783, and
also, incidentally, two and a half times as much as was received from
feus in the Ancient Royalty.[55] Then, in 1798, began the feuing of
ground to the east of St Andrew's Square, ground obtained from
Lord Alva in 1793-94 and now free from restrictive agreements. Income from land sales abruptly leapt upwards, topping £4,000 in
1798 (for the third time in the town's history) and this time expenditure rose less than proportionately. York Place, Albany Street, Duke
Street and Elder Street were built very rapidly, often in large
'parcels', and the capital account position at last began to improve,
sales receipts exceeding expenditure by almost £4,000 between
1798 and 1802. The deficit had been halved. Total expenditure to
date was £70,000, total receipts were £66,000. Moreover, the
profitable and enchanting prospect of Robert Adam's Charlotte
Square was now to be glimpsed, feuing rather slowly, it is true, but
something of a promised land nevertheless to architect, builder,
Town Council and citizens alike.

26. Balconies, E Register Street. The textured stone gives life to the plain façades of such Edinburgh tenements.

   The clouds of war which darkened the general economic prospect
of the last years of the eighteenth century did not damp the 'spirit
of improvement' in Edinburgh; and the Town Council no doubt
entered the nineteenth century with buoyant and not unreasonable
hopes of an ultimately successful financial outcome to the city's great
development schemes.

V

Extensions Southward

In the middle of 1784 discussions began between the Town Council and representatives of the 'six Districts on the south side of the City'.[1] There were three questions to decide. First, on what terms were the inhabitants of the southern districts to assist financially in the building of the South Bridge? Secondly, under whose management should the bridge be built? Lastly, to what use should the profits, if any, be applied? Agreement seems to have been reached on all three questions with comparatively little difficulty. The southern districts were to contribute financially by means of a cess levied in proportion to that levied elsewhere in the city on the basis of valuation in the southern districts mutually agreed or decided by arbitration.[2] In return, the town was to build a reservoir for water in Heriot's Gardens or Bristo Street, and to supply water to individual houses on the same terms as in the Old Town. Secondly, the bridge was to be built out of general revenue, and any deficiency was to be made up by a general rate on the whole city (the rival proposal was for toll charges on the use of the bridge). Building was to be in the hands of ten commissioners, responsible to the Town Council. And lastly, although the Council was sympathetic to the view that 'it would be extremely palatable to the Citizens of Edinburgh if the money to be made by the proposed Communication was to be alloted as a fund for a new University', they thought nevertheless that 'the good Town should be permitted to apply the profit to any public purpose they thought best'.[3] In May 1785 the South Bridge Act was passed in these terms, except that the anticipated profits were now earmarked for the University, and the Bridge Commissioners became 'likewise Commissioners for building a New College'.[4]

27. Buccleuch Place, built about 1800. The slates, cobbles, and astragals are details which add up to a satisfying architectural synthesis.

111

While the necessary Bill was in Parliament, some opposition arose. The inhabitants of Leith, not unreasonably, objected to being taxed in order that the inhabitants of the southern districts should enjoy an easier way of getting into and out of town. Others objected to the line from the Tron Church, preferring that the road to the bridge should leave the High Street from the back of the Guard House.[5] The Lord Provost went to London in April in order to help matters forward. And the opposition evidently died down or was overcome, for in July workmen were employed to lower the level of the High Street at the Tron Church by five or six feet, and on 1 August 1785 the foundation stone of the bridge was laid.

Only a few details regarding the building of this bridge have survived. Land and property were bought, as in the case of the Exchange and the North Bridge, at prices determined by a specially empanelled jury of fifteen. Numerous old buildings were demolished, including 'a brewery and brewing house, kiln and stables' lying 'on the east side of the road through Adams Square', the property of John Adam.[6] The Trustees paid the very modest sum of £250 for the area between Niddry's Wynd and Marline's Wynd, and £250 for the area fronting the Cowgate 'lately the fish mercate'.[7] The east side of Niddry's Wynd, at the foot of which Robert Adam's mother had lived in the 1750s, disappeared, as did Marline's Wynd and Peebles Wynd. So did the Black Turnpike at the head of Peebles Wynd, at one time 'nearly the most sumptuous building in Edinburgh'.[8]

The new bridge or viaduct which was thus driven through and over one of the most populous parts of the Old Town was a very substantial piece of civil engineering, over one thousand feet in length. The foundation of the central pier is said to have been dug twenty-two feet deep, and the whole structure, although not so high as the North Bridge, was made up of no fewer than nineteen arches. The contract, with Alexander Laing, architect and mason, is dated February 1786, and the bridge was built very quickly, being open for foot passengers in July 1788. The building cost was £6,446. According to Stark,[9] the ground on each side of the bridge was subsequently sold by the Town Council for a total of £30,000. Examination of the City Chamberlain's accounts suggests a lower, but not a very much lower, figure; and the conclusion would seem to be that

the venture was a profitable one. It is, however, worth remarking that in 1788 the Trustees were authorised to receive $2\frac{1}{2}$ per cent annually on the valued rent of all rateable property in the Royalty for a period of four years; and that in 1792 they were 'owing considerable sums of money'.[10]

In the course of 1786 the Trustees became involved in a dispute with Robert Adam. What happened is not quite clear, but certainly Adam prepared two plans for the southern approach, including in them preliminary designs for new university buildings.[11] Each plan provided for a straight street flanked by 'colonades', and in one of them there is a semicircular crescent laid out to face the University. The plans differ principally in the width of the street and in its relation to the Tron Kirk. An elevation was also prepared, which provided 'one connected design, every separate House makes only a part of the whole'. According to the critics,[12] the Trustees' plan was for a bridge over the Cowgate running in an oblique line from the North Bridge ('contrary to the plans laid before Parliament'[13]), and allowing only twenty feet between the road and Niddry's Wynd, the road even so being so far west as to cause the gable of the Tron to intrude into the street. There was no proper provision for drainage.

[29] *Robert Adam. Design for South Bridge, arch over the Cowgate, about 1786. soane MUS.*

(a)

[30] *Robert Adam. Designs
for South Bridge development,
1786, with terraced shops and
dwellings.*
   (a) W *side elevation*
   (b) *back of* W *side, from
      Blair Street*
   (c) *central block on* W *side*
   (d) *elevation of proposed
      dwelling house*
SOANE MUS.

(b)

(c)

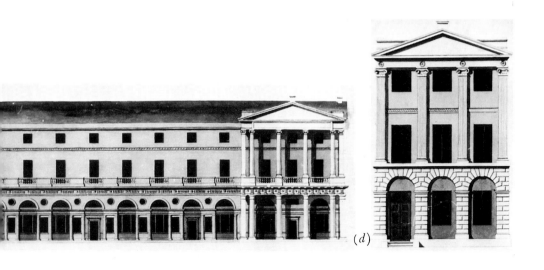

(d)

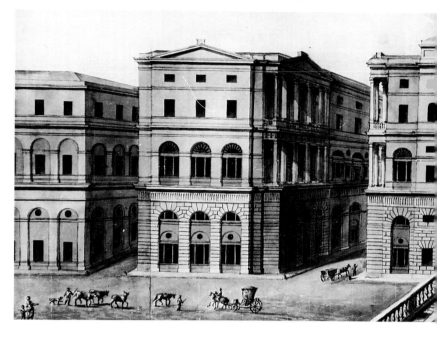

Also (in what are undoubtedly Adam's words) 'the Trustees' intention of taking some House in the New Town as a Model, to repeat it through the whole length of the Street, would have too much sameness and produce a very unpleasing and tiresome effect especially as there is no House already built in the New Town that an Architect would chuse as a Model for a Shop to imitate, far less to repeat it through a Whole Street'.

While Adam argued about the superiority of his own plans, the bridge and street were being formed. But this was not the end of the matter, for Adam finally went to law against the Trustees. In 1789 he claimed that he had received only £500 out of a total of £1,228 7s owed him by the Trustees 'for making drawings and designs and for expenses and trouble' in connection with the bridge over the Cowgate and the whole 'southern approach'. In November Henry Dundas handed down a decree arbitral which gave Robert Adam an additional £500 in respect of this claim. It is not clear whether Adam had been asked to prepare plans which were subsequently rejected,

or whether the South Bridge and approach as finally built was a compromise between his plans and the Trustees'. It is certain only that Adam's plan was for development on a larger scale than the Trustees were prepared to consider.

Much the same has to be said of James Craig's *Plan for Improving the City of Edinburgh*, published in 1786.[14] This plan, of which the publication was 'unavoidably delayed', seems to have been a major although unsolicited contribution to the debate on public improvements. Craig's reputation was much dimmed from what it had been in 1767, and it is doubtful if his opinion carried much weight in the later 1780s. His plan nevertheless deserves examination, for it contains four important suggestions:

1. The intersection of the High Street and the road from the North Bridge should be opened out to form a large octagonal space containing the Tron Kirk in the south segment, the aim being 'to prevent the accidents to which both carriages and foot-passengers would be liable, if the entry to so great

[31] Robert Adam. Impression of South Bridge and the Cowgate, 1786. Adam's proposals were not carried out. soane MUS.

117

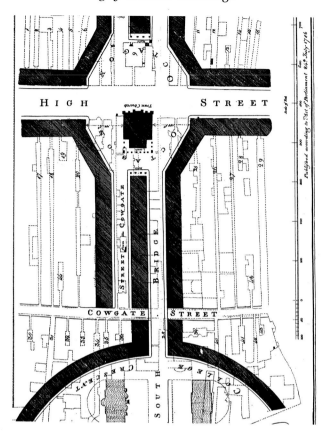

[32] Craig. Plan for an octagon and crescent at extremities of South Bridge. 'Plan for improving the City of Edinburgh', 1786.
ETC

a thorough-fare was at right angles to the High-Street'. The buildings in the Octagon were to contain shops at ground level. Also, an arcade was to be added to the south side of the Tron Church below window level, so as to 'make an agreeable shade in summer, and a shelter from rain'.

2. There should be a south-facing crescent centred on the line of the North Bridge and extending five hundred feet from the west end of the University area to the east end of the Royal Infirmary, in order to provide 'an elegant approach to the area'.

3. A new road should be laid out from Lauriston and George Square, passing south of the University across the Pleasance

and thence between Arthur's Seat and Calton Hill towards
Musselburgh. 'I have walked over the course of this road,
which is the most picturesque and elegant approach that
possibly can be to any city whatever; and to make it still
more beautiful, clumps of planting would greatly embellish
the scene upon the south side of the Calton-hill, and the
north side Arthur's Seat; at the foot of this hill by St.
Anthony's chapel, there are springs of fine water, which are
allowed to run into the kennels and wastes. At a very small
expense, a fine sheet of water may be made, which might
afford some pleasure to the angler in summer, and exercise
to the skaiter in winter.'

4. A set of public markets should be laid out near the existing
flesh-markets,[15] namely, a fish market, a poultry egg and
butter market, and a green market. These should be 'all
designed with arcades for shelter from the weather, and a
well in the centre of each'.

None of these proposals for re-planning along the route of the new
South Bridge was accepted. They would have been expensive, because
they all required the demolition of existing properties, not all of
which were ruinous or inconvenient, and demolition was, as a rule,
for the sake of securing more open space. Craig recognised the
problem, and claimed that experience showed that wide and more
handsome streets feued at proportionately higher prices. It seems
likely that he had a rather cavalier attitude towards existing properties. Whether his proposals were ever seriously considered by the
Town Council is not recorded; but they are interesting and original,
showing a lively sense of the activities and pleasures of city life, and
it is significant that they should have been put forward at this time.

Had the proposals of either Adam or Craig been executed, they
would have constituted, along with some other proposals made at
the same time, the largest scheme of public improvements carried
out in Edinburgh in the eighteenth century. But they were destined,
some to be deferred until after the Napoleonic War, others never
to be carried out at all. Nevertheless they deserve notice, because
they show that the splendid ambitiousness of 1752 had not been lost
thirty-four years later, and indeed was now linked to hopes of

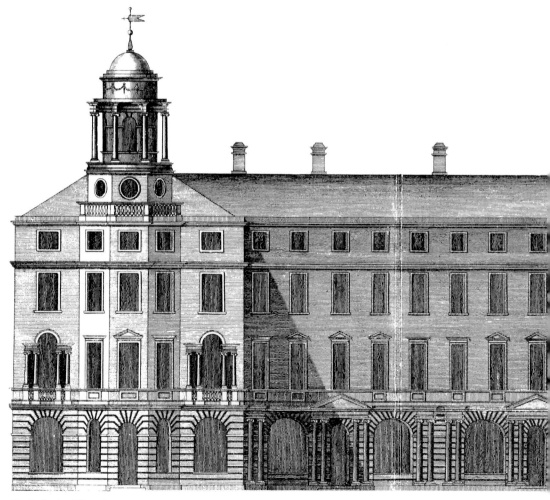

*[33] Craig. Elevation of the
proposed octagon at the Tron.*
E T C

immediate practical achievement which the first generation of planners had hardly been able to entertain.

The idea which had to be left for the nineteenth century to realise was that of 'an easy and commodious communication from the Lawn Market to the New extended Royalty'.[16] The motive was provided by the steady development of the New Town westwards. At least as early as 1781 proposals were afoot for a 'bank' or 'bridge' of communication to lead south from Princes Street, and late in 1782 an advertisement appeared informing builders that they would be allowed to lay down earth and rubbish 'dug from the foundations of houses or otherways on the west side of Princes Street where the foresaid embankment is proposed'. In 1786, possibly earlier, this rubbish and earth had to be deposited 'according to instructions issued' and some of it was carted and deposited at the expense of the town. In February 1786 the Town Council resolved to procure a credit for the purchase of houses on the north side of the Lawn-market with a view to driving a road through to the New Town, and throughout the spring and summer properties were being bought in the neighbourhood of Baxter's Close, Reid's Land and Morocco's Close.[17] But nothing more is heard of the scheme after 1786,[18] and the Mound was left to grow, 'according to instructions', at the rate of many thousands of cartloads of earth a year.[19]

The only one of the 1785-86 proposals on which an effective start was made before 1800 was for the building of a university, and a bridewell and prison. The need for the former was very great, for the latter beyond dispute. The House of Correction, alongside the Charity Workhouse near Bristo Port, was a low, wretched building, far too small. Prisoners, including debtors, were incarcerated in the Tolbooth in the High Street, a building, 'not accommodated with ventilators, with water-pipe, with privy', all parts of it 'kept in a slovenly condition; but the eastern quarter of it (although we had fortified ourselves against the stench) . . . intolerable.'[20] An Act of 1782 made some provision for replacing both the prison and the bridewell, and in 1785 the sum of £10,000 was mentioned as the probable cost. One of the advantages specified was that the Tolbooth, 'constituting a third of that cumbersome mass of buildings the Luckenbooths', could then be demolished, and that the rest of the

Luckenbooths could quite easily follow suit, turning the High Street – 'already one of the noblest in Europe' – into 'the grandest in the world'.[21] Thus even the building of a prison was to contribute to the visual splendour of the city! In the event, however, the prison remained for the meanwhile where it was, and only the new Bridewell on Calton Hill was built, to a design by Robert Adam, between 1791 and 1795.

The new University was a far grander project. The student population in the second half of the eighteenth century was in the neighbourhood of one thousand, and among the professors were several of the most eminent scholars of the day. The fabric of the University, however, left a great deal to be desired: 'What is called the College is nothing else than a mass of ruined buildings of very ancient

[34] Early 19th c view of the Mound.
KAY

123

construction.'[22] In the ruins (a picturesque exaggeration, for not all the buildings were old and dilapidated) classes were held, the library was accommodated, and some of the professors lived. At least as early as 1767 an 'intended plan of rebuilding the College'[23] was spoken of – 'people are warm in approving of it'[24] – and it was thought to raise money by subscription; but nothing came of the idea, except that the Town Council paid David Henderson ten guineas for making a plan 'of the new intended College'.[25] In 1785, however, after the North Bridge and after the American War, came new proposals, first put forward in the *Scots Magazine*. Details of what was desirable were given. There should be a Chapel, a Hall, space for the library (which has 'advanced rapidly' of recent years), space for a Museum, and also 'a common Faculty-room'. A 'sufficient number of large and commodious Teaching-rooms', it was noticed, would also be needed, and residential accommodation for the Principal and some professors. As to accommodation for the students, 'there never were but a very moderate number of chambers for the students to dwell in; and for many years past there have been none, it having been found necessary to employ these for other purposes. Such accommodations, however, are by no means looked for; nor is it necessary, as the students live promiscuously with the other inhabitants . . .'[26] Equally fortunately, there was no need to look for a new site: 'No better site for a College can be required than the site of the old one.' It was central, it was near the Royal Infirmary, and in nearby streets students were customarily 'accommodated with lodgings'. All that was needed was the will to begin, and £40,000.

This scheme must no doubt have been widely discussed, and much preparatory work done before the actual proposal to build was laid, somewhat abruptly it would seem, before the Senatus. At a meeting of that body specially convened on 19 October 1789, the Principal, Dr. William Robertson,

> stated to the meeting that when he and several of the Professors were at breakfast at the Lord Provost's house some days ago, his Lordship had informed them that the Town Council had come to the Resolution to have the foundation stone laid of a new building for the University, designed by Mr. Robert Adam Architect, on the 16th day of next month.

The Town Council, explained the Lord Provost, had been en-
couraged·to come to this resolution by the 'prospect of a liberal
contribution from the publick, and of aid from Government, which
the Right Honourable Henry Dundas, Treasurer of the Navy, had
undertaken to use his utmost influence to obtain . . .'[27]

Forms to be signed by those promising to subscribe are dated 2
November 1789, and open with the following words:

> Whereas the Buildings in the University of Edinburgh are
> extremely mean and inconvenient, some of them in a very
> ruinous condition, and all of them unsuitable to the flourishing
> state of that Seminary of Learning, in which not only a great
> part of the Youth of Scotland, but many Students from different
> places in the British Dominions, as well as from Foreign
> Countries, are educated; and whereas a PLAN for building a
> NEW UNIVERSITY has been prepared by Robert Adam,
> Esquire, of London, Architect, which has met with general
> approbation: We Subscribers . . . etc.

Early in 1790 the Trustees (who included the Duke of Buccleuch,
Henry Dundas, Robert Adam, and the Lord Provost) resolved to
advertise in the London newspapers for subscriptions, 'expressing
the Hope . . . that an Undertaking calculated for the commodious
Education of the Youth of both Parts of the United Kingdom, and
highly ornamental to the Capital of Scotland' would receive support
from 'every Friend to the Prosperity of the Country'.[28]

The design for this very large building was supplied by Robert
Adam, but his final designs differed in several ways from the building which stands today at the corner of Chambers' Street and South
Bridge. It is, indeed, inaccurate to describe the University as an
Adam building: the internal arrangements are not by Adam at all,
and no single elevation is exactly as he intended. On the other hand,
the University retains many important features of Adam's design.
The general style of the four sides which enclose a single court is
strongly reminiscent of Adam's original plan. The main departure
from Adam's plan – and it is a very substantial one – is that this
single court replaces a proposed transverse forecourt leading to a
square quadrangle beyond. This would have been an interesting
arrangement, but the forecourt would have been possibly somewhat

[35] Robert Adam. East front
of University. An original
watercolour, after Adam's
design.
EUL

dark – better suited to lie under Italian than Scottish skies. The east
front, however, except for the dome, which is not the one he designed, is pure Adam; the great portico has been described as
'possibly the noblest'[29] of all his works, bold in character, essentially
simple, the six great columns each a single monolith of Craigleith
stone, three feet in diameter and twenty-two feet high. (Doubts

126

were expressed at the time whether they could be safely transported across the North Bridge; and erecting them safely into position was a formidable task.) The elevation within the court facing the main gate is also almost exactly as Adam planned it, and the opposite, west-facing elevation within the court is very largely according to Adam's designs. The remaining elevations, except for that facing

Chambers' Street, are largely the work of Playfair, who was commissioned to complete the building after 1815. The interior is almost entirely Playfair's work. The chief difference between the instructions for the interior given to Adam and those given to Playfair was that Adam had to arrange accommodation within the College for no fewer than eleven professors as well as the librarian and the Principal. His successor was instructed to allow – and at the last moment – only for 'chambers' for the Principal.

The foundation stone was laid with all due ceremony on 16 November 1789. Promises of money rapidly came in, and in 1790 a subscription list was published. The total sum promised was £15,366 This was a very encouraging start. The principal subscribers were as follows:

The Lord Provost, on behalf of the City £400 per annum for five years.

The Writers to the Signet 200 guineas per annum for three years.

The Faculty of Advocates 100 guineas per annum for five years.

The Royal Society of Edinburgh 100 guineas per annum for five years.

The Earl of Hopetoun 100 guineas per annum for five years.

The Earl of Wemyss £100 per annum for three years.

These subscriptions totalled over one-quarter of the total sum then subscribed. The rest of the money came from a great variety of people. The aristocracy was particularly prominent. Forty-two titled persons subscribed their names, scarcely one of them promising less than £50, most of them one hundred guineas. After these the principal groups of subscribers were merchants (fifty-six), members of the Royal College of Physicians (forty-four) and advocates (thirty-seven); there were also many Writers to the Signet, bankers, and excise officials, while the list includes a sprinkling of bakers, joiners and wrights. Some contributions were in kind – a log of mahogany, sold for £3, five hundred bags of Cousland lime, sold for £28 16s. 4d., and two stots which realised £34 12s. It is an interesting list, reflecting the character of a society still far from rich, dominated by a land-owning aristocracy, committed overwhelmingly to the business of agriculture, of trade, and of government,

28. One of the six columns of Craigleith stone that support the portico of the University. The columns are monoliths, a conceit that suggests the flamboyance and scale of Adam's fancy.

still sufficiently small and close-knit for all kinds of persons to join together in a common cause.

Building began in 1789. At first, Adam and his clerk of works, John Paterson, did not find it easy to arrange contracts with masons and carpenters whom they thought suitable at prices which they regarded as reasonable. Members of the Town Council and the Board of Trustees tried for many months to secure jobs in building the College for themselves and their friends, and Paterson required the Lord Provost's support to meet the attacks of one disappointed mason in particular, Alexander Reid.[30] There was also considerable last-minute discussion of details – in particular, it was felt that the houses which Adam had planned for the professors were 'too magnificent' in a scheme supported by voluntary public contributions. The Trustees continued to look about for money, inviting the various Presbyteries throughout Scotland to secure subscriptions from their members. And by the summer of 1791 it was anticipated that 'several apartments' would be ready for use in a few months.[31]

This hope was realised; but it was the end of progress in the eighteenth century. In 1792 Robert Adam died; and with the out-

[36] The Quadrangle, the University, as it might have appeared in one version derived from the Adam/Playfair plans.
EUL

29. The Quadrangle, the University.

K

129

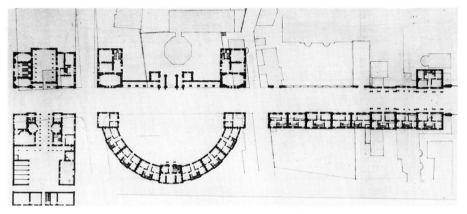

break of war in February, 1793, building operations were first slowed and then halted completely. Men and materials were increasingly required for war purposes; money became scarce and dear; prices rose; and a succession of bad harvests made food dear and the calls on charity heavy. (In 1795, according to Cockburn, 16,000 persons in Edinburgh depended on public or private relief, and the exact quantity of food which a family should consume was specified by public proclamation.) In 1789 the Trustees had quite reasonably looked forward to an adequate income from charitable donations, always with the possibility that they could fall back on government aid. But the 1790s was a very disappointing decade by comparison with the buoyant 1780s, and in 1799 a petition was at last addressed to Henry Dundas, who had 'undertaken to use his utmost influence' to secure government aid ten years before.

Few trustees have ever drawn up a sadder document. All the money, they say has been spent, and they have been 'obliged to contract a considerable debt, upwards of £5,000,[32] to different tradesmen'. Some accommodation has been made available, but work has had to stop, 'leaving a considerable part of the east and north fronts unroofed, and the beams and joisting exposed to the injury of the weather; the College area being at the same time embarassed with sheds, stones and other materials . . .' As a result, the thirteen hundred students of the College suffer 'in many respects . . . greater inconveniences than were felt during the miserable state of the old buildings.' The Trustees, the document continues, have been 'averse

130

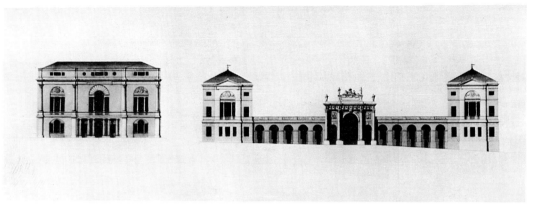

from troubling his Majesty's ministers with any application respecting a matter of this sort, while the public at large requires so much of their attention . . .' But the present situation having continued for 'several years', the new building 'raised to its present situation at a great expense, is likely soon to become ruinous . . . the rafters and other timber are going fast to decay', while 'some of the tradesmen are beginning to grow clamorous, though promised interest for their money; while the Trustees do not yet know from what funds either principal or interest is to come'. Observing, however, that 'the Proprietors of the Forth and Clyde Navigation are now enabled by authority of Parliament to pay up their debt to Government of £50,000; and that this sum, as they are informed, is to be applied for public works in Scotland', they presume to ask for some help in the admirable task of completing the unfinished and decaying buildings.

Alas! their hopes were in vain. Dundas's reply is not recorded; but the Trustees made a renewed application for help, in very similar terms, in November 1800. Pitt's war finance could not find room for expensive public works, and the wells of charity were dry, or appropriated to other purposes. An income tax had been instituted, there was heavy government expenditure overseas, investment in agriculture was proceeding at an exceptional rate, and prices, especially food prices, were moving erratically at exceptionally high levels. Above all, the price of consols, the inverse of a safe rate of return on investible funds, was very low. Money, in a word, was scarce

[37/38] Robert Adam. South Bridge proposals, 1786. The colonnaded building shown on the plan, and in elevation above, is apparently an early design for the University. Of interest also is Adam's proposal for a crescent facing the College.
soane MUS.

and valuable, in spite of currency depreciation. In such circumstances, university building had to wait. A grant of £5,000 was made 'applicable to putting the incomplete buildings of the University in a state of security as far as possible'; but for many years the gaunt walls, the unglazed windows and the bare rafters of Adam's great design stood bleakly beside the South Bridge, a forlorn reminder to passing citizens of the relentless pressure and the costly ebb and flow of a great Continental war.

[39] South Bridge, looking N. *An amateur drawing, about 1800.* EUL

30. Doorway in Elder Street. Here, again, the dressing of the stone, & the railings, are conceived in terms of Edinburgh's slanting sunlight giving decorative play.

VI

Public Works 1800-30

When the nineteenth century began, the South Bridge, the most recently completed major project of public improvement in Edinburgh, had been in use for over twelve years; work on Register House had been stopped for about the same length of time; and the new University building had lain uncompleted, going slowly to ruin, since 1793. Private building, alone, survived the first impact of the war, but between 1793 and 1800 even private building was going on at a very markedly slower pace than before. It revived somewhat, partly as a result of the start of feuing in Elder Street, Greenside Street, Duke Street and Albany Street, between 1800 and 1805, and in 1810 and 1811 its level was again above the normal for the war years.

Public building revived gradually from 1806, and it began again in the High Street, just across from the Merchants' Exchange which had been the first great project of the eighteenth century. Pressure on the accommodation for the Supreme Courts of Scotland in the old Parliament Buildings beside St Giles had been growing, and in 1806 and 1808 two Acts of Parliament authorised the conversion of the old buildings. The work was given to Robert Reid, and was carried out between 1807 and 1810. Radical alteration of the interior was essential. It is not so clear that Reid had also to destroy, as he did, the curious façade of the old Parliament House, erected between 1632 and 1640. Only prints of it remain; and while no architectural masterpiece, it certainly seems to have been a design of character. Reid replaced this by an extended Ionic elevation which originally embraced the west and south-west sides of Parliament Square and later (after the terrible fire of 1824) was continued on the east side.

31. Staircase and vestibule, the Signet Library.

133

It is a competent piece of work, but monotonous and rather undistinguished. To those who knew the old building and revered its 'Scottish architecture' Reid's design was a nonentity, stripping the scene 'of all its historic interest'[1]; and for them the contrast was all the more painful. In his *Memorials* Cockburn expresses some of the indignation felt at the time:

> The Parliament Square (as foppery now calls it, but which used, and ought, to be called the Parliament *Close*) was then, as now, enclosed on the north by St. Giles Cathedral, on the west by the Outer House, and on the south, partly by courts, and partly by shops, above which were very tall houses, and on the east by a line of shops and houses of the same grand height.[2] So that the courts formed the south-west angle of the Close. The old building exhibited some respectable turrets, some ornamented windows and doors, and a handsome balustrade. But the charm that ought to have saved it, was its colour and its age, which, however, were the very things that caused its destruction. About 170 years had breathed over it a grave grey hue. The whole aspect was venerable and appropriate; becoming the air and character of a sanctuary of Justice. But a mason pronounced it to be all '*Dead Wall*'. The officials to whom, at a period when there was no public taste in Edinburgh, this was addressed, believed him; and the two fronts were removed in order to make way for the bright freestone and contemptible decorations that now disgrace us.[3]

But this criticism goes too far. Moreover, excellent work was done inside the building. Reid was commissioned in 1807 by the Society of Writers to the Signet to arrange accommodation for their library in the reconstructed building in Parliament Square, and in 1812 the services of William Stark were also obtained for this purpose. Two large rooms were designed, of which the upper was for the Faculty of Advocates. Both are very fine, lined with Corinthian columns, the upper being no less than 136 feet long and lit by a central saucer dome; it is possible that this room gave a hint for the later-designed University Library. The Writers to the Signet paid about £10,000 for the building of the lower hall, which has an ingenious system of central heating,[4] and paid the architects £755. The upper hall was

32. Parliament Square. Reid's concept is a close copy of Adam's University.

purchased from the Faculty of Advocates by the Writers to the Signet for £12,000 in 1826.

The year after work began in Parliament Square there was passed an Act for New Buildings in the City of Edinburgh. The essence of this scheme was the building of a new gaol. This was an old proposal. An Act of 1781 had empowered the magistrates to build a new gaol, and an Act of 1790 had provided for the building of a Bridewell and House of Correction on Calton Hill. This latter proposal was carried out, the foundation stone being laid in 1791 and the building completed in 1795. Semi-circular in plan, it was designed by Robert Adam, replacing the old House of Correction in the Canongate. But the project for a new gaol hung fire, in spite of the condition of the old one, which was acknowledged to be atrocious; cramped, dark, squalid and insanitary. Part of the difficulty was choosing a suitable site. That preferred in 1812 was just east of Liberton's Wynd. This was a Wynd between the West Bow and Parliament Close. The site had the advantage of proximity to the Law Courts, but it was objected to, particularly by those who had seen the new modern gaols at Oxford, Chester and Lancaster, as too small and surrounded and overhung by other buildings. It was accordingly suggested that 'part of the sloping bank, on the south side of Princes Street, betwixt the Mound and Canal Street' should be used, having 'all the advantages desirable for the purpose'.[6] The originator of this scheme, which achieved some popularity in the town, did not think that there need be any loss of amenity; a Court of Justiciary should be built fronting the street so as to hide the gaol on the lower ground behind, and in any case no injury could result to the houses nearby, because 'this part of Princes Street is now in a great measure composed of shops and houses of public accommodation'. Mercifully, this plan to thrust the largest gaol in Scotland on the notice of every visitor to the town and of every citizen who walked along what was supposed to be the handsomest street in Europe, was abandoned in favour of a scheme which, although better, was still far from ideal. This was to site the gaol just to the west of the Bridewell on the south slope of Calton Hill. 'It was a piece of undoubted bad taste to give so glorious an eminence to a prison. It was one of our noblest sites, and would have been given by Pericles to one of his finest edifices. But

33. The interior, the Signet Library. Compare Playfair's Upper Library (facing page 193)

[40] *Plan of Central Edinburgh, about 1827, showing various phases of New Town development. To the right of Craig's town is his St James's Square scheme; upper right, Playfair's scheme for the N of Calton Hill; across Queen Street there is the*

19th C series of Circuses and Squares by Reid and others; to the left, the linked curves of the Earl of Moray's development.

BROWN/WOOD

[41] Robert Adam, The Bridewell, with Archibald Elliot's 'feudal fortress of romance' – the new gaol – in the background.
shepherd

34. The Governor's house, Calton Jail, with the romantic ironwork of Waverley Station.

in modern towns, though we may abuse and bemoan, we must take what we can get.'[7] An Act of 1814 specified the new site. But fresh difficulties arose. There was a dispute, to begin with, about finance, for this was a national gaol, to house serious offenders from all over Scotland (how the old gaol had ever done this, no one knew; except that such a large number of serious offenders in the eighteenth century were hanged or transported), and so it was not clear how much of the cost should be met by the city. In the event, an Act of Parliament laid down that of the total estimated cost of £27,495 the city should provide £8,000. This money the magistrates promptly borrowed from Sir William Forbes and Co., and building began in 1815. It was said to resemble 'a feudal fortress of romance'.

A second difficulty, however, was more formidable. The Calton Hill was not easily accessible. No properly made road went near

the proposed site; from Leith Street the approach was 'up a steep, narrow, stinking, spiral street'[8]; and even the route to the Hill from the Law Courts in the High Street was largely by devious and narrow streets. The obvious solution was to drive a way through 'the mean line of houses' which blocked the east end of Princes Street, bridge the deep ravine of the Low Calton, and construct a road along the south face of Calton Hill. This plan had been suggested, apparently by John Paterson, Adam's clerk of works at the University, in 1790; but it had been given up on the grounds that valuable properties would have to be acquired and demolished, and that there would be difficulty in securing permission to drive a road across the burial ground on Calton Hill. Certainly the undertaking was a formidable one; but the magistrates now resolved upon it, as part of a further extension of the Royalty. Commissioners were appointed, nineteen in number, by Acts of 1813 and 1814. Those appointed included the Lord Provost and three other members of the Town Council, an ex Lord Provost, the two Members of Parliament for the City and the County, and a string of persons in powerful politico-legal positions such as the Lord Advocate, the Solicitor General, and the Lord Chief Baron of Exchequer. As a provisional financial arrangement it was agreed that the city should contribute £12,000 from its general revenues towards the cost of the road and bridge, the 'road districts', i.e., the trustees of the city's turnpike trusts, £26,000. Should this prove insufficient, it was further agreed that the city would stand ready to pay an additional £10,000 raised by assessments, and after that, if necessary, an additional £5,000. It is perhaps significant that the Act of 1814 empowered the trustees or commissioners to take up at interest any sum not exceeding £50,000. In the event, all these figures were to be greatly exceeded.

The Commissioners began by appointing Mr Robert Stevenson as 'engineer' for the scheme, and at the same time, late in January 1815, they resolved to borrow £37,000 in five moieties of £7,400 each from the Bank of Scotland, the Royal Bank, the British Linen Bank, Sir William Forbes & Co. and Messrs Ramsay Bonar & Co. The security they offered consisted of the funds provided by the Act, principally the £18,000 which was to come from the Leith Walk Toll, and the £12,000 liability of the City of Edinburgh. In

35. Steps up Calton Hill, with Nelson Monument in background.

139

the event, £25,000 of the money borrowed from the banks was raised on the personal security of the Commissioners.

The next step was to purchase properties on the line of the proposed development. Most of these were bought at from fourteen to eighteen years rental. The largest transaction involved the property belonging to William Butter – possibly the same William Butter who had been a contractor for some of the New Town – situated at the east end of Princes Street. The rental in this case was £609 and the purchase price was £12,000, but it was agreed that the Commissioners should pay only the interest on this sum, at 5 per cent, while William Butter was alive. Within a year, by the end of 1815, the Commissioners had spent £22,991 on properties purchased (including the £12,000 owing to Butter), and they calculated that another £11,838 would be required for this purpose. Their total resources at the time being £37,000, it was obvious that more money would be needed, for the estimated expense of the bridge was put at £15,000, of excavations (including the removal of the old Calton burying ground, which was in the line of the road) at £12,000, and of laying the road at £4,352. More assessments – including one on the city for £10,000 – and more borrowing ensued, and in six months the total funds were stepped up by at least a notional £40,000 – notional, because of this amount £30,160 was the estimated value of the land now in the Commissioners' possession and at some future date to be feued by them. But the estimated expense of the work to be undertaken was rising as fast as the Commissioners' resources. Between December 1815 and June 1816 estimated cost rose by £40,000.[9] So once again the Commissioners turned to the banks; would they lend another £33,500? The banks were reluctant; each had already lent £7,400. But, said the Commissioners, if the banks refuse to lend, 'not only must this noble Work be stopped, and employment be withdrawn from many hundreds of workmen, at a time when such employment is so much required',[10] but the land already bought will remain on the Commissioners' hands, a liability instead of an asset, and the Commissioners will consequently be unable to repay any of the £37,000 already borrowed – and where will the banks be then? Presumably seeing no other hope of the return of their money, the banks accepted

[42 a & b] Waterloo Place. The Waterloo Place/Regent Arch scheme under construction (a) looking w along Princes Street, (b) looking s E towards the gaol and Salisbury Crags.
EUL

140

these arguments, and lent £22,500 at 5 per cent on the security of various assessments.

Meanwhile, detailed plans had been maturing. James Gillespie, Richard Crichton and Archibald Elliot all submitted designs for the bridge and buildings in November 1815, and Elliot was then chosen to be architect for the scheme. A month later, however, Stevenson submitted a report which had an important influence on the appearance of this part of Edinburgh, and which is interesting as showing the concern for visual effect entertained by one who was not an architect but a civil engineer. He pointed out that if no buildings were built on the bridge, those passing over would be able to look north to Leith Walk, 'one of the greatest thoroughfares in town' or south to 'the curious City scene on the southern side of the bridge'. The bridge should therefore not be built (as must have been suggested) 'after the manner of Pultney Bridge Bath' but should be left open for the sake of the views it would command, 'it being very desirable that the interest and attention of the passengers and strangers should be kept up in the same agreeable style of variety all the way from Gayfield Square to the Register office'.[11]

The contract for the bridge, designed by Elliot but in accordance with Stevenson's ideas, was signed in the summer of 1816, and work proceeded. But in 1817 the Town Council found itself involved in legal proceedings regarding amenities at the east end of Princes Street. The trouble arose from an agreement dated 16 January 1817, which allowed three feuars to erect buildings immediately to the west of the north abutment of the North Bridge; that is to say, on the steeply sloping ground now occupied by shops and the North British Hotel. This might have been allowed to pass, had not the Town Council agreed that the east front of these buildings might be as little as twelve feet from the west side of the North Bridge, and that the buildings might rise three stories above the parapet of the bridge. No sooner did the effects of this decision begin to be seen than protest arose. Cockburn was one of those who protested, and he gives the reasons as follows:

The new street along the southern side of the Calton Hill disclosed some glorious prospects, or at least exhibited them from new points. One of these was the view westward, over the

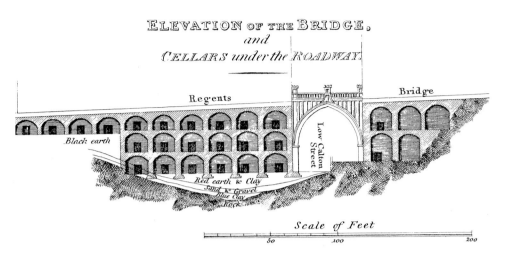

ELEVATION OF THE BRIDGE,
and
CELLARS under the ROADWAY.

Regents   Bridge

Black earth

Low Calton Street

Red earth & Clay
Sand & Gravel
Blue Clay
Rock

Scale of Feet

50   100   200

North Bridge. But we had only begun to perceive its importance, when its interception by what are now called the North Bridge Buildings raised our indignation; and we thought that the magistrates, who allowed them to be set agoing in silence, had betrayed us. We were therefore very angry, and had recourse to another of these new things called public meetings, which we were beginning to feel the power of.[12]

Besides public meetings and legal proceedings there were negotiations, and as a result of these it was agreed in the spring of 1818, after six months of wrangling, that there should be 'such a reduction of the Buildings as will restore the Communication of view between the Calton Hill and the Eastern Division of Princes Street'.[13] As the buildings were by this time mostly built and tenancies arranged, this decision meant some demolition and reconstruction, as well as compensation. In the event, the top storeys were removed from three buildings, while a fourth was built one storey lower than originally planned. Compensation to the feuars was agreed at just under £3,500. The Commissioners approved these alterations, on the ground that the North Bridge Buildings 'materially interrupt the effects the Commissioners had in view in laying out that [Calton Hill] approach'.[14] It would not be easy to parallel this costly reconstruction of newly-built property (wise as it no doubt was; the buildings which remained look ugly enough in all conscience in contemporary prints) simply for the sake of a public view.

[43] *Waterloo Bridge. One of the designs, illustrating the technical problems of the site, and method of construction.* ETC

143

Protest about the North Bridge Buildings reached the Commissioners officially in November 1817. Two weeks before this they had had some excellent news. Feuing of the areas which they had already bought to the north of the bridge had begun in July, and in reply to a total price asked for all the lots of £15,500, a Mr Peter Lorimer had come forward with an offer of £15,000 for the whole area, plus £10,000 for the grounds to the south of the bridge. Now, in October, Lorimer came forward with an offer to take the building areas to the east as well for another £10,000. He made only two conditions. The total of £35,000 was to be paid in three annual instalments from 1819 to 1821; and he was to be 'at liberty to carry a terrace from Waterloo Place to Leith Street if I shall deem it advisable to do so, provided my plan shall meet with the approbation of Mr. Elliot'.[15] This offer, and the conditions, were accepted with alacrity, and it suddenly began to look as if the Commissioners' worries were over.

Who Mr Peter Lorimer was, or whom he represented, we do not know. £35,000 was a very large sum to be bound for in the way of business, and Lorimer must have had a good deal of capital, or rich friends or partners. Certainly he seems to have had business ability, for he brought this large transaction to a successful conclusion. It was not easy. He was certainly helped, in August 1818, by securing the contract to build the new Post Office buildings in Waterloo Place. But the essential difficulty he faced was that his ability to get on with the work and perform his contract was limited by the progress made by the Commissioners in carrying out the public parts of the scheme. It was of the utmost consequence to Lorimer that the bridge should be completed – as at one time promised – by Whitsunday, 1820, so that work could be expedited on the houses, which Lorimer had undertaken under heavy penalties to deliver finished in a specified time. The Commissioners met this date – indeed, the bridge seems to have been usable in 1819 – but early in 1820 Lorimer was complaining that he was unable to sell his buildings 'because no road is made or is likely to be made passable and free from interruption and encumbrances'[16] for many months. The roadway was littered with building materials, sheds, and rubbish dug from the foundations, and it can hardly have attracted prospective residents. But work on the road was hindered by the reappearance of financial

36. Waterloo Place, cutting through Calton burial-ground.

difficulties. Once again, the Commissioners were running out of money; in January 1820 they seem to have been unable rather than unwilling to meet a bill for £4 2s. And once again they turned to the banking house of Sir William Forbes, which lent another £3,000 on the security of a specific city assessment. The Commissioners scraped through, with the help of a new Act in the summer of 1821 authorising them to raise more money; and Lorimer, too, paid over his £35,000, and may be supposed – though there is no proof of it – to have made a profit. In January 1822 the Commissioners recorded that 'the works are brought to a close'.[17]

Almost exactly seven years had thus been required to build the eastern approach to Princes Street. It was a fine achievement of civil engineering, the bridge, over a very deep ravine, being fifty feet high and carrying an open screen in the centre of which, on each side of the bridge, is a simple Corinthian 'triumphal' arch.[18] The road is lined by strictly symmetrical buildings of a severely classical style, and the screen walls further east, which continue the formality of the road where there is no room for buildings, are diversified with columns and niches between them. Prominent among the buildings is the Waterloo Hotel. Designed by Elliot, this hotel was erected in 1819 to the orders of the Edinburgh Waterloo Tavern and Hotel Company, created in 1818 with a capital of £22,000 in £25 shares. The prospectus stated: 'Although the Metropolis of Scotland is said to boast of more elegance and splendour than most Cities of Europe, yet there has never existed a Tavern where more than fifty persons could be entertained with ease or comfort, nor has it ever had an establishment like the Tontine of Glasgow, where Strangers could see the manners of the people, and mix with the Society of the place.' The Lord Provost and Sir William Forbes were both on the Committee of management, and the Town Council took £1,000 of stock as soon as the shares were marketed. This venture, along with the new Post Office building, must have been of material assistance to the success of the whole scheme.

Waterloo Place is grand and severe, and not altogether unworthy of its name. The financial operation which made it possible likewise had elements of grandeur. The following is an abstract of a final statement prepared in 1830.

37. The Regent Arch, Waterloo Place.
ETC

RECEIPTS AND EXPENDITURE, CALTON BRIDGE SCHEME

30 January 1815 to 31 January 1830

Receipts		Expenditure	
Bank Loans	£37,000	Property purchased	£65,992
Further Bank loans	22,500	Road making	27,110
Interest received	1,630	Bridge building	12,329
Materials sold	1,900	Rents	218
Rents	1,023	Mr Elliott	1,650
Areas sold	36,685	Mr Stevenson	500
Contributions etc.	26,351	Interest on money borrowed	10,238
Sir William Forbes 1821 loan	3,000	Legal expenses	8,494
Promissory notes from time to		Bank loans, repayments to:	
time discounted by the		the Bank of Scotland	16,063
Commissioners	12,000	the Royal Bank	24,544[19]
Cash received by drafts on		the British Linen Bank	12,526
account with:		Sir William Forbes & Co.	41,898[19]
the Bank of Scotland	16,018	Ramsay Bonar & Co.	12,484
the Royal Bank	25,993	Special loan (1821) repayment	
the British Linen Bank	12,440	to Sir William Forbes & Co.	3,000
Sir William Forbes & Co.	41,918	Expenditure on gaol	1,876
Ramsay Bonar & Co.	12,422	Moneys borrowed	12,000
Odds and ends	93		
		In hand	51
Total	£250,973	Total	£250,922

Three features of these accounts deserve comment. The first is that of the £66,000 spent on properties, only £39,000 is satisfactorily accounted for in the Minute Books. This may, or may not, be an accident. The second is the size of the overdrafts which the banks permitted the Commissioners. No bank lent more than £11,900; yet the drafts on the Royal Bank exceeded this by £14,000 and those on Sir William Forbes & Co. by the enormous sum of £30,000. Of a certainty the banking system of Scotland was mobilising capital on a large scale in those days for public works in Edinburgh. The third point is the relative smallness of the payments made to the engineer and the architect. Stevenson, who from the start of 1815 until the spring of 1819 worked without payment while himself paying an assistant, received less than £900, having engineered a bridge and a road valued at over £39,000! Elliot, with almost £1,900, was much better treated – also, he did not have to wait four years for payment, as he received £200 in 1816. Even so, this £1,900, which included £100 per annum 'for management' was hardly a princely return.[20] Professional men employed in operations

[44/45] Waterloo Place, looking E. In the Ewbank engraving, the old Theatre Royal, demolished in 1859, is on right. The lithograph, about 1950, is by Leonard Rosoman, ARA

of this kind were still the residuary legatees in matters of payment, unless they were very famous.

The building of Waterloo Place and Waterloo Bridge was thus a very great scheme, requiring a larger expenditure in seven years than was needed in laying out the essentials of Craig's New Town in the course of a quarter of a century. It was at bottom a scheme of improved access, but questions of beauty as well as of utility were involved, and the architect and the Commissioners strove not unsuccessfully to adorn the city as well as to make it easier to enter and to leave. But the scheme of 'the bridge to Calton', as it was called at the time, was far less ambitious than the contemporaneous and closely related 'Calton Hill Scheme'. This was nothing less than the laying out of 'a New Town between Edinburgh and Leith', occupying 'between two and three hundred acres, and forming nearly an oblong square',[21] calculated to out-do the splendours of Princes Street, George Street and Charlotte Square.

There were to be three principal feuars – Heriot's Hospital,[22] Trinity Hospital and Mr Allan of Hillside – and early in 1811 the Lord Provost (who was an interested party because the city was also involved in the feuing in a minor way) succeeded in persuading the principals to bind themselves to 'a joint plan for building'. The area in question lay along the slopes of Calton Hill and to the north of it, bounded approximately by Easter Road on the east and by Leith Walk on the west. By March 1812 the ground had been surveyed and a plan was advertised for; it was ordered that advertisements were to appear in newspapers in London and Glasgow, as well as Edinburgh, twice a week for a month, then once a week for another month, then once a month 'till further orders'. Prizes, awarded according to the judgment of the majority of proprietors, were on an equally generous scale – three hundred guineas first prize, one hundred guineas second prize. By the closing date for the competition, 1 January 1813, thirty-two plans had been received, and it was resolved that they should be publicly exhibited, 'that the general opinion of the public may, if possible, be known'.

The exhibition of plans was duly staged and a good deal of trouble taken over it. It was not very public – tickets of admission were sent to the principal inhabitants, and there were complicated rules and

38. Waterloo Place, from Register House.

regulations which must have kept attendance down to a few hundred. Even so, no consensus of opinion seems to have emerged, for late in March the Commissioners resolved to ask for reports on the plans from the following:

Wm. Stark, architect at Drumsheugh.

James Gillespie, architect, 21 Union Street.

John Paterson, architect, Canaan.

Robt. Burn, architect, Edinburgh.

Wm. Burn, jr., architect.

Robt. Reid,   ,,   .

Robt. Brown,   ,,   .

John Baxter, jr.,   ,,   .

Reports, by such as accepted the invitation, were to be submitted within fourteen days, and the Commissioners added that they would not be bound by the reports. The invitation was accepted by Gillespie, Paterson, Wm. Burn, Reid and Baxter. The Commissioners then appointed Baron Clerk[23] and Gilbert Innes, Esq.[24] to report on the architects' reports, which were necessarily very brief and which differed from one another in numerous particulars.

Not surprisingly, Clerk and Innes were unable to solve the Commissioners' difficulties for them by pointing to any one of the plans as conspicuously the best; 'some of them have noble features and parts that would have a good effect in execution, but at the same time they have such defects, as to render it unwise to adopt them'.[25] The two referees, however, made one definite recommendation which was important: 'The observations offered by the late Mr. Stark', they wrote, 'deserve the utmost attention, and as far as practicable should be assumed as a rule for forming the plan of the buildings along Leith Walk, and in particular the preservation of the pine trees in the front of Greenside House should not be forgotten or omitted.'[26]

Stark's 'observations' were later expanded and published, in June 1814, as a *Report . . . on the Plans for laying out the Grounds for Buildings between Edinburgh and Leith*. His views were evidently not called forth by any specific request by the Commissioners or magistrates but seem to have been the result of extended personal interest and reflection. It may be asked why did he not accept the Commis-

39. Calton Hill, from Calton burial-ground. The circular monument commemorates Professor Dugald Stewart. Behind, to the left, is Craig's Old Observatory, with Playfair's City Observatory behind, again.

sioners' invitation of March 1813 to report on the plans which had
been submitted. The explanation is almost certainly that he was by
then seriously ill; he died in October, 'too young to have done much'.[27]
But his Report clearly influenced Playfair, whose plan for this area
of Edinburgh was later adopted.

Stark's Report is indeed a remarkable document. It is brief (a
mere fourteen pages), ill arranged and somewhat repetitive, and
the writing is awkward and stilted. It is concerned not with questions
of actual building but with the principles of town lay-out, and the
discussion of these is startlingly modern; the twentieth century has
still to assimilate much of what Stark knew. His essential position
is that the architect has to appreciate and then exploit the merits of
his site, not impose something upon it; and the excellence of the
architect's opportunity varies with the attractiveness of the site.
Thus it is central to his arguments to insist that 'the Calton Hill is
an object of public interest, considered either as a leading feature in
the general scenery of Edinburgh, or as a striking and attractive
spot, affording a succession of the most splendid and diversified views
that are to be found assembled in the immediate vicinity of any large
city, and within the compass of a few minutes walk'.[28] Basing himself
on this sort of consideration, he lays down two general principles.
First of all, symmetry of plan is of little value; attractive on paper,
it tends in execution to be merely monotonous; convenience and
scenic effect are more important.

It were sacrificing too much, perhaps, to scenery, to make it a
cause for giving up elegance or convenience in the arrangement
of the building, or even for incurring any considerable loss of
ground; although this last falls to be a matter of calculation; for
beauty of site will be found most probably a vendible commodity. It may indeed be attended with a sacrifice of another
kind, though that surely will not be deemed of any importance;
it may injure the symmetry of the *ground* plan, and disturb the
harmony and measured allotment of streets, squares, and
crescents. Yet it were easy to shew of how little consequence
all this is, except upon paper.[29]

40. Regent Terrace on the slopes of Calton Hill.

And, in case the reader should miss the application of these remarks
to James Craig's once much-vaunted plan, Stark goes on:

150

To a stranger occupied in the examination of the present New
Town, it would import little to be informed, when looking along
George's Street, that it is precisely parallel to Prince's street
and Queen's Street; or, if admiring Charlotte Square, to be told
that it forms the exact counterpart upon the ground plan to
St. Andrew's Square.[30]

On the contrary, streets should follow the natural contours of the
ground, and if this makes them other than straight, so much the
better; there is, 'in a *bending* alignment of street, much beauty, and
perhaps the most striking effects'.[31] And by following the contours
of the ground, variety will be achieved: 'among the qualities we value
in the distribution of a town, variety and unexpected change of form,
both in the streets and buildings, are by no means the least acceptable'.

Secondly, Stark is particularly insistent on the value of standing
trees. Trees 'enrich and give interest to the whole surrounding
scene'[32]; they should be used to 'adorn a square or public walk, or
give interest and picturesque effect to a church'.[33] And in this argument he calls to his aid an apparently extensive acquaintance with art
and architecture:

> It seems to be now admitted to have been a prejudice, that trees
> and town buildings are incongruous objects. They must surely
> be admitted to assimilate well together, since our best landscape
> painters, Claude and the Poussins, never tired of painting them,
> nor the world of admiring what they painted. From the practice
> of those great masters, whom we must regard as unerring
> authorities, of constantly combining trees and architecture, it
> might be inferred to have been their opinion that there could
> be no beauty where either of these objects was wanting.
>
> Were it asked, to what circumstance does Grosvenor Square
> owe its beauty and attractions? the answer would surely be, to
> its architecture and its trees. Leaving it, and proceeding to
> others which have *not* the advantage of this fine accompaniment,
> for example to Fitzroy Square, built with stone, and magnifi-
> cently ornamented by Mr. Adam, even in winter we feel the
> change. Would the view of the Colleges of Oxford excite the
> same sensations of pleasure, if the gardens and the trees were

*41. Hillside Crescent. Note the
Greek key decoration of the railings, to tie in with the Doric
columns.*

151

away? Or the scenery of the Mall, or the Bird-Cage Walk, or the streets of the towns in Holland? Even in Amsterdam, a town built in a quagmire, the street views are delightful, from the effect of the rows of lime trees, notwithstanding the ridiculous encasement of their stems in green sentry boxes.[34]

And Stark applied these principles to the particular case of Calton Hill. The fine double row of elms extending two hundred yards along Leith Walk, their existence totally ignored in all the plans submitted, should be a prominent feature of the proposed New Town. An esplanade or terrace should be built along the faces of the hill, both north, east and south, at a moderate elevation, because it is from this height that the views are the finest – the Old Town 'exceedingly grand', Arthur's Seat and Holyrood House, the gay and animated scene of Leith Walk, Leith itself in the distance, and the shipping in the roads. Lastly, nothing is to be gained, as in some of the designs submitted, by carrying the buildings all over the summit of Calton Hill; such buildings would be inaccessible, and the area would be much better used as a public walk.

'Beauty of site will be found most likely a vendible commodity'; 'among the qualities we value . . . variety and unexpected change of form . . . are by no means the least acceptable'; 'assemblages of *trees* might be well worth preserving' – here were precepts of town planning which came from a different world, apparently, from that inhabited by those who had already submitted plans. Stark obviously had affinities with the eighteenth-century artist, still more with the eighteenth-century aristocrat laying out his estate and preparing to admire the view which would be partly his own creation.

Stark's observations, the Commissioners noted, 'had given universal satisfaction'.[35] But their novelty gave rise to delay. After an expenditure of almost £900,[36] the Commissioners were still without an acceptable plan, and almost three years later they were seemingly no farther than resolving that 'an Architect of eminence and taste' should make out a plan 'suited to the varied and picturesque state of the ground'.[37] Their search for a suitable person, however, was by that time nearly at an end, for in February 1818 William Playfair was appointed architect for 'the proposed New Town between Edinburgh and Leith'.

[46] *CaltonHill , in use as a*
public walk, mid-19th C. *The*
Nelson Monument (1815)
represents an inverted
telescope.
EUL

153

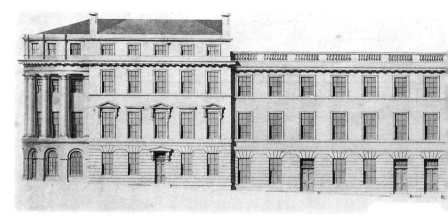

[47] *William Playfair.*
Elevation for Leopold Place.
E U L

Playfair produced his plan in April 1819, backing it up with a Report of which 1,000 copies were printed, and in August a second Report was added. Plan and reports follow the ideas and the advice of William Stark almost to the letter. The aim, says Playfair, is a happy union of foliage and building, and this will be furthered by careful preservation of the elms which so much adorn Leith Walk; there will be a terrace half way up Calton Hill, but the top of the hill will be left as a garden; strict attention is paid to the nature [lie] of the ground, for 'a tame monotony will be sure to result from a complete uniformity of plan; a fact but too well exemplified in many parts of the New Town of Edinburgh'.[38] Thus far, Playfair is the merest echo of his master. There are, however, a few original touches. The terrace is to have houses only on the upper side, so as not to obscure the view for those walking or driving along[39]; in the more utilitarian part of the town there will be markets faced by 'Fourth rate Houses' and so 'completely screened'; half way along London Road there will be a crescent 'of great size' with three streets radiating off it – 'the good effect of the diverging of several Streets from a Central point has been long felt and acknowledged particularly in the Piazza del Popolo at Rome'.

As was to be expected, this elaborate version of Stark's plan – for such it was in essence – met with much the same enthusiasm as had greeted the original, and was accepted by the proprietors, after some small modifications had been made, in December, 1819. Work on

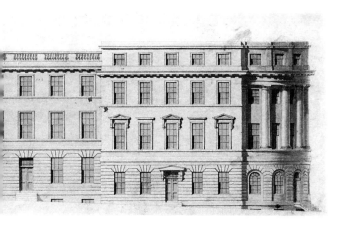

the foundations of the roads started almost at once. Playfair had estimated in the spring that road-building would cost £5,489, and it had been agreed that the Trustees would pay the first £3,000 and that all expenditure thereafter would be met equally by Heriot's Trust and by Mr Allan, one of the feuars. In the event, the total cost was £7,495, and this caused a dispute about payment, which was however settled without too much difficulty. Playfair also had his financial disappointments. He had been paid a fee of £100 on appointment as architect. When the contract was signed he was paid £300 for his drawings and surveying work, and the arrangement was made that he would receive a payment of £5 5s. for each house elevation required by purchasers of sites. But in 1821 he informed the Commissioners that he had prepared elevations for houses in Leopold Place, Royal Terrace, Calton Place, Hillside Crescent and Elm Row at a cost to himself (in materials, assistants' time and so on) of £44 1s. and had received in payment forty guineas. The Commissioners agreed that he should have more for general superintendence; but details are lacking.

This scarcity of commissions for elevations, already noticeable in March 1821, no doubt foreshadowed the imperfect success of the whole scheme. Playfair had, indeed, forseen the danger when he wrote his second Report in August 1819. He explained in that Report that he had deliberately kept a high proportion of the Calton Hill area as open space, because 'there is a formidable rival to contend with, in the Buildings which are now going forward at the western end of the present new town. There a Circle of fashionable and wealthy people has been collected', and there they will tend to stay. If the Calton Hill area is to compete, it must have something unique to offer, and that is provided by the gardens, 'the main spring by which the whole may be set in motion'. It was, however, too late. The centre of gravity of the New Town was already shifting westwards, and although the terraces on Calton Hill were built and remain as splendid ornaments of the town, making an excellent use of an exceptionally fine site, the great bulk of the newly planned area, intersecting streets, circus, octagons, open spaces – all this lying to the north of London Road was never built as planned. Only London Road itself, with Hillside Crescent and the three streets radiating from it (unlikely, alas! to remind anyone of the Piazza del Popolo in Rome) remain to bear witness to this part of Playfair's plan.

One disadvantage faced by the Calton Hill / Easter Road development was the fact that this area was somewhat cut off from Craig's New Town, not only by distance, but also by the intrusion of public buildings – Register House, the new Post Office in Waterloo Place, and the somewhat decaying theatre on a site which had once been part of Shakespeare Square. These were now added to, perhaps to the further disadvantage of residential developments in the neighbourhood, by the building of the Royal High School.

The building of this new High School, and along with it the building of Edinburgh Academy, resulted from long and complicated negotiations which, in the later stages, turned into a rather fundamental division of opinion. The original idea, put forward in 1822 by a Committee of Subscribers to the plan of a new school, was for a 'Seminary separate from and altogether independent of the High School of the City'.[40] The subscribers were persuaded, however, to accept the idea of a new school 'connected with and primarily on the same footing of [sic] the present High School, under the patronage of the Magistrates' and – as the subscribers had originally proposed – 'on the north side of the town'.[41] It was agreed in the autumn of 1822 that the Town Council would build this school. William Burn was engaged to prepare drawings, the site of the present Edinburgh Academy, proposed by the subscribers, was accepted, and the contract

42. The High School.

156

was advertised. Twelve estimates were received, ranging from
£15,200 to £19,423. This was a blow, for it had been supposed
from the beginning that £12,000 would suffice. But a more serious
difficulty now arose. Merchant Councillor Blackwood moved for
delay on the grounds first that only 1,000 boys in Edinburgh were
taught Latin and this was too small a number for two schools, and
secondly that the method proposed to raise money for the new
school, namely a two guinea entrance fee, would exclude all poor
children from the new school and confine them to the old High
School – 'the effect would evidently be to create a separation between
the different classes of the Community, thereby destroying what has
heretofore been one of the proudest Characteristics of the Scottish
system of education, and attended with consequences of the most
beneficial kind, both to persons of all ranks individually, and to the
general character of the Nation.'[42] This delaying amendment was
accepted, although at the same time a loan of £9,000 was arranged
with Sir William Forbes and Co., and Thomas Hamilton was asked
to prepare an alternative plan to that of William Burn.

In the following few weeks, however, the Town Council changed its
position. In a long report submitted in April, a Council Committee
acknowledged that the existing High School, rebuilt on the old site
in 1717, was overcrowded, and inconvenient for the majority of its
700 pupils who came from the New Town. The Committee argued,
however, that to site a new school near Canonmills would be 'most
exceedingly inconvenient for the inhabitants at large',[43] however
convenient it might be for pupils in the New Town, and that in any
case a second school would so reduce numbers at the old school that
'its progress to ruin will be incalculably accelerated'.[44] There should,
therefore, be only one school, in a central position, 'fitted up with
every accommodation so as to obviate the complaint of crowds'. (It
was not thought that the existing teaching staff was inadequate;
with classes of 'nearly 200' and 'upwards of 200' the pupils' conduct
and progress had been 'the theme of general approbation and
praise'.[45]) As for a site, what about the North Loch? 'The aspect and
name of the North Loch are apt to create a prejudice against it;
but . . . it is capable of being levelled up, drained, embellished, and
planted, so as to be rendered quite healthful, dry, and ornamental to

*43. The hall, the High School.
Note the verve of the early
cast-iron capitals.*

157

the City.'[46] Alternatively, the Excise Office in St Andrew's Square, once the house of Sir Laurence Dundas, might be acquired. In all this the Committee of Subscribers found nothing new except the proposed site in Princes Street, 'subject to a servitude', as they pointed out, 'which the inhabitants of that street have, with the utmost determination, maintained against schemes much less likely to be objected to'[47]; and they called on the Town Council to implement the promise which it had undoubtedly made eight months before, to build a new school at Canonmills. The Council admitted a change of mind, but claimed that there had not previously been enough time to reflect; and in May it was decided to build a new High School. Negotiations to obtain the Excise Office fell through, and so the Calton Hill site, 'the only place in the New Town, now left, to which the High School can with any propriety be removed'[48] was chosen two years later, in 1825. Hamilton was asked to prepare a plan, the total cost on no account to exceed £20,000. The town presented the site and made a promise of 'one or two thousand pounds'; for the rest, the public was to 'come forward with subscriptions for the balance'.[49]

The original subscribers, Scott and Cockburn among them, went ahead despite the Town Council, and the Edinburgh Academy, designed by William Burn, was opened in October 1824. The oval assembly hall is very fine, and the elevation simple and pleasing, although the columns which support the Doric portico are perhaps rather wide for their height. As for the High School, work began late in the summer of 1826. The contractor, unfortunately, ran out of money and discharged all his workmen in the spring of 1828, and then, very inconveniently, died. The school was finally completed in the spring of 1829 at a total ultimate cost of £24,200 – not an excessive sum for a building which has been described as 'the noblest monument of the Scottish Greek Revival'.[50] Of this sum, slightly less than £4,300 was raised by public subscription.

The Royal High School lies on the south side of Calton Hill, and is not visible from the New Town. (The best view of it, in fact, is from the Canongate churchyard, where Adam Smith lies buried.) But the Calton Hill supports other buildings, or fragments of building, which are visible all over Edinburgh. The hill is, indeed, littered with buildings of one sort or another, mostly of classical

44. The gateway to High School.

158

shape and form, a seemingly fanciful arrangement of harmonious compositions which forms a pattern constantly and wonderfully changing as one looks up or across at the hill from different parts of the city. Everything there was built between 1776 and 1830. There is the Old Observatory, designed by James Craig and given – it is said upon the passing suggestion of Robert Adam – the appearance of a fortification. Built between 1776 and 1792, this is the only building certainly by Craig which still stands. It looks a little like a converted castle, with a strong hint of domestic gothic, and is really rather extraordinary. Nearby is the New Observatory, a striking, cruciform structure in Roman Doric, with pillars and pediments and a prominent dome in the centre; designed by Playfair, it was begun in 1818. Also by Playfair is the monument to Dugald Stewart, which, like the Burns monument by Thomas Hamilton a little further down the hill, takes the form of a small, circular temple. Above them rises the tall column of the Nelson Monument, a somewhat gothic design of dubious architectural merit by Robert Burn. The only part of the gaol which remains is the governor's house, designed by Archibald Elliot. Castellated and battlemented, it is rather absurd; yet it adds piquancy and variety to the scene.

But the most prominent, the most ambitious, the most remarkable structure on the Calton Hill is the National Monument, 'the pride and poverty of Scotland'.[51] The scheme for a great memorial to those fallen in the Napoleonic War was mentioned at least as early as 1817. In January 1822 an appeal was launched for £42,000 'to erect a facsimile of the Parthenon', an appeal signed by, among others, Sir Walter Scott, Francis Jeffrey and Henry Cockburn. There were to be 'catacombs', and at one point it was suggested that the Monument might be a burial place for the famous and the great, a sort of Scots Westminster Abbey on the top of Calton Hill. But alas! sixteen months later only £16,000 had been subscribed, although a Parliamentary grant of £10,000 was hoped for. The promoters were disappointed, especially as they regarded this 'restoration of the Parthenon' as a matter not merely of Scottish concern but of international concern, 'a splendid addition to the architectural riches of the empire'.[52] They determined nonetheless to make a start, and appointed C. R. Cockerell as architect in 1823.

45. Craig's Observatory, Calton Hill.
46. National Monument, Calton Hill.

159

Cockerell was the leading authority on classical architecture, and no better choice could have been made; but the Committee felt that a resident Scots architect was also necessary; and they appointed Playfair. This appointment did not appeal to William Burn, who was a friend of Cockerell, to whom he wrote as follows:

> To give you any idea of the proceedings of parties in regard to the National Monument, would be to unfold a system of jobbing and illiberality of which you cannot entertain the slightest conception. . . . Mr. Gillespie there is nothing he would hesitate about and therefore his conduct surprises no one, but I confess I felt no little disappointment that Mr. Playfair should have taken the step he has done. . . .[53]

However it was arranged, Playfair became the resident architect, and Cockerell had little more to do than supply the master drawings, for which he received three hundred guineas. The contract, signed in 1826, was for £13,300. The workmanship was of the very highest quality – 'The masonry is as good as can be, and the columns look like each of one stone'[54] – while the cost of the raw materials (finest Craigleith stone) and of handling them was also very high: 'It takes twelves horses and 70 men to move some of the larger stones up the hill.'[55] By 1829 the money was finished and the work came to a 'dead halt'. What had been accomplished was only a fraction of what had been planned, but it looks well – better, perhaps, than if it had been finished: 'When the sun shines and there is a pure blue sky behind [the pillars] (a rare event you will say) they look most beautiful, but surprisingly small.'[56]

These varied and extensive operations on and around the Calton Hill, costly, elaborate, picturesque and important as they were, were gradually overshadowed, in the early 1820s, by a discussion which was to be of even greater consequence. What to do about the *Earthen Mound* had been a matter of debate in the 1780s, and in 1786 the Town Council had begun to buy houses on the north side of the Lawnmarket with a view to opening a communication between the High Street and the extended Royalty. This scheme petered out after nine years, and nothing further was done until after the war. Some of the tenements bought by the Town Council being demolished, however, an open space appeared between the foot of Lady

Stair's Close and Dunbar's Close; and this piece of open ground was bought by the Bank of Scotland in 1800 for £1,350. For a hundred years the Bank had been in Bank Close, a narrow alley opening from the south side of Parliament Square. The building occupied by the Bank, about midway between the Lawnmarket and the Cowgate, was 'a three-storeyed house with attics and with small windows that did not open – the upper half glazed and the lower a square of wood which when pushed along two grooves allowed of fresh air being admitted'.[57] The Bank had been looking for fresh quarters for some time; and a site between the New Town and the Old had obvious attractions. Robert Reid and an architect called Richard Crichton were employed, and by 1802 over seventy men were at work. Finding secure foundations was a problem, for the Mound was

[48] A vision of the Calton Hill complex completed. The building below the Monument is the High School.
EUL

M   161

'travelled earth'; but the building was completed by 1806. What was built then is scarcely visible now, for Reid and Crichton's design almost disappeared in the extensions and embellishments made in the 1860s. The original elevation was somewhat square, with a large shallow bow to the north (still visible), a cupola, and a retaining wall. To modern eyes it may seem not inelegant, and the site is certainly a fine one, which the Bank improved by purchasing and demolishing a number of nearby 'lands'. But no one seems to have liked what was built. A 'prominent deformity', Cockburn called it; 'really an eyesore' said Sir John H. A. Macdonald. Some may think these remarks more applicable to the present building. But, along with Parliament Square, the original did nothing for Reid's popularity, and a sigh of relief must have gone up ten years later when he failed to secure the job of completing the University.

The siting of the Bank had important consequences, for it ruled out or made more difficult certain lines of approach up the Mound to the High Street. But it made no difference to what could be planned lower down, and by 1820 the idea of a range of buildings running north and south along at least some part of the Mound near Princes Street gained ground, and during 1821 plans for these buildings were prepared by Wilson and Hamilton, and by Playfair. It seems that provisional agreement about Playfair's plans in outline was reached, but nothing further is heard about the general scheme, probably because of the onset of depression in 1825.

One particular proposal, however, was proceeded with. It was agreed in 1822 'that it will be of great advantage to obtain a Public Building at the north end of the Mound according to the Plans of Mr. Playfair now approved',[58] and that the site should be offered jointly to the Royal Society of Edinburgh, the Society of Scottish Antiquaries, the Institution for the Encouragement of the Fine Arts and the Board of Trustees for Manufactures and Fisheries. In the event the feu was taken by the Board of Manufactures and the other three societies became the Board's tenants.

A detailed plan by Playfair existed at the end of 1822.[59] 'The building is to be of Grecian Architecture from a design by Mr. Playfair', wrote the secretary to the Board for Manufactures to the Institution for the Fine Arts, 'and evinces in a high degree the pure

[49] *Reid and Crichton. The Bank of Scotland prior to its extensive alteration by David Bryce in 1868-70.*
EUL

classical taste and Scientific attainments so conspicuous in that Gentleman's professional labours'.[60] Five estimates for building were received in the autumn of 1822 and the lowest, for £13,850 by John Inglis, was accepted. The Board (which obtained its finance from the central government under a clause of the Treaty of Union of 1707) was to meet the cost by a cash credit of £10,000 from the Royal Bank, where £10,000 belonging to the Board was held until October 1824, and thereafter by setting aside current savings. All did not go well. Alterations to the plan added £1,290 to the expected cost early in 1824. Much more serious, the contractor complained that the supply of stone from the Culallo quarry in Fife, which Playfair had recommended as saving £1,000 by comparison with the best Craigleith stone, was intermittent and inadequate and was hindering the work. The Board took a high line, and loftily reminded the contractor that he had bound himself to finish the work by 1 February 1825. But a month later Playfair confirmed that Culallo stone was no longer to be had in sufficient quantity; stone from the Earl of Moray's quarry at Dalgety, also in Fife, might therefore be used. This did not solve the problem. Supplies from Dalgety were also inadequate, and it was thought that the best of the stone was in any case going to Moray Place. There was nothing for it but Craigleith Quarry – 'in Craigleith Quarry, and no other, they met with a stratum of excellent solid stone of a suitable colour'[61] – and the additional cost would have to be faced; another £854.[62] The contractor was now well behind schedule – the building was half finished instead of finished in February 1825 – and he began to be 'in great want of money'. By the middle of 1826, however, sixteen months behind schedule, work was virtually completed, and in October 1826 completion was formally acknowledged. The total cost was £16,879, 22 per cent above the estimate, and there was an additional item of £570 for railings. Playfair received 5 per cent of £16,879 less the £854 for Craigleith stone, a payment to him of £800.

This Royal Institution was, however, a very poor affair by comparison with the elaborate building which stands at the side of Princes Street today. It was only two-thirds of its present length, had no side projecting porticos, and presented on its Princes Street front a single and not a double row of columns; it was, in fact, if contemporary prints are to be trusted, somewhat square, heavy looking, and ill-proportioned. The opportunity to think again was given to Playfair five years later, in 1831, when the Board of Manufactures decided that the available accommodation was inadequate; and Playfair's second thoughts were a great deal better than his first. Agreement to enlarge the building southward by sixty feet was reached between the Board, the Town Council, the Proprietors of Princes Street and Tod's Trustees (a group we shall meet again later) early in 1832. (The only dissentient seems to have been William Burn, Playfair's fellow architect, who published a letter 'expressing his disapprobation of that Building being further extended; and not only this, but recommending that the present Building should be taken down, and erected with such enlargement or improvement as may be found necessary, on a more elevated position at the south end of the Mound'. The Board expressed indignation at 'the extraordinary nature of [this] unsought advice'.[63]) Playfair produced a plan late in the summer of 1832, extending the

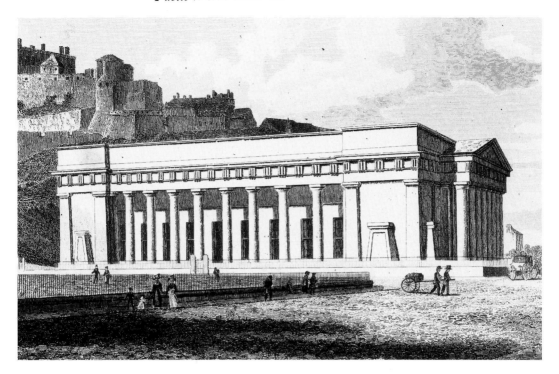

building by sixty feet and also adding the side porticos. Contracts were invited, and the lowest, for £15,414, was accepted in December. The foundations, which caused trouble, were completed twelve months later, and the building was finished twenty-four months after that, in December 1835. But the contractor was paid not £15,414, but £17,008. The extra money was for 'alterations'. These 'alterations' were probably the front row of eight pillars which extend the main portico of the building forward into Princes Street. This feature of the design first appears in an elevation by Playfair dated 28 March 1834. The building as it stands, long, fairly elaborate with its fluted columns, perhaps a little over-decorated, is thus the result of two separate building operations and three successive designs. Its total contract price was just over £29,000, but this was exceeded by almost £5,000, and the final cost to the Board of Manufactures, including furnishing, painting, railing and paving, was just over £40,000.[64]

[50] *Playfair. The Royal Institution, now Royal Scottish Academy, in the 1820's.*
E U L

In the meantime, in the thirteen years which elapsed between Playfair's first plan for the Royal Institution and the final completion of that building, the most far-flung and complex of all the improvement schemes of the early nineteenth century was discussed and set in motion. This scheme had three related parts: to use the Mound as a line of communication between Princes Street and the High Street; to construct a new road southward from the High Street; and to join the top of the High Street with the western end of the New Town and the western approaches to Edinburgh.

Discussion first took definite shape with the publication in 1824 of *Prospectus of a Plan for opening a Road from Main Point, West Port, to the High Street of Edinburgh. Plan by Thomas Hamilton, junior.* Main Point, West Port, was a junction of roads known then as Bread Street, Cowfeeder Row, Laurieston and Portsburgh; it still exists, only Cowfeeder Row has become High Riggs and Portsburgh has become West Port. Hamilton's plan involved building a road round the south of the castle and a bridge over the deep depression where King's Stables Road now runs, lowering the level of the High Street and beautifying St Giles. He put the total cost of road and bridge at £19,000, adding £26,000 for property purchase etc., giving a total expenditure of £45,000. But he reckoned that feuing the improved area would make the scheme 'nearly pay for itself'. The Lord Provost called a public meeting in March which agreed to the proposals, and added that 'William Burn, Thomas Hamilton and Robert Wright Architects should unite in their endeavours to bring about the adoption of a General Plan for the feuing of the grounds belonging to the different proprietors in the vicinity of the projected improvements'.[65] Within a few weeks an addition to the plan had been put forward and accepted, the Southern Districts 'expressing much anxiety that the improvements proposed should embrace a communication from the Lawn Market to the South'.[66]

This fresh proposal raised new issues, and plans multiplied. In December 1824 Robert Stevenson submitted a plan 'for a road through the Grassmarket'. A few months earlier a Mr Leslie had produced 'a new plan for an approach from the West'. But already, in June, Burn and Hamilton in collaboration had put forward proposals for two roads leaving the High Street at 'nearly the same point' going respectively south and west, and also suggesting 'an opening to the Mound in nearly a direct line with Hanover Street, down through Miln's Court'.[67] (The direct line with Hanover Street was already ruled out by the building of the Royal Institution, centred on Hanover Street.) These proposals were too much for the Improvements Committee, which pointed out that the purchase of a great deal of property on both sides of the High Street would be required. Nothing daunted, Burn and Hamilton prepared a careful plan which they backed up with a fairly lengthy report in November.

The basis of their plan was acceptance of the line of the Mound as it was at the Royal Institution (not far from a straight continuation of Hanover Street) for direct, almost due north and south entry to the High Street. The corollary of this was rejection of the winding approach by Bank Street which is used today. They then argued that 'as the Earthen Mound must continue to be the great leading access from the North, it is perfectly obvious that the more directly several streets [coming from south and west of the High Street] can be brought towards this point, the more generally useful and advantageous will they become'. They therefore proposed forming a large open road junction at the top of the Lawnmarket. This would cost a lot of money. On the other hand, 'a great part of the property to be thrown down for the West Road, and other improvements on the Castlehill, consists of wooden tenements crowded together, and almost ruinous'; their plan would 'bring into an improvable state property at present almost without value', destroying principally 'the wreck and rubbish of past centuries, sinking fast under the pressure of their own weight, receptacles of filth and hot beds of contagion'. No doubt with an eye on Stevenson's proposal, they congratulated themselves on preserving the Lawnmarket, 'interesting for its antiquity, and its striking characteristic features.' And they concluded by estimating that the south and west approaches combined would require an expenditure of £152,000 but that the net cost, after allowing for profits from feuing improved properties, would be only £24,000.[68]

This report the Improvements Committee accepted; and to carry the proposals out it recommended an assessment of 2· per cent on the city for ten years, adding that the assessment might, if necessary, 'be continued for a few years longer'. The scheme was still being considered as a whole. But from this time the twin problems of how to join Princes Street to the High Street and how to break out of the High Street with roads leading south and west became separated.

Controversy about the Mound was on the whole less complicated and less acrimonious. An Act of 1816 had authorised the Town Council to erect buildings on the Mound in accordance with a plan to be agreed between them and a group of feuars in Princes Street. Such a plan was agreed shortly afterwards, and another, this time by Playfair, was agreed in July 1822. Early in 1825, however, the influential Faculty of Advocates took a hand in shaping policy. First, the Faculty let it be known that they did not agree that a direct line up the Mound from the Royal Institution was better than Bank Street. They then, in a subsequent communication, objected – very properly and wisely – to an open-ended assessment of the kind recommended by the Committee, and, of the utmost importance, they asked for a guarantee that the Princes Street 'gardens' and the Mound would be preserved as a largely open space.

> The propriety of reserving the whole ground in front of Princes Street from being covered with ordinary buildings was impressed on us the more forcibly from our having discovered that very serious designs were in contemplation, or rather in progress, for actually applying it to this purpose. Now, if the Mound and the south side of Princes Street were to be built upon without restriction, a more fatal injury would be inflicted upon the City, than Edinburgh could almost receive from any other proceeding. We therefore considered it as of prodigious consequence to put an end to all doubt upon such a subject.[69]

The Town Council had argued that it had an agreement with the Princes Street Proprietors guaranteeing the preservation of the gardens, but, as the Faculty wisely pointed out, 'this is a contract which the *Public* has no right to enforce, and which the parties thereto may abandon or alter'.[70] And the Town Council conceded the point.

47. *Side elevation, Royal Scottish Academy.*
Overleaf 48. *Rear façade Royal Scottish Academy.*

There can be little doubt that this was a crucial moment in the city's history. Attempts to secure the ground south of Princes Street for building had been repeatedly made. The Princes Street Proprietors

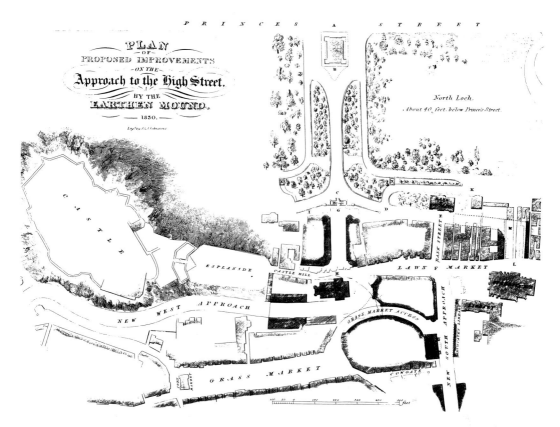

had warded off most of these attempts, but their conservative influence was declining as the Princes Street houses were converted
into shops and business premises. That the Faculty of Advocates at
this juncture took a strong line and more or less demanded an
assurance on the open spaces question as the price of their agreement
to the Improvement Bill which the Town Council was preparing was
decisive. From the spring of 1825 the future of the Mound is discussed within the framework of the idea that the ground between
Princes Street and the Old Town should remain, more or less completely, an open space.

The Improvements Bill brought forward in 1825 was rejected in
Parliament. Two years later, another one was under consideration.
This made no mention of the projected road between Princes Street

[51] Plan of proposed 'im-
provements', the Mound.
Hamilton's proposals of 1830.
E T C

49. The Mound, with
New College in middle distance.

[52] '*Mr Trotter of Dreg-horn's Plan for Improving the Mound*' (1834).
ETC

and the High Street, but proposed that the road southward should run from Bank Street to Bristo Port (the present line of the George IV Bridge) and not from further up the High Street. This line was preferred because the levels were easier, because less demolition of property was necessary, and as 'interfering less with the character and existing thoroughfares of the ancient city'.[71] This proposal ran counter to the Burn and Hamilton idea of a road junction at the top of the Lawnmarket, and strengthened the case for using Bank Street as an exit to Princes Street. The Bill also contained a clause securing the Princes Street gardens area east of the Mound 'henceforth as a pleasure ground'.

This Bill settled some questions, but there was still room for discussion about the proper use, not of the gardens, but of the Mound itself. In 1829 there appeared Alexander Trotter's *A Plan of Communication between the New and the Old Town of Edinburgh*. Trotter proposed to level the Mound for a distance of 485 feet south of the

170

Royal Institution and build there, in line with the Institution, two
rows of shops and warehouses with a continuous palace front and
an arcade for pedestrians between them – what he later described as
'a *Rue des Marchands* in the interior of a splendid Edifice'. Plan and
elevations were by Archibald Elliot, and the buildings were to be
heated 'by means of Boiling Water applied through Horizontal
Tubes'.[72] Trotter's argument was that 'the high prices given for
shops in the finest situations of the New Town' were destroying the
residential character of the principal streets and squares, and that
this character could be preserved by providing a dignified, central
shopping area; the Mound, in Trotter's view, was 'a situation
peculiarly adapted to this purpose'.[73] He added, however, that if
building on the Mound should be deemed inadvisable or impracticable, then the Mound should be lowered so as not to detract from the
imposing effect of the Old Town and Castle as seen from Princes Street,
a view which would be much improved if 'no longer intercepted by

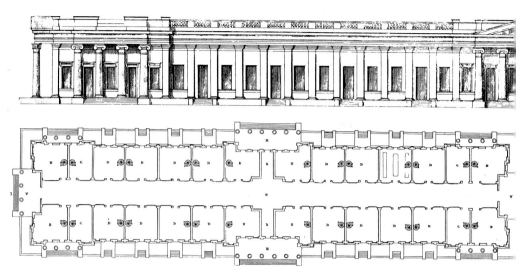

the inclined surface of an unseemly mass of earth'. Lastly, the road to the High Street should pass behind (north of) and not in front of the Bank of Scotland and enter the High Street opposite St Giles.

This scheme was well received, and it was left to Hamilton, in a *Report relative to Proposed Improvements on the Earthen Mound*, published in 1830, to expose its weaknesses. He made two points, one economic and one aesthetic. First, 'the great extent and value of the property which would be effected by deviating so greatly as Mr. Trotter does from the present line of communication by Bank Street would occasion such an expense as to render their [sic] execution altogether unadvisable'.[74] Secondly, the proposal to enter the High Street opposite St Giles would not improve but would 'very materially alter and injure the present aspect of that singularly picturesque part of the Town . . . the spire, which towers upwards of two hundred and fifty feet above the valley of the North Loch, would when fully exposed, be found in reality to be little more than one-half of that height; consequently it must lose much of that importance which has hitherto characterised it.'[75] Instead, Hamilton proposed the route now used round the front of the Bank to Bank Street, arguing that this route, although steeper than that proposed by Trotter, was much cheaper. He also advised levelling the Mound except for that part

used for the road, and argued that, suitably planted and ornamented, it might be transformed 'at a comparatively small expense' from 'an unshapely and deformed mass' into something 'highly ornamental, and not altogether unworthy of the city'.[76]

[53] Elevation and plan of proposed Arcade on the Mound, drawn by Elliot according to Trotter's proposals, 1834. E T C

This was almost the end. Another plan, this time by Playfair, was produced in December 1831, of which the principal features were the preservation of the upper parts of the Mound as 'road-way and pleasure-ground' coupled – as in Trotter's plan – with a good deal of building on both sides of the road lower down. These proposals did not appeal to Tod's Trustees, who owned the land further up the Mound, and they sought advice from Burn, who severely criticised the proposals. Like Hamilton when he criticised Trotter's proposals, Burn used both economic and aesthetic arguments. Buildings on each side of the Mound, he pointed out, would require exceptionally deep and costly foundations because they would stand on 'made-earth', and this would render the financial success of such a speculation exceedingly problematical; he calculated, in fact, that the cost would be three times any possible return. On aesthetic grounds, his view was equally decided: 'in reference to their situation between the Old and New Town, I can look upon [the proposed buildings] in no other light than as destruction of the yet grand and magnificent opening still preserved in that situation, and which at little expense might be formed to give importance to the whole City, increased value to the adjoining properties, and the most imposing feature this City yet possesses'.[77] Poor English and questionable economics, this was yet the embodiment of very good advice. How to join the Old Town and the New was the trickiest problem of all, and the idea that it should chiefly although not entirely be left to nature was undoubtedly the correct one. What had once been the peculiar opinion of 'gentlemen and prominent citizens' was now also, on the whole, the opinion of professional architects. Playfair, of course, was for altering nature a good deal. But he had a fondness for large schemes, and it was perhaps in his nature that he should have wished to build more where he had already built the Royal Institution.

The Town Council seems to have been unconvinced by these arguments, and from March 1831 to March 1832 the Council struggled to persuade Tod's Trustees to agree to Playfair's plans. But the Trustees would not agree to any offer in the way of compensation which the Town seemed willing to make, nor would they agree 'to be bound to continue the line [of building] on their ground, and to complete the buildings within a reasonable period'.[78] So, the Town Council being unwilling to proceed without prior agreement, nothing was done. Only at the end of 1834, when the High Street was being lowered (it proved impossible to lower it by three feet, as planned, because of cellars below the street and houses without foundations), Bank Street was also lowered, the slope of the hill reduced, proper pavements provided, and some improvements made to the roadway on the upper part of the Mound. These works seem to have been completed in the spring of 1835.

While all this was going on, a major battle was being fought over the proposals to build new approaches south and west of the High Street. The plan put forward by Burn and Hamilton in 1824 and accepted by the Improvements Committee was embodied, with little change, in an Improvements Bill of 1825. This measure was designed to empower the magistrates to build a road westwards from the Lawnmarket, to build a road from the Mound or Bank Street southwards, with a bridge over the Cowgate, to rebuild parts of Lothian Road, the High Street and the Lawnmarket, and to open a new street from Adam Square to Brown Square. The bill was brief, and the powers which it sought to convey to the magistrates were specified in a general and summary fashion. It encountered opposition in Parliament, and failed to pass.

This failure led to second thoughts, and in 1826 a much more limited and therefore much cheaper scheme was put forward, one, moreover, by which 'the characteristic features of the ancient ridge on which the Old Town is built would not be disturbed'.[79] This scheme had three parts:

1. lowering and levelling the High Street;

2. 'widening the approach to Castlehill by the removal of the decayed Wooden Tenements upon the North Side, straightening that side of the Street, by which a view of the Castle will be given from the High Street, which has been so long desired, and replacing those tenements by houses in the old Flemish style of architecture, or whatever style appears most consonant with the character of this ancient part of the City of Edinburgh, which is so much identified with the history of former days.'

3. 'the opening of a street from the head of the West Bow, and carrying it along the South Bank of the Castlehill, to communicate with that part of the Town, to the West of the Castle, which was increasing so rapidly. . . .'

These measures, it was claimed, would serve to prepare the way for 'the South Approach'.

Clearly, items one and two were merely a smoke screen to facilitate the passage of item three, the only item of real substance in the proposals. Efforts were made to justify retention of the western approach proposal when so much else proposed in 1825 was being abandoned. All traffic approaching Edinburgh from the north and west gathered at Main Point, Portsburgh. But from there the approach to the Old Town led 'only into obstruction, terminating in a steep ascent, inaccessible to stage coaches and heavy carriages'.[80] Moreover – and this was a more persuasive consideration – the areas of Lauriston, Lochrin, Orchardfield and Fountainbridge were 'in a manner insulated from the northern districts', and these areas, it was alleged, were now 'a populous neighbourhood . . . the seat of a great city.' The proposed new road would make an easy communication to the High Street, incidentally restoring the old part of the town to life; it would be scenically attractive, overlooking 'Heriot's Hospital, the College, Arthur's Seat, and the Pentland Hills; thus commanding one of the noblest views in the City'; and it would be cheap to build, for the route 'does not trench upon any ancient buildings of interest. The district over which it extends is in a state of rapid decay . . .' In fact, the west approach could be done for little over £15,000, and the whole scheme, including lowering the High Street and one or two odds and ends, was to cost a mere £25,364. This could be covered by a £25,000 assessment, or 20/- per cent per annum, which on a rental of £25 ('undoubtedly above an average') would be 3/- payable by the landlord and 2/- payable by the tenant, in each case for only five years. Compared with the South Approach, reckoned to cost over three times as much as the West Approach, the expense was trifling. Now was the time to do it, 'as the wages of labour and the prices of materials and property, are now considerably less than formerly'. Besides, 'a great and opportune relief, by the demand thus created, may be given to these, whether of the class of proprietors or of labourers, who are now suffering from the pressure of the times. It has, indeed, been in many quarters of the country proposed, and in some carried into effect, that public works should be undertaken, expressly for the public relief . . .'

On this basis, there appeared in 1827 proposals for a new Improvements Bill.[81] These proposals, however, went considerably further than the suggestions of 1826, for in addition to the west approach there again appeared the south approach, this time by Bank Street to Bristo Port, 'by which a great deal of property will be saved'. The Burn and Hamilton proposal for a large-scale street junction in the Lawnmarket was thus finally jettisoned in the interests of economy, but the idea of a south approach was preserved. In addition to these two main items it was proposed to take powers to do a great number of things: to make, for example, a new western approach to the Grassmarket, 'which, on market days particularly, broad as it is, can with difficulty, or rather cannot at all, contain the crowd of cattle, market goods, and buyers and sellers, resorting to it'; to continue the Bristo Street line into St Patrick's Square; to improve St Giles and secure 'a site for a Church in the line of the new improvements'[82]; to empower the College Commissioners 'to open up the narrow streets to the North and West of the College', and to join South Bridge into the new Bristo Street line to the south.[83] To pay for these and some other improvements, it was proposed that there should be an assessment of one per cent on proprietors and one half per cent on tenants of houses of £10 and upwards of yearly rent for at least twelve years, these assessments to be continued possibly for another six years if required, along with some additional assessments on the chief beneficiaries and non-assessment of a few individuals.

This scheme was very similar to the Bill which had been flung out of the Commons in 1825, but it was declared by its supporters to include only those proposals on which 'the public voice was most generally united', and those who framed the new proposals may have hoped that the extraordinary confluence of advantages described in their own Report and in that of 1826 would disarm criticism. If so, they did not have to wait long to be disillusioned. It was promptly argued that the new Bill proposed heavy taxation for an indefinite period, gave powers to exempt persons not named in the Bill, allowed non-assessment of the southern districts who were nevertheless to be the chief beneficiaries, and all this in times so hard as to cause 'an alarming depression of property in Edinburgh'.

The most notable expression of opposition to the Bill was a pamphlet published in 1827 entitled *Considerations submitted to the Householders and Shopkeepers of Edinburgh on the Nature and Consequence of the Edinburgh Improvements Bill*. This pamphlet is stated to be 'by a Committee of the Inhabitants', but it bears all the marks of having been written by a single hand. Avoiding petulance but calling a spade a spade with a contemptuous disregard for the laws of libel, the writer of this anonymous pamphlet possessed a style which any eighteenth-century pamphleteer might have envied.

'The burdens on the inhabitants of Edinburgh are more severe than in any other city in the kingdom' – such is the opening sentence. And now, the writer goes on, there is to be a new tax to support involvement in 'an immense, complicated, and precarious SPECULATION without limit'. This speculation, moreover, is for the sake of a sectional advantage. West of St Giles there is not only no 'populous neighbourhood' as described in the Report of 1826, there are almost no buildings of value. But there is a powerful motive for going on, and this motive the Report proceeds to lay bare as follows:

4. Some speculative individuals purchased ground in that district, to the west of the Castle; and as they found that their purchase would yield no return, unless they could succeed in obtaining a road to the High Street, they boldly proposed to assess *the whole inhabitants of Edinburgh*, to build a Bridge, to

carry *their* Road along the Castle Rock, till it reached the Lawnmarket at the Bow. The Committee wish to avoid every appearance of personality; they therefore abstain from naming these individuals, who, however, have made themselves pretty generally known by their unwearied activity in going round to the different Meetings, and exerting themselves in promoting the present Bill, in which several of them are named as Commissioners . . . This project, too, though it threatened at one blow to demolish the picturesque beauty of the Castle, and could be of no conceivable advantage to any part of the Town except the High Street, was in some degree beneficial to the Propositors of the Union Canal, as it afforded a convenient passage from their basins to the Old Town . . .

5. On hearing of this scheme, the inhabitants of the Southern Districts put in a claim *for themselves*, and proceeded to demand *another Road and Bridge* should be made from the High St. in a southerly direction, without which (say the western projectors) they 'dropped a hint' that they would oppose the West Road altogether. The South approach was also acceptable to the propositors in the High Street, who saw the advantage of obtaining two additional entrances, without paying more than a very trifling proportion of a general assessment on the whole city.

6. Things having advanced so far, architects were employed who exerted their ingenuity in preparing magnificent and gorgeous plans. Every feature of our ancient and venerable city was proposed to be demolished, to give place to a heterogeneous mixture of modern buildings, in the *Flemish* style. The architects, of course, laboured heartily in their vocation, and proposed to involve the town in a speculation of building and feuing, exceeding £270,000 . . .

7. The very complication and extent of the speculation created a *new interest* to support them. For the *Incorporated Trades* of the old town saw in them a productive and ever-enduring job, where the public was to be their paymaster . . .

8. On the other hand, the wealthy classes inhabiting the New Town, and various others, viewed these measures with no small

[54] Terminus of Union Canal, sw of Castle, near Main Point, Portsburgh. EWBANK

degree of distrust. Land owners, professional men, annuitants, capitalists, families resorting to Edinburgh for education, or for the comforts of polished society, all asked in vain for the *principle* which could condemn them to pay a heavy tax for the benefit of individuals holding property in obscure districts, to which they were utter strangers . . .

Although inveighing chiefly against the west approach – 'one of the most palpable jobs ever attempted to be palmed upon any community'[84] – the writer also entertained the darkest suspicions about the south approach. It was not only unnecessary and liable to injure rents on the existing South Bridge; it also led to nothing but the Meadow Walk. 'The proprietors of feuing ground in the south-western quarters, and of George Square, Lauriston etc. have formed great expectations of the additional value which that [south] approach would give to their properties; but the same Approach will enable the Town Council to *dispose of the Meadows as building ground,*

and convert an agreeable promenade into a lucrative speculation.
To the inhabitants of the New Town in general, (who would pay
two-thirds of the expense of it) this Approach is a matter of *total
indifference . . .*' Why not extend the Royalty and tax everybody?
And as for the excuse about providing work for the unemployed, the
schemes proposed would merely 'bring over a horde of poor Irish,
who would drive out the native labourers to make room for them,
and ultimately become a permanent burden upon the inhabitants of
this city'.[85]

This pamphlet makes it plain that we have here a classic case of the
old economic problem, so prominent on a national scale in American
history, of who is to pay for public improvements. The conflict in
Edinburgh was between the wealthy inhabitants of the New Town,
who, like the rich men of Boston and New York, opposed 'western
improvements', and those with commercial interests in the areas in
question who stood to gain most by the proposals. It is clear enough
that the argument that the New Town inhabitants would pay most
was correct; they paid most in rates anyway. On the other hand it
was undeniably outrageous that the southern districts should pay
nothing. It also seems to be clear that there was no consensus of
popular opinion in favour of the proposals. The Wards of Police were
consulted in 1827, and the outcome was extensive conflict of opinion.
'Here', as the pamphleteer complained, 'the matter ought to have
rested. But self interest never sleeps.' And it appears to be true that
the principal demonstration of public support for the proposals was
a rowdy meeting of would-be beneficiaries who thrust the scheme on
a complaisant magistracy.

At all events, a Bill on the lines of the 1827 proposals was prepared.
Its expenses were underwritten to the tune of £2,755 by those who
supported it – the abortive Bill of 1825 had cost the Town Council
several thousand pounds, and they did not choose to take the same
risk twice – and petitions against the Bill were unavailing. The
Preamble to this Bill – the Act of 1827 – was as follows:

> Whereas it is desirable that a Communication should be made
> from the West End of the Lawnmarket of the City of Edinburgh
> to the Country on the West, by a Road along the South Ridge
> of the Castlehill, and a Bridge over the Road at the Back of the

Castle of Edinburgh, and that another communication should be made from the Lawnmarket opposite the South end of Bank Street, to the Country on the South, by a New Street and Bridge over the Cowgate towards Bristo Port:

And whereas it is expedient, for the sake of improving the Communication between different Parts of the said City, to level, widen, and otherwise improve the Earthen Mound and Bank Street:

And whereas it is expedient to improve the Access from the West to the Grassmarket, by widening the same on the North Side of the Building called the Cowmarket, situated therein, and from the East by opening a Communication from the Grassmarket to the Lawnmarket:

And whereas, in order to make the said Communications and Improvements, it is necessary to level, pave, and otherwise improve the Lawnmarket, and certain Parts of the High Street, and of the Street called the Castlehill of the said City:

And whereas it is desirable that Powers should be given to widen the Street called the Castlehill, by removing certain Houses and Buildings on the North Side thereof; etc.

An extremely important section forbade building on the Meadows or on Bruntsfield Links. This was inserted by the Committee of the House of Commons which dealt with the Bill, and was accepted by the Town Council only because the Bill would otherwise be lost. (The argument of the opposition was that this enforced upon the city a sacrifice of good building land of very great value.) Also, the Bill provided that there was to be no building on the south side of Castlehill, no building south of Princes Street east of the Mound, 'excepting always a Public Theatre or Playhouse', and no development on the lands of Orchardfield (the area south-west of the Castle, through which the west approach would pass just before reaching Lothian Road) without plan and elevations being approved by the Commissioners. There were to be eighty-two of these Commissioners,[86] including eight members of the Town Council and numerous lawyers (Henry Cockburn among them), two members of the banking family of Bonar, and William Burn the architect. The assessments were as proposed earlier in the year, with the additional provision that the

181

Commissioners could recover ten per cent of the annual feu duty of properties newly disposed of in the 'improved area', for twelve years, provided the properties were disposed of within twelve years of the completion of the scheme – an early example of a 'betterment' provision.

Commissioners were duly appointed, and they began their work in the usual manner, that is to say by borrowing against the security of the assessments and properties to be acquired. They borrowed twenty thousand pounds from the Bank of Scotland, the same from Sir William Forbes and Co., the same from Ramsay Bonar and Co., and the same from the Commercial Bank; a total of no less than £80,000. Late in 1828 work began on the foundations for the King's Bridge, to span the low ground at the foot of Castle Hill, on the line of the west approach.

The Commissioners at first concentrated their attention on the two bridges required – the small King's Bridge for the west approach and the much larger 'new south Bridge' (King George IV Bridge, as it is called today) which was required to span the deep depression of the Cowgate on the line from Bank Street to Bristo Port. In January 1829, the King's Bridge was contracted for at a price of £3,638, and in March, a contractor was found willing to build the south bridge for £14,749. Hamilton, who was architect to the scheme, protested that this bridge could not be built for less than £18,000. No attention was paid to this warning, with the result that a year later the contractor had to be released from his contract, and another undertaker found. This wasted time, but does not seem to have caused the Commissioners any direct financial loss. In the summer of 1830, indeed, they were planning to spend some £12,000 on additional roads and approaches around the Lawnmarket. And then, in January 1831, it was suddenly resolved to stop the entire works in a fortnight. At the end of the month it was resolved to go on for a fortnight more. But the Commissioners met only once, to conduct formal business, between February 1831 and February 1832. The explanation is simple. They had run out of money.

This situation they had foreseen towards the end of 1830, and in December there had appeared a *Report to the Commissioners for the City Improvements by the Committee appointed by them to consider the*

most expedient mode of providing means for completing the Improvements.
The main purpose of this Report seems to have been to exculpate
the Commissioners and to lay the blame for the current difficulties
principally upon the shoulders of the public which, according to the
Report, had manifested 'a determined purpose . . . that both [ap-
proaches] should go on together',[87] thereby landing the Commission
in the all too familiar predicament of having bitten off more than it
could financially chew. It was admitted that there had been a certain

*[55] An early photograph,
about 1860, showing the Cowgate arch of George IV Bridge.*
Yerbury

183

amount of financial miscalculation; but even for this the Commission accepted little responsibility. The new taxes, the Report explained, had brought in less than expected, chiefly because of 'the great fall in rental . . . during these years'. (The fall cannot have been much between 1827 and 1830, when business conditions in Scotland were not very good but were fairly stable.) Against this, expenses had risen because the new south bridge had been enlarged to seventy feet in width with three arches instead of one; not enough had been allowed for interest on borrowed money; above all, the allowance made for 'incidents' had been too little – by £14,000.

This did not add up to much of an explanation. The Commissioners had known perfectly well when they began work that they were to build two approaches at once – that was the essence of the 1827 Bill. They also had known the financial provision, and they had not complained of its inadequacy. Yet in two years they had reached a situation, with neither bridge built and therefore neither approach open, in which they had assets of £7,240 and 'immediate engagements' of £10,233. The financial estimates – they can hardly be described as accounts – which they now produced were as follows:

FINANCIAL SITUATION AS AT 9 JULY 1830

	Expenses incurred	Expenses to be incurred	Total
Miscellaneous	£11,111	£13,481	£24,592
South and East Grass-market Approach	23,523	73,243	96,766
West Approach	27,421	47,096	74,517
High Street		5,260	5,260
Interest		20,000	20,000
Total	£62,055	£159,080	£221,135

	Returns received	Returns to be received	Total
South Approach	£ 512	£56,072	£56,584
West Approach	1,452	43,001	44,453
Total	£1,964	£99,073	£101,037
		Deficit	£120,098

Thus the *net* outlay on the scheme, already, in two years, just over £60,000, was not expected to increase; but a further £97,000 had to be spent, according to this reckoning, in order to secure the completion of the scheme and thence the total anticipated return of

£101,000. And in order to find the necessary money the Commission bluntly proposed an assessment on the city of another £50,000, to be raised by adding 50 per cent to the existing assessments, prolonging them for five extra years, and roping in the Middle, South and West Districts. The pamphleteer of 1827 must surely have smiled a bitter smile: had he not written, 'if the sums levied be found inadequate to complete the project, does not every one see that the public *must*, of necessity, hereafter consent to a fresh assessment, one or more . . . it is a mere delusion to hold that [the citizens] are bound only for a twelve years assessment'?

It was now, of course, a question of throwing good money after bad, or of losing everything through non-completion of the scheme. Almost inevitably, the former alternative was chosen, and in 1831 there appeared a *Report to the Commissioners for the City Improvements by the Committee for obtaining the new Act of Parliament*. This Report, like the previous one, was chiefly designed to exonerate the Commissioners and justify an additional assessment. All the old arguments were repeated, but there was included a report by Hamilton which dealt in some detail with problems of feuing. Hamilton's aim was to rebut statements which had been made by opponents of the scheme. Criticism had been levelled at the assumption in the original plans that the average feuing price of improved property in the hands of the Commission would be 25/- per foot. Hamilton claimed that this was a modest figure. It might be

> perhaps the maximum feu-duty that, even in the most speculative periods, has been obtained for the most fashionable situation in the close outskirts of Edinburgh, such as Lord Moray's grounds. But in Princes Street, the sites . . . have cost about the annual rate of 180/- per foot . . . In St. Andrew's Square prices nearly as high have been obtained; and central property in George Street cannot at the moment be had under a price equivalent to 65/- or 70/- per foot in front . . .[88]

This argument seems very weak. Comparisons with George Street and Princes Street were beside the point, for the new approaches were not going to make available feuing ground in the middle of the town. They were going to offer feuing ground on the outskirts, and the comparison with Lord Moray's grounds was therefore relevant; but to admit that in an equivalent situation 25/- per foot had been obtained only during a fever of speculation did nothing to strengthen Hamilton's case. The other point which he argued concerned the time which would be required to feu the ground:

> The [opponents] estimate the average time of feuing the remaining 1480 feet along the South Bridge and in Bow Street at Martinmas, 1840; meaning that it will not be all feued until after Whitsunday, 1850, nor all paying feu-duty until after Whitsunday; 1853. I look in vain for any thing that ever happened in this city to justify these conclusions; it is as if one were to believe that, if by any means feuing grounds were to be created in Castle Street . . . it should remain unoccupied for twenty years.[89]

The best that can be said for this is that Hamilton was not much of a logician and not much of an historian, however good an architect he may have been. Once again he was comparing central areas with the new peripheral areas with which he was concerned. And had he looked at the records, he would have found that not twenty years but twenty-five years had been required for building to spread from the east end of Princes Street and St Andrew's Square to Castle Street. Of course, a great deal turned on the influence of the trade cycle, which repeatedly and violently disturbed the British economy throughout the nineteenth century and which made nonsense of so many business calculations of the time. The boom of the mid-1820s, which had reached its peak in 1825, had favoured real-estate development and had, indeed, been the background to the early stages of thinking about the west and the south approach. The later 1820s were by comparison lean years, and yet by 1830 it seemed reasonable to expect that conditions similar to those of the mid-1820s would soon reappear; the idea of a seven to eleven year long cycle had not yet entered anyone's head, and it was certainly unfortunate that the sustained business upswing of the 1830s did not begin until 1833.

50. George IV Bridge. The upper level road system was not all gain. Here the steeple of mediaeval Magdalen Chapel is dwarfed by the new level of buildings.

In the event, the Act was obtained without much difficulty. It contained three principal sets of provisions. First, the number of Commissioners was reduced from about fifty-four to twenty-one. Secondly, powers were given to raise an additional £65,000 by means similar to those authorised by the 1827 Act, and to borrow

up to £65,000. Thirdly, Bank Street and Castle Street were not to be widened, and the preservation of the Princes Street gardens was again guaranteed, as was the ruling that there should be no building of any kind in all time coming on the Meadows or on Bruntsfield Links. In a sense, this final group of items was, in the long run, by far the most important of all.

The new Commissioners took over, but throughout 1831 and 1832 the works were almost at a standstill. Progress was made on King's Bridge and this was virtually finished by January 1833, but apart from this the main effort was a review of Hamilton's plans and accounts — accounts which he was very slow in producing and plans which he was very loath to part with. There was little building activity because, evidently, there was little money. The new assessment could not produce funds overnight. And although the Commissioners had powers to borrow £65,000, from whom were they to get the money? For once, the banks do not seem to have been complaisant, and without bank assistance nothing could be done. The Commissioners turned to the only other source, and by an amending Act of 1833 they were authorised to borrow up to £95,000 from the Commissioners for the Loans of Exchequer Bills for Public Works. In a word, the Government came to the city's rescue.

The financial situation was now as follows:

COMMISSIONERS' INCOME AND EXPENDITURE
27 July 1827 to 11 November 1838

Income		Expenditure	
Assessments (1827 Act)	£38,425	Property purchased	£16,606
Assessments (1831 Act)	11,194	Operations on Castlebank	11,430
Bank loans	57,261	King's Bridge	5,399
Exchequer loan commissioners	95,000	Property purchased for sites	
Sundries	3,832	for city churches	9,695
		Sundries	4,220
Total	£205,712		
Sale of materials etc.	5,439	Total	£47,350

The Exchequer Bills were received in August 1833, and work on a full scale was resumed. The contractor for the George IV Bridge unfortunately died late in the year, and in 1834 Hamilton resigned as architect to the Commissioners. Despite these set-backs, the bridge was usable in the summer of 1834 and might have been completed 'but for the demand for workmen for the harvest'.[90] Work on

51. King's Bridge, with the barracks of the Castle in the background.

lowering the High Street was then begun, and improvements were started on Bank Street. The architect to the scheme was now George Smith, appointed at the end of 1834 under the novel arrangement of receiving an annual salary – £200 per annum paid half yearly; he was in addition to receive three guineas from each feuar for a plan and elevation. The ground plans for feuing the area of Orchardfield, however, continued to be those of Hamilton. This was important, for the Orchardfield area was the scene of development which amounted to the creation of a new town in miniature. A large part of this area belonged to John Grindlay and Grindlay's Trustees, who had been prominent among the guarantors for the expenses of the 1827 Bill,[91] and who provided £3,000 towards the building of King's Bridge, the rate of payment depending partly on the rate of feuing of the ground. The Commissioners exacted the promise, however, that the elevations of buildings on streets leading to Lothian Road 'shall be similar to the buildings now erected at Downie Place' (four or five storeys in height with polished ashlar on the first storey); and the ground plan for feuing (Hamilton's) was to be approved by the Commissioners. In this way, formal, unified planning of the area was secured in this case also.[92]

Throughout 1834 and 1835 the Commissioners were tremendously active in purchasing property, in feuing, and in dealing with problems about claims, levels, retaining walls, railings, drains, wells, curb stones, and gas pipes. Between 11 November 1833 and 9 July 1835 they spent £20,516 on the purchase of property for the south approach, and no less than £22,092 similarly for the west approach. Even at the end of all this, however, with a total expenditure of £81,259 in twenty months, the work was not finished. In the autumn of 1835 they were still working at the head of the West Bow, and in August 1836 they were working on drains in connection with Castle Terrace. Indeed, there seemed no end to their operations. And the final Minute Book of the Commissioners has as a first entry an estimate showing that £26,568 was still needed to complete the work in hand. What were called 'tangible funds' amounted to only £12,836; this was insufficient even for a partial completion of the works, reckoned to cost £15,500; and in any case, there were debts amounting to £19,055. The capitalised value of feu-duties receivable amounted to the magnificent sum of £3,290 – so much for Hamilton's feuing calculations of 1831. The Commissioners had, it is true, other assets; and of course there were always their prospects. But emergence from the wood was not yet.[93]

By comparison with these extensive and extraordinary operations, other works being carried on in Edinburgh in the early nineteenth century seem small. Yet there were several other projects – two in particular – which were certainly large having regard to the sums involved and the income of the city, and which were of permanent importance.

But before considering these two major works – Register House and the University – it is worth glancing at three churches which were built between 1810 and 1830, all of which are still prominent in the city and which possess considerable historical and architectural interest. The first of these is St George's, in Charlotte Square. It had from the first been intended that a church should occupy the site looking down George Street, and when he designed the elevation for Charlotte Square Robert Adam designed a church for this site. For some reason – on the score of expense, it is sometimes said – Adam's plan was not utilised when, in July 1810, the Town Council began to consider building. It was decided to raise money by letting seats in the unbuilt church for fifteen years in advance on a cash payment basis, but as this would not provide sufficient, resort was had, as usual, to the banks. Robert Reid, who had been chosen as architect, stated verbally that £18,000 would be the sum required. Accordingly, the Town Council approached 'the different Bank and Banking Companies to know to what extent they would be willing to accommodate the Town',[94] and specifically asked the Bank of Scotland, the Royal Bank and Sir William Forbes and Co. for £6,000 each. Sir William Forbes and Co. returned an 'immediate answer', agreeing 'with much pleasure',[95] but the other banks declined. The Commercial Bank was then asked, and agreed; and with the hope of 'the loan of a considerable sum' from the Incorporation of St Mary's Chapel, the Town Council went ahead. Contracts were signed in May 1811, and in June St Mary's Chapel produced the desired £6,000, which was deposited with the two co-operating

[56] Robert Adam. Design for St George's Church – 'It is certainly a pity that the Adam design was not used'.
scots mag. 1814

52. St George's Church, as designed by Reid.

banks. All should have been well. But in the spring of 1813 money began to run short, and it was belatedly discovered 'that no specific estimates of the cost of this church had been originally taken from Mr. Reid'.[96] When asked, Reid estimated that an additional £7,875 would suffice; £15,800 had already been spent, so the total was now to be £23,675.[97] The banks obliged, requiring, however, personal

security; and the church was finished early in 1814. It is internally a small and rather plain building, but the façade is moderately imposing, and certainly one of the most notable features of the Edinburgh skyline is the dome of St George's, a coffered dome sheathed with copper, which supports a small gilt 'temple', also domed and carrying a cross at the top, about 150 feet above the ground. The dome is pleasing, although the church itself, taken in isolation, can hardly be called a distinguished building. It was scarcely completed when unfavourable comparisons began to be drawn between Adam's plan and Reid's achievement – 'each part appears to have been designed with the same cool and deliberate bad taste which characterises the whole plan'.[98] This is unjust, but it is certainly a pity that the Adam design was not used. It might almost be said that the New Town has suffered a twin misfortune in its churches, for St Andrew's is the right church in the wrong place, and St George's is the wrong church in the right place. Another church built in this period is St Stephen's, at the foot of St Vincent Street, begun early in 1827 according to designs by Playfair, and opened for worship at the end of 1828. The contract price was £18,975. It is an extraordinary design, making good use of a difficult site. The dark cavernous portal beneath the tower seems to swallow up the steeply descending street, and the imposing flight of steps which goes up beneath the portal leads, rather surprisingly, into the gallery. Its style, as was remarked at the time, is certainly unique, and the arrangement does credit to the architect's ingenuity.

St John's Episcopal Chapel – now St John's Church – is in complete contrast to St Stephen's. The site, at the west end of Princes Street, was obtained not without opposition from the Princes Street Proprietors, for it was open ground on the south side of the street, used then as a market garden. Designed by William Burn, work on the church began in the spring of 1816 and it was ready for use two years later. The style has been described as 'a free rendering of English Perpendicular',[99] following in some respects, particularly in the charming fan vaulting of the roof, carried out in this case in plaster, the example of St George's Chapel, Windsor.[100] As originally designed, the tower was to carry a high, lantern-like, openwork crown. When only partially constructed, this crown blew down in a

53. 19th century Fan vaulting of the nave, St John's Church.

191

gale in January, 1818, and was never replaced. For this act of God there is reason to be grateful, for the proportions of the church as it stands are admirable. It seems to have made in its day a striking contrast with the neighbouring church of St Cuthbert's, which according to a contemporary, looked 'so like a huge stone box, that some wags have described it as resembling a packing-case, out of which the neighbouring beautiful toy-like fabric of St John's Church has been lifted'.[101] St John's was built at a cost of £18,013, raised partly by donations and partly by subscriptions of £20 shares which paid interest at five per cent. This was reduced to three per cent in 1819. The largest shareholder was Sir William Forbes, who was also a member of St John's, and who is buried, like Sir Henry Raeburn, in the small churchyard to the south of the church.

St John's looks so small partly because it is so well proportioned. Register House, on the other hand, is a very large building. Much of it was completed before 1800, but what had been built soon proved inadequate for the purposes for which it was intended, and in 1822 an Act was obtained in order to complete the building 'according to its original plan but with certain modifications'. In August, Robert Reid, described as 'Surveyor of the General Register House', was directed by the Trustees to prepare plans, and in October the building contract was signed. Work went on at a leisurely pace, and then in 1827 another Act was obtained, more money being needed because the Trustees 'had found it expedient to alter, and in some respects to enlarge, the original plan or design'. The final result is externally very close to the original design, but Reid made some important internal modifications. In particular, the large double stairway leading to the gallery and north room is his, and so is the style and decoration of the large north room itself. There was some controversy at the time about the 'freeze' in this room,[102] and it must be said that the total effect is somewhat ponderous. The accounts were fully settled in 1834, total expenditure being put at £38,776. It was agreed at the start that Reid's remuneration should be five per cent of total expenditure.

One other large building begun before the war remained to be completed after its end; the University. And as the war drew to a close, discussion about what to do about 'the college buildings' was

54. The cavernous doorway to St Stephen's Church.

192

renewed. In 1813 application was made to the Lords of the Treasury
for money, but without success. In 1815 the Town Council and the
College jointly addressed another petition to the Government for
aid, 'which aid', the Town Council Minutes significantly add, 'it was
now understood the Lords of the Treasury were disposed to grant'.[103]
This hope was not in vain. A Committee of the House was set up to
consider the matter, and it was from the start sympathetic to the
University case. The Committee was struck by the increase of
student numbers (they had risen, according to the Town Council,[104]
from 1,000 in 1768 to 'at least 2,000' by 1815), an increase which
the Committee note was due to 'the Celebrity of [the College's]
Professors and particularly by the high estimation in which the School
of Medicine is held all over Europe'.[105] The University had at one
time raised £30,000, but this sum had proved 'quite inadequate'.
And the Committee advised the Town Council and the College to
produce a modification of Adam's plan so as to reduce the expense,
and suggested that it would be reasonable to plan for completion on
the basis of an additional £70,000 or £80,000. A few weeks later,
towards the end of June 1815, almost on the morrow of the battle
of Waterloo, the Government made an initial grant to the University
of £10,000, 'with prospect of the like sum annually for seven
years'.

The Town Council lost no time, and on 9 July 1815 the following
notice was sent out:

> Architects are hereby invited to give in plans for finishing the
> College of Edinburgh, on a reduced scale, leaving out the south
> front, and the cross building, which formed the small court in
> the original plan, – regard being always had to the part already
> executed, and to the preservation of the architecture of Mr. Adam
> as far as practicable.
>
> A premium of One Hundred Guineas will be given for the
> Plan which shall be approved of.

The last date for the submission of plans was 15 February 1816. In
August 1815, however, the rules were altered so as to allow architects freedom to do as they pleased with regard to the south front

55. The Upper Library, the University.

and the cross buildings. Plans were submitted by nine architects:

William	Adam	(Edinburgh)
William	Burn	(,,)
Richard	Crichton	(,,)
Archibald	Elliot	(London)
Thomas	Hamilton	(Edinburgh)
James	Milne	(,,)
Robert	Morrison	(,,)
John	Paterson	(Greenhill Cottage)
William	Playfair	(Edinburgh)

Robert Reid had prepared plans for the Lord Provost in 1810, and in a curious letter written in August 1816, which incidentally throws some light on the architectural practice of the day, he gave the reasons why he now declined to enter the competition.

> Mr. Reid . . . humbly conceives that the commission he holds as architect and surveyor to His Majesty in Scotland, and the experience he has had in conducting and adjusting the accounts of extensive public works, in a certain degree points him out to the Commissioners as having some claim to the appointment in question. But . . . Mr. Reid at the same time wishes it may be distinctly understood, that he does not desire to be concerned in carrying the designs of any other artist into execution; for he has long adhered to the resolution of the most respectable in the profession, to accept of no professional business, where he is not exclusively and confidentially employed.

There is no record of a reply to this communication having been made.[106]

The problem now was to choose one of the nine plans. The professors of the University were consulted, and their opinions are preserved in a document entitled 'Reports of the Professors' Opinions on the Plans'. The preface of this Report contains the ominous remark, 'If there was a difficulty in arranging the Reports etc. of the several Architects on their respective Plans . . . there is certainly more difficulty in arranging the Reports or Opinions of the several Professors thereon.' Yet although these opinions varied a good deal, it is easy to see that the plans of Burn and Playfair were by far the most popular. Of Burn's proposals not a great deal is known. His elevations were seemingly more ornamental than those of Playfair, and although he claimed to have 'adhered most faithfully to the *whole* of Mr. Adam's *exterior* elevations of the buildings'[107] his plan required a rather different dome above the east front, because he located the library on the two upper floors above the main entrance, and wanted a dome to admit light. Nor did his arrangements of internal accommodation find as much favour as those of Playfair.

[57] *Playfair. The University; drawing of acanthus leaves as a detail for a Corinthian capital.* EUL

Over five thousand of Playfair's plans and drawings are still in the possession of the University, and there is also his extremely business-like *Report concerning the Mode of completing the New Buildings for the College of Edinburgh*. Unlike Burn, he proposed to retain the original Adam dome – a dome which was in fact never constructed – and this intention counted strongly in his favour; as David Hume, Professor of Scots Law, remarked, 'it is hardly just, indeed hardly decent, to the memory of Mr. Adam, that this [east] front, which is marked with his name as architect, should receive its finish and decoration from any hand but his own'.[108] Playfair also retained Adam's idea of having at each corner of the court a 'circular corner' or quadrant, with arches on the main floor and columns above, and an open passageway behind – a development of the idea to be seen in William Adam's design for Hopetoun House, and which gives a Palladian flavour to the interior of the court. Playfair was, according to his uncle Professor Playfair, the only competitor to retain this feature of the original Adam design, except for William Adam.[109] Playfair also scored with the compromise proposal that there should be a chapel but not a very large one; said the Professor of Chemistry, 'it would be unnecessary waste of the very best part of the building,

[58/59] *Adam & Playfair. The University, Museum front.*
Adam's original design (above) *and Playfair's modified version* (below).

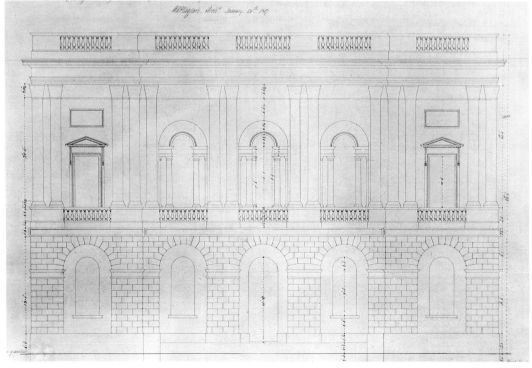

[60] *William Playfair.*

were the western side of the court [as in Burn's plan] to be devoted to this purpose . . . the plan proposed by Mr. Playfair, of fitting up the large apartment on the ground floor of the library for a chapel [is] the preferable one.'[110]

What decided the matter, however, was the superiority of Playfair's proposals for the museum and library. 'The show-rooms of a school of science', wrote the Professor of Hebrew, 'ought to be its library and museum, and these are of unequalled beauty in Mr Playfair's plan'.[111] The museum, occupying the main part of the west side of the College, was a large room, ninety feet by thirty-four, two floors in height, lit from above by two domes and a small central lantern. It is now somewhat altered. The library was on two floors. On the ground floor it was divided into a sequence of five almost separate rooms; two outer rooms, two inner circular rooms lit from above, and a central rectangular room, fifty-seven feet by sixty. This arrangement was repeated on the upper floor, the two circular rooms becoming galleries round a well which let the light pass to the lower library from the two great domes above the roof. Playfair described his upper library as a single room, the different sections of which were linked together by the use of columns; 'the several divisions are in a manner thrown into one great room. A person, therefore, standing at either extremity, has the whole range before him, extending to a distance of 190 feet . . .'[112] This was certainly an exaggeration, for the various sections of the upper library were, in spite of the columns, largely cut off from one another. Nevertheless, the arrangements for the library, its large overall size dictated by 'the absolute necessity of appropriating to this department every portion of space that can possibly be obtained . . . the number of books . . . amounts to 50,000 volumes . . . increasing at the rate of 1,000 volumes per annum'[113] – these arrangements commanded widespread, almost universal, admiration: 'Mr. Playfair's plan for the library bears the stamp of genius, and combines every advantage that could be desired – at once commodious, elegant and even magnificent. In short, when finished, it would unquestionably be the boast of our northern metropolis.'[114]

The opinions of the professoriate appear to have been shared by the Committee to which plans, by Government order, had to be sub-

56. Detail of the Upper Library.

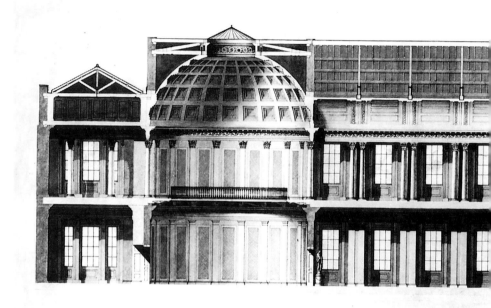

mitted – a committee which included the Lord Provost, the Principal of the University, William Dundas M.P., Sir John Marjoribanks and some others – and Playfair was appointed architect in 1817. Work on the College, recommenced in the summer of 1815, gathered momentum after the laying of the foundation stone of Playfair's plan in March 1817. Playfair's plans were certainly a continuation of the work of Adam. In some respects his designs followed those of Adam very closely – for example, the east-facing front of the court is almost as Adam designed it.

Numberless changes were made, however, both internally and externally. The disappearance of the cross building is of course the major one, resulting in internal proportions of the quadrangle which Adam never envisaged. The depth of the east range was also increased, so that the main entrance to the University – the so-called 'domed vestibule' – has become rather tunnel-like and gloomy.

As the work progressed, alterations were made in Playfair's own plans. The original proposal for a flight of steps running continu-

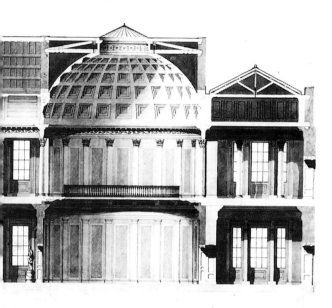

ously round the whole of the court was abandoned at an early stage. The elevations of the south fronts of the building, both within the court and facing College Street, were made more handsome, although the south face of the south range is still somewhat dull and a great deal less interesting than Adam's original design, which included an upper colonnade.[115] Most important of all, the upper library was radically altered. The domes and the circular openings and rooms beneath them disappeared, and the central upper room with its high arched roof was extended east and west, lit now by windows on each side. This alteration was in principle suggested by Robert Hamilton, Professor of Public Law,[116] in 1816: 'A light from above . . . is at no time the best . . . Mr. Playfair's library would be much improved, by lighting these two rooms from the south side, and by giving them the whole oblong area included in the plan . . . With this alteration, Mr. Playfair's design would be very grand indeed, and, in my humble opinion, perfect: And it is not foreign to observe that by leaving out the domes, there would, I learn, be a considerable saving

[61] Playfair. The University Library, original design – 'Mr Playfair's plan for the Library bears the stamp of genius'.
EUL

199

in expense . . .'[117] Thus there should go to the Professor of Public Law some of the credit for the creation of the room which is one of the greatest glories of the University, which is one of the finest achievements of late classical architecture in Britain, and which can stand comparison, although it is in quite a different style, with the justly celebrated Wren Library at Trinity College, Cambridge. There is no foreshadowing of this magnificent room in the extant plans by Robert Adam.

The Government's promise was of £10,000 per annum until the completion of the building. Work on the College during 1817 was principally on the foundations, and expenditure in that year amounted to only £3,367. Of this total, Playfair received a 'percentage' of £250, out of which he paid £80 to his principal clerk, £10 to a temporary clerk, and £25 for stationery and drawing materials. Not a great deal was done in 1818, but in 1819 large scale operations began, and for the next nine years, with little serious interruptions, work on the College went steadily forward. In January 1823, after receiving a total of £80,000, the Commissioners produced their first exact estimate of the total final cost. They would need, they calculated – or rather, Playfair calculated – another £37,043. The Treasury accepted this figure, and the annual payments of £10,000 continued for three more years. The Commissioners then asked, at the end of 1825, for another £16,043, £9,000 above their estimate of less than two years before. The Treasury demurred, pointing out that provision had been made for only £7,043. The Commissioners replied that the building was externally complete except for the roofing of the south wing, that it would be a great tragedy to be held up for want of money at this point, and that more money was needed because 'the general expense of the work has unavoidably increased, owing to the great rise in the price of labour' [118] The words can hardly have been written when the boom of the 1820s collapsed, and prices began to fall. This did not solve the Commissioners' troubles, and the Treasury – possibly glad of an excuse to curtail public spending in a year as depressed as 1826 – awaited further information. This was supplied in February 1827. The building, the Commissioners wrote, was virtually complete except for lowering the court and providing steps within the court, except for

[62] *Playfair. The University. Plan and elevation of Venetian window and Corinthian columns in Museum front, w side of Quadrangle.*
EUL

200

fitting-up the library, and except for adding the dome or 'spire'. The whole thing could be finished – for another £16,889. The Treasury refused to consider this figure, and after four years of reflection – during which the Commissioners were able to draw on previous grants – supplied a final moiety of £6,000. In addition, however, £2,717 was released from a grant of £5,000 made by George III to preserve the new buildings in 1801.

The University was thus built with public money to the tune of £121,000. This was about £11,000 short of the sum asked for. An estimated £6,000 was saved by not adding the dome, which had been so prominent a feature of Adam's original plan.[119] No less than £23,000 was spent on the Library. In 1826-27 over £4,000 was spent on pulling down old houses nearby 'to secure free light and air, and to secure the Buildings against danger from fire'.[120] Even so, no attempt was made to improve the surroundings of the University on anything like the scale suggested by Craig in 1786, by Robert Adam in one of his original plans, or by the Improvements Act of 1827. Chambers Street has since then been created, but orderly planning for the area as a whole has still to be put into execution.

[63] *The University. Adam's east front, as built.*
shepherd

[64] *'I have stood,' wrote Cockburn, 'in Charlotte Square and listened to the corncrakes in the dewy grass.'*
kirkwood, 1819

202

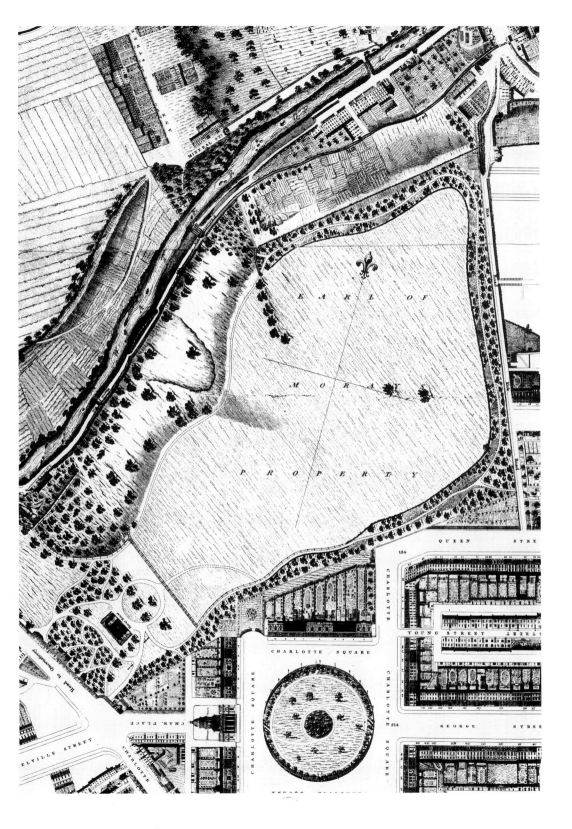

VII

Private development after 1800

When the nineteenth century dawned, Charlotte Square was the most westerly part of the town and of the Royalty. Three sides of the square were still unbuilt, but on the north stood a few houses. Beyond them was open country. North and west of the square, says Cockburn, there lay 'an open field of as green turf as Scotland could boast of, with a few respectable trees on the flat, and thickly wooded on the bank along the Water of Leith . . . That well-kept and almost evergreen field was the most beautiful piece of ground in immediate connection with the town, and led the eye agreeably over to our distant northern scenery . . . I have stood in Queen Street, or the opening at the north-west corner of Charlotte Square, and listened to the ceaseless rural corn-craiks, nestling happily in the dewy grass.'[1]

The land so described did not belong to the city. Most of it had at one time been in the possession of Heriot's Hospital, but over a long period of years the Trustees had disposed of the greater part of their property in this neighbourhood. They retained a good deal, however, and were one of the four important superiors in the lands immediately north and west of the New Town; the others were the Earl of Moray, Sir Francis Walker, Hereditary Usher of the White Rod in Scotland, and Henry Raeburn, the painter, who was knighted in 1822.

The lands belonging to the Trust were by far the most extensive of these holdings. They stretched uninterruptedly from the gardens north of Queen Street to a line joining Silvermills and Canonmills, bounded on the east by Broughton Street and on the west by Wemyss Street and St Stephen Street. The Earl of Moray's property was adjoining on the west. It was a smaller area, bounded approximately

57. View across Dean Valley to Eton Terrace.

by Charlotte Square and Queen Street on the south, Church Lane on the east, and on the other sides by Queensferry Street and the Water of Leith. These Moray lands had once been owned by Heriot's Hospital, but had been feued by the Hospital at various times between 1648 and 1756. The property of Sir Francis Walker lay further west still, on the west side of Queensferry Street. It was bounded by Queensferry Street itself, Lynedoch Place Lane, Belford Road, and Palmerston Place, but Alva Street and the south part of Stafford Street were not included. This land had been feued by Heriot's to a variety of people between 1702 and 1763, and was then gathered into the hands of the Walker family by a series of dispositions dated between 1787 and 1809. The Raeburn lands, unlike the others, were almost entirely west of the Water of Leith, forming a triangle with the bridge at Stockbridge as its apex, and the three sides formed by Dean Terrace, Ann Street and Raeburn Place. East of the Water, the only Raeburn property was a small piece of ground which later became India Place. This was feued by Heriot's to Robert Raeburn in 1758, and passed to Henry Raeburn in 1821.

These four properties were developed for the most part independently of one another and at slightly different times. The earliest development outside the strict confines of the New Town was not in this area, however, but to the east of Queen Street, where, beginning in 1799, the Heriot Trust feued ground for the building of Duke Street, Elder Street and York Place. These streets were largely built between 1799 and 1804, Elder Street being chiefly remarkable in that it was entirely built by two local builders, John Reid and John Young. It was a few years after this that Heriot's major development began, down the slope to the north of Queen Street; but discussions about it had been going on for several years before 1800. This area was not entirely owned by Heriot's, for in 1785 some thirteen acres had been acquired by David Stewart, variously described as a 'banker' or 'merchant' in Edinburgh, Lord Provost from 1780-82; and in 1791 Stewart acquired another acre of ground, 'exposed to public roup within the Exchange coffee house'[2] in March of that year. Stewart seems to have been a man of substance, for in 1790 he offered to purchase his feu-duty 'and as much more superiority as would entitle him to a freehold qualification for which exclusive

58. Doorway in Duke Street.

of the value of the feu he was willing to pay Three hundred Guineas'.[3] This offer was refused.

The idea of a joint plan for the feuing of this whole area was first put forward by Stewart in a letter to the Trust noted in their Minutes in June 1792:

My Lord,

In consequence of what passed between the Committee of the Governors of George Heriot's Hospital and me I have with the assistance of Mr. William Sibbald your Surveyor made out a plan for building on the ground lying to the north of Queen Street the property of the Hospital and myself – This plan I now take the liberty of transmitting to your Lordships for the inspection of the Governors who I request will take it into their consideration with as little loss of time as possible – I believe this matter is already before the Committee . . .

Six months later it was reported that a 'sketch' had been made out 'by Mr. Sibbald the Good Towns Superintendent of works', and that there was good prospect of the Hospital feuing according to this plan 'upward of Fifteen thousand pounds Sterling'.[4] Over two years later, in 1795, the Trust noted that Sibbald was working on a plan for this area. Perhaps the Governors were in no hurry, for it was said that the matter 'had already lain over some years'.[5]

The earliest dated copy of a plan for 'the ground north of Queen Street' is in the Heriot Trust archives. It is dated 1796, and is described as 'by David Stewart Esq.'. This plan, reproduced on p. 207, is rather in the nature of a sketch, but it is interesting because it contains the two main features of the final development – a circus (this became Royal Circus) and a square (Drummond Place) joined by a straight street running east and west (Great King Street). It it also possible to identify the street which became Royal Crescent; and the gardens, which already existed and were in the hands of six private owners including David Stewart himself, are also shown although not quite as they now exist. The circus and square are also further south, i.e. further up the hill, than in the final plan. It is clear, however, that the main features of the planning of this area had been worked out by Stewart and Sibbald by 1796.

While the plan was being modified in the following years, two

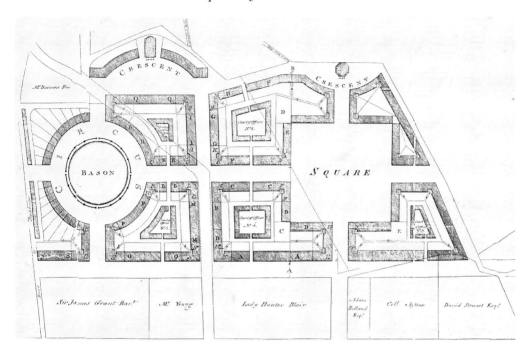

important changes took place. First, the city became involved in the proposed development when in 1797 it acquired five acres of ground adjoining the 'planned area'; and in 1800 Stewart disappeared from the scene, bankrupt. (Financial pressure may have lain behind his request in 1799 for permission to build on the garden ground belonging to him between the east end of Queen Street and Abercromby Place; this request was refused by the Trustees of Heriot's Hospital.) John Morrison, W. S., became trustee for the creditors of Stewart, and it was he who took part in the final negotiations carried through in 1801 and 1802. In December 1801 it was moved in a meeting of the Heriot Trustees 'that a plan on a large scale should be made out with all possible despatch by Messrs Sibbald and Reid from the Sketch or plan now presented to the Governors'.[6] This may have been the plan which existed in 1796 and which was ordered to be engraved 'and a thousand copies to be cast off'.[7] Reid and Sibbald certainly lost no time, for in February 1802 'a plan of the joint ground belonging to the good Town and Mr. Stewart and the

207

Hospital on the north of the Gardens of Queen Street, made out upon a large scale, as recommended at last Meeting was produced in Council and approved of'.[8] These references are the first in which the name of Robert Reid appears in this connection.

The feuing of the ground could now begin, and between 1803 and about 1823 this part of the New Town was very largely built. The progress of building was, very roughly, from the Queen Street gardens northwards into the open country, down the green hill towards the still unspoilt Water of Leith, 'a clear running stream, with plenty of roaches and eels'.[9] Building began in Heriot Row, which was largely completed between 1803 and 1808. An elevation of Heriot Row by Robert Reid, signed January 1803, faces p. 210; the Row as built does not quite correspond to this elevation. Heriot Row was followed by Northumberland Street, built between about 1807 and 1819, and, at much the same time, Jamaica Street. Abercromby Place came next, begun in 1814 and almost completed by 1819. Great King Street was somewhat later, between 1814 and 1823; and then, after the war, came India Street (1819-23) and Royal Circus (1820-23). For this last, Playfair's elevations were submitted to the Trustees in January 1820.

All this area, excluding only the building already completed in Heriot Row, was developed in a uniform manner, controlled not only by the street plan of Sibbald and Reid, but also by a Contract, dated 1806, between the City of Edinburgh, the Governors of George Heriot's Hospital, and the new owners of David Stewart's lands, namely George Winton, James Nisbet and Thomas Morison, described as 'Architects in Edinburgh', and Maxwell Gordon and John Morison, both Writers to the Signet. The main clauses of this contract are to the following effect:

First.   The houses in Heriot Row and at the west end of Abercromby Place to be two storeys plus a basement or sunk storey, not to rise more than 33 feet above street level, except for the projecting houses which are to be limited to 51 feet.

Second.   The houses in Dublin Street, Howe Street, India Street, Pitt Street and other streets running north from Abercromby Place and Heriot Row shall not

59. Heriot Row.

208

overtop the projecting houses mentioned in the first clause.

Third. The houses in Drummond Place, Great King Street, Royal Circus etc. shall not exceed 46 feet except for the projecting houses; in Northumberland Street they shall not exceed 33 feet. Also 'the roofs of all the houses in the different streets, Rows, Squares etc. shall not exceed one third of its [sic] breadth' i.e. there were to be no high-pitched roofs.

Fourth. 'That no storm windows nor any raised Breaks in the roof in imitation of French roofs or otherwise shall be allowed' except in Cumberland, Spencer, Dundas, Pitt, Nelson, Duncan and Jamaica Streets.

Fifth. 'That the houses in all the foresaid places, except in Jamaica Street, Nelson Street, London Street, King Street, Dublin Street, Scotland Street, Duncan Street, Dundas Street, Pitt Street, Howe Street, Saint Vincent Street and India Street shall be built as follows:– the sunk storeys shall be of broached ashlar, or rock work, and all above to be polished, droved or broached ashlar, and shall have blocking courses fifteen inches high, and the slates not to project above 3 inches over the said blocking courses'.

Sixth. 'That in the foresaid places there shall be sunk areas in front of all the houses with a good iron railing and foot pavement of the following dimensions' [details follow, varying as between different streets], and 'water closets shall be allowed to be built, but these shall not project farther from the back wall than five feet, nor be higher than six feet above the level of the parlour floor;· and further it is hereby expressly stipulated that the ground marked in the plan for stable ground shall be applied to no other purpose than for stables, and coach-houses, or washing houses, or other offices for the use of the occupiers of the front tenements alone . . .

60. *Drawing-room in Heriot Row.*

Seventh.	'That the common sewers shall be executed agreeable to a plan to be made out by the said William Sibbald and the Purchasers shall be taken bound not only to make and construct the common sewers and lay the side pavements with a sufficient rail and to causey the streets, but also to keep the whole in good and sufficient repair, in all time thereafter, at the sight and to the satisfaction of the Dean of Guild of the City of Edinburgh, and his Council for the time being, all to be made and constructed in a manner to be pointed out by the said William Sibbald . . .'
Eighth.	Feus in the different streets are to be disposed of at not less than the following prices per foot in front:

Seven shillings. Bellevue Crescent, Cornwallis Place, Drummond Place, Great King Street, London Street, Mansfield Place, Royal Circus.

Five shillings. Abercromby Place, Heriot Row, Dublin Street, Duncan Street, Dundas Street, Howe Street, India Street, Nelson Street, Northumberland Street, Pitt Street, Saint Vincent Street, Scotland Street.

Four shillings. Royal Crescent, Fettes Row, Cumberland Street, Jamaica Street and Spencer Street.

Ninth.	'a street shall be made [northwards] in continuation of Hanover Street'.
Thirteenth.	The Royalty shall be extended over all the grounds referred to.

[66] Reid. Elevation for Heriot Row, 1803. Heriot Trust

Fourteenth. The City binds itself 'in order that [these streets] may be sufficiently supplied with water . . . to lay a main pipe of seven inches diameter to the South boundary of the lands of Bellevue', and the Hospital binds itself 'to lay a main pipe of the like diameter from the main pipe in George Street to Heriot Row facing Queen Street . . . before or so soon as any house in the said Heriot Row shall be finished . . .'[10]

Fifteenth. 'That from these main pipes, water shall be distributed along the several streets and other places by service pipes at the expense of the respective proprietors or their feuars . . .'

This contract is notable for containing the first detailed set of regulations for building in Edinburgh over a large area. (What had been specified for building in the New Town in the eighteenth century was, by comparison, undetailed and perfunctory.) A high degree of

uniformity was the prime requisite – uniformity which yet allowed
variations in decoration and in the design of doors and windows.
Water supply is arranged for, but the feuars are to pay a very large
share of the cost, as well as being wholly responsible for the construction of sewers, streets and pavements. The price differences as
between different streets (corresponding to differences in the regulations about railings, sunk areas and pavements) are also interesting;
generally speaking, these differences reflect the importance in the
plan (not obvious at first sight to anyone on the ground) of the
main axis of London Street and Great King Street.

It is almost unnecessary to say that when it came to carrying out
the plan difficulties were encountered. Some areas sold disappointingly
slowly; stances in Great King Street, for example, were repeatedly
put up for sale throughout 1810, with only meagre results; late in
1813 the roadway itself was still not made. In the case of Great King
Street this was because many houses and sunk storeys remained unbuilt. The fault, however, was sometimes that of the superiors; as
when the feuars in Heriot Row and Northumberland Street declared
in 1805 that the plan which had induced them to take their feus
provided for immediate completion of the communication by Hanover
Street, and accordingly petitioned that the road (Dundas Street) be
made 'possible'. Nine years later Robert Dundas W.S. complained
similarly that the road from Queen Street to Howe Street was 'in
bad repair and not made to its proper breadth'.[11] Defective water
supply was also a source of trouble. The feuars in Royal Circus complained in 1821[12] that they had feued 'upon the faith that there was a
water pipe laid down Howe Street of sufficient size for supplying the
whole adjoining grounds with Water'; but they now found the pipe
to be 'two small', and asked the Governors for a contribution of £40
to pay for opening up the road in order that the feuars might lay a
new pipe. Complaints about building contrary to the regulations were
also not infrequent. A more serious matter was the objection made
by feuars in Great King Street in 1812, to the effect that Mr Lauder,
skinner, was erecting 'some buildings . . . at or near Silvermills . . .
for the purpose of a new manufactory with a steam engine, on a
large scale for manufacturing and preparing Shoe Leather, Sheepskin,
Buff Leather and glue, all of which would be offensive, noxious and

61. Nelson Street, from
No. 20 Nelson Street.

212

disagreeable to the Neighbourhood . . .'[13] The Solicitor General advised an interdict, which early in 1813 Lord Meadowbank refused to grant. Nothing more is heard of this intrusion of modern industry – or rather the apprehension of the intrusion of its smell – into the genteel and well-ordered arcady of Reid and Sibbald's New Town.

After the Heriot Trustees, Sir Henry Raeburn. Raeburn's lands were in the country, most of them quite separate beyond the Water of Leith. In this neighbourhood, in 1760, the foundation stone of St Bernard's Well had been laid by Provost Drummond's brother, the occasion giving rise to a tribute to the provost by James Wilson:

> Great Drummond improveth what nature doth send;
> To country and city he's always a friend.[14]

Many years later, in 1789, the present circular Roman temple on a rusticated base, designed by Alexander Nasmyth, was erected 'at the sole expense of Francis Garden, Esq. of Troupe, one of the senators of the College of Justice'.[15] It is a charming eighteenth-century fancy

[67] *Royal Circus from India Place.* *Ewbank*

62. Drawing-room, 20 Nelson Street (courtesy, Professor and Mrs D. Talbot Rice).

213

on the very banks of the Water of Leith, and its immediate surroundings are still rural although there are houses everywhere beyond the trees. But one hundred and fifty years ago it was not so. The only houses nearby were those of the little old village of Stockbridge. It was probably here, in the house beside his father's yarn-boiling premises, that Raeburn was born in 1756.

It was a pleasantly situated little spot. Immediately behind the house ran the mill-lade, at that time pure and limpid. To the north was a beautiful fruit orchard, covering the ground where Saunders Street now stands. To the south was a fine grass park, extending south and west to where it was bounded by the Earl of Moray's pleasure-grounds of Drumsheugh. India Place and Mackenzie Place are built upon this park.[16]

In 1778 Raeburn greatly increased his property by marriage, and in 1813 he began to lay out and feu the ground for what we should nowadays call a housing estate, adjacent to but separate from the city. Raeburn Place was built first; Dean Street was begun in 1816; and Ann Street, possibly named after his wife, in 1817. India Place, east of the Water of Leith, and St Bernard's Crescent were later, the

63. Houses in Ann Street.

214

former begun in 1823 and the latter not until 1825. Before these dates, the earlier development in Ann Street, Dean Street and Raeburn Place was virtually complete. Of these, the most interesting is Ann Street, a small, charming street with fairly deep and narrow gardens fronting the houses; Georgian houses seldom had much front garden, and the effect is all the more unusual in that in spite of the modest proportions of the street as a whole the east side is arranged with a palace front, a central pediment surmounting a set of three-storeyed houses flanked on each side by lower houses which project forwards at the end of the street. It is an almost unique experience to walk down Ann Street – originally, as it were, a village street – on a summer day and see – like a Greek temple in a cottage garden – the form and symmetry and elegance of the houses set off by the little informal gardens, the green shrubs and trees, the roses nodding on their stems.

If Ann Street was to some extent informal in its setting, the next development was far more a continuation westwards of the older urban rectilinearity of Craig's New Town. The centre of life of the New Town was always moving west. Thus the line of Shandwick Place was planned as early as 1801 and agreed to in 1813 by the city, the Heriot Trust, and another feuar named Maitland. Shandwick Place, Coates Crescent and Atholl Crescent were almost entirely built by 1825. But the principal developer was at first Sir Francis Walker. Like Raeburn, Walker began feuing in the last years of the war, but progress was slow. Perhaps the centre of gravity of Edinburgh life had not then moved sufficiently far west for the most westerly streets of the town to achieve a ready popularity; and of course the approach to the Old Town via Castle Terrace was not opened until after 1830. Coates Crescent and Melville Street, where the earliest houses were built, were not far advanced by the time that feuing began in nearby Stafford Street, owned by Lord Alva, in 1819, nor was the whole scheme much further on when houses began to be built in Walker Street in the autumn of 1822. Melville Street was the principal feature of the plan, and in it the Walker family built their own house. The house elevations, except for the handsome centrepiece which looks down Stafford Street, follow a regular and simple design by Robert Brown, dated 1814, and the street was to a

64. Ann Street.

215

large extent built in 1825 and 1826. The feuing plan for the whole area was made out by Gillespie Graham – it existed in 1826, but there must have been a plan before this – and the Hospital, as superior of the lands, had an interest in it. Both Sir Francis Walker and the Hospital seem to have had a high opinion of this plan, for both were prepared to make sacrifices in order to see it carried out. In the midst of early building, Graham decided that it was an object of first rate importance that certain houses and grounds should be acquired for the purpose of opening suitable approaches from the east, and that such purchases should be made without delay and with the greatest privacy. Accordingly, late in 1825 the Hospital bought four houses in an unfinished state in Lynedoch Place from James Milne, architect (probably a builder) for no less than £4,402 10s. This purchase was not a profitable one. Almost four years later, in 1829, the Hospital decided to make the houses habitable and sell them, for the prospect of feuing on a large scale was still 'very remote, joined to doubts how far the other feuars in Lynedoch Place would consent to the houses being pulled down, as deviating from the plan of feuing'.[17] But the houses were now valued in their unfinished state at only £2,669! Gillespie Graham was no doubt doubly at fault in this transaction – first in entertaining too grand an idea of what would be a suitable eastern approach to 'the lands of Coats', and secondly in paying too much (in a boom year) for the properties. On the other hand it is to this streak of grandiosity and magnificence in Graham's mentality that we owe so much – the splendid breadth and spaciousness of Melville Street, for example, the wide and handsome intersection of Melville Street and Walker Street. The plan had admirable features, but it matured slowly; as late as 1850 nothing had been built between Melville Street and what is now Belford Road; and ten years later Manor Place was still the western edge of residential Edinburgh.

Graham's talents were to find a yet finer expression. The last of the post-war Georgian developments on the west side of Edinburgh was the development of the Earl of Moray's properties, 'the lands of Drumsheugh', feued and built on principally in the years from 1824 to 1827. This area, the centre line of which is now the site of Randolph Crescent, Ainslie Place and Moray Place, was in 1822, when the scheme for its feuing was finally set out, a blank between on the one hand Craig's New Town and the Hospital's development round Heriot Row and Royal Circus, and on the other Sir Francis Walker's gradually unfolding scheme centred on Melville Street. The Earl of Moray's feu, indeed, was slowly built up to and surrounded by new houses – except of course on the west where it was bounded by the Water of Leith – between 1807 and 1820.

Charlotte Square, in particular, was rapidly filling up. Building on the north side had continued at a slow pace for some years, but in 1807 fresh Articles and Conditions of Roup and Sale were issued by the Town Council (purchase money was set at no less than twenty-eight years' purchase of the feu-duty), and during the next thirteen years this square was almost completed, the south side being built last between 1811 and 1820. The plan followed was Robert Adam's, but departures from it were numerous. The principal deviation, of course, was by the Town Council itself when it scrapped Adam's plan for a church and adopted the cheaper but very much inferior design by Robert Reid. In the houses themselves, also, changes were made. The north side is very much as Adam designed it, but the east and west sides follow his intentions less accurately. For the east side north of George Street, Robert Reid even went so far as to make out a complete modified plan, and when his proposals were challenged by proprietors in the Square the defence offered was that not a single house in the square had been built in exact conformity to Adam's original plan. Some variation was perfectly allowable; by the 1807 articles of sale 'builders are to conform to the elevation, excepting as to placing the doors, which the purchasers shall have liberty to make convenient for themselves'. This was standard practice. It was another matter when windows were made less high than in the plan by at least a foot, when square doors were built arched, centre houses were built with two doors instead of three and without a centre door, and pavilioned houses appeared with gables and roofs three feet higher than originally intended.

It was perhaps these experiences in Charlotte Square and the litigation which they gave rise to (in 1811) which decided the Earl of Moray to produce the extraordinarily detailed 'Articles and Conditions of Roup and Sale of the Grounds of Drumsheugh', dated 7 July

1822. These articles represent the furthest development in this period of the policy whereby a feuar laid down what was and what was not to be built. The Town Council had begun this policy in the eighteenth century but the regulations then made were not elaborate and their enforcement was rather feeble. In any case, these Town Council regulations applied only to Craig's New Town, and in no way affected building on the thirteen acres which the Earl of Moray was now to feu. The most important clauses in the Articles affecting the Earl's property are as follows:

> *Quarto.* That the houses to be erected on the several lots, shall be built on a regular plan, conform to an elevation prepared by the said James Gillespie, approved of by the said Earl . . . and the whole of the fronts as well as the ornamental parts to be done of polished Craigleith, Redhall, or Maiden Craig stone, or stone of an equal colour and quality, as shall be approved of by the architect for the time; that the said James Gillespie, and failing him, such other architect as the said Earl or his foresaids may appoint, will furnish the builders with working elevations, and a set of drawings of the full size for the mouldings, and for which the said James Gillespie, or other architect for the time, shall be entitled to five guineas from the proprietor of each lot; that the under part of the building in the sunk areas below the rustic work, and the courses of the ashler [sic] above the belt of the rustic work, shall be thirteen inches high; and that the range of the buildings may be properly connected, the ashler is to be tusked twelve inches at least, which will preserve a uniformity in the heights of the buildings; that the whole of the chimney stalks shall range with the fronts, and by no means come nearer the fronts than the edge of the platform, nor shall the roof be made higher than represented on the elevation; that the depth of the breaks or projections shall be the same as shown by the ground plan, described on the same sheet with the elevation; that the ground, marked stable-ground, on said ground plan shall be applied to no other purpose than for stables, coach-houses, or washing houses; and the said stable ground shall be sold to those only who wish that accommodation; but in order to give access to the back ground of the stances adjoining the

65. Well-disciplined, domestic Georgian architecture in Malta Terrace.

[69] *Mr Gillespie Graham and Mr Thomas Hamilton, from Crombie's 'New Athenians', 1847*

stable ground, there will be a lane of four feet preserved for that purpose; that the elevations of the stables shall be built according to a plan, to be prepared by the said James Gillespie or other architect, to be named as aforesaid; that there shall be no storm windows allowed, or any raised breaks above the line of the roofs in front of the said buildings; and in respect the said Earl has resolved to preserve the beauty of the bank on the south side of the river, between the boundary walls of the feus, on the north of the property and the river, and to reserve the same as pleasure ground, for the benefit of himself and his feuars, as represented on the said ground plan, and to which the feuars shall have access in common, upon paying a proportion of the

66. *St Bernard's Crescent.*

219

original expense in laying out the said bank as pleasure ground, and also of the annual expense of dressing the said piece of ground, and keeping it in proper order. It is hereby declared, that the feuars of those lots whose back ground is connected with the said pleasure ground, shall not have it in their power to build stables and offices of any description on the said back ground, or to raise the north boundary wall of their respective feus higher than three feet from the surface of the ground, which shall be formed on a regular slope, as shall be directed by the said James Gillespie, or other architect . . .; and they shall be taken bound to place and keep in proper repair a light iron railing, on said north boundary wall, in order that the view of the river and bank may be preserved to the feuars on that side of the property; but it is hereby further declared, that the proprietors of any flat or flats in any of the houses to be built on the said grounds, shall not have the privilege of walking in any of the pleasure grounds on the property without permission of the said Earl and his foresaids, and on procuring such permission, paying a proportion of the original expense of laying out the pleasure grounds, and of the annual expense of keeping them in proper order . . .; . . . that minor alterations may be made upon the elevations, as shall be suggested for the better internal arrangement of the plans, such as altering or transposing the position of a door or window, keeping down windows for balconies, provided the same are previously approved of by the said Earl or his foresaids, and the said James Gillespie . . .; that all the sunk areas shall be twelve feet in breadth, and shall have a foot pavement ten feet in width, except those in St. Colme St., Glenfinlas St., Forres St., and Darnaway St., where the areas will be ten feet in breadth, and the foot pavement nine feet in width; that the walls enclosing the back ground shall not exceed in height nine feet, and the height of the stables, coach houses, or washing houses, shall not exceed twenty-six feet to the ridge of the roof; that the feuars will have the power and liberty to erect on the back ground attached to their respective houses, such out buildings as they may consider necessary to afford additional conveniency, but on this express condition and

67. Lord Moray's Pleasure Grounds: a path above the Water of Leith.

provision only, that such outbuildings are in no case, or on any account whatever, to rise higher than the walls enclosing the back ground, or nine feet, the roofs thereof to be flat and covered with lead . . .; that the feuars on the north side of the property, and on the east and south of Moray Place, will be taken bound to keep the back elevation of their respective houses of the heights, and on a level with, the front elevation, and to build them of neat, hammer-dressed stone, laid in regular courses with belts and breakings, and a cornice and block course on the top, as shown by the elevation; that the windows in the back of these houses must be placed in a regular and uniform order, and according to elevations furnished by the said James Gillespie, or other architect to be appointed as aforesaid; and it must be understood that no projections from the back of the houses shall be allowed higher than nine feet from the level of the ground.

Quinto. That the purchasers shall be at the sole expense of forming, causewaying, and paving the streets in front of their respective buildings and meuse lanes opposite to, or in any way connected with, their properties, and shall also make and construct the common sewers, agreeably to a plan to be made out by the said James Gillespie, or other architect to be appointed as aforesaid; and the purchasers shall be bound to enclose the areas in Moray Place and Ainslie Place, and to lay them down in shrubbery and walls, as shown by the plan; and they shall be further bound to enclose these areas with parapet and retaining walls and iron railings in a suitable and handsome manner, according to drawings and directions to be given and furnished for executing the same by the said James Gillespie, or other architect to be appointed as aforesaid, and which shall not be more expensive than those adopted in the Royal Circus; and the feuars shall have the exclusive privilege along with the said Earl and his foresaids of using the same as ornamental pleasure ground; and they shall also be bound to make the roads and streets delineated on said plan, it being hereby declared, that the said Earl and his foresaids are to be at no expense whatever in enclosing the said areas, nor maintaining the same, the

68. Lord Moray's Pleasure Grounds: a path in Doune Terrace Gardens, with Randolph Cliff behind.

purchasers taking the whole burden thereof upon themselves, and the feuars shall be bound not only to make and construct the said streets, lanes, roads, causeways, common sewers and side pavements, parapet walls, retaining walls and railings, but also to keep the whole in good and sufficient repair in all time thereafter, at the sight and to the satisfaction of the said Earl . . .

These provisions are interesting in several respects. There is the obvious fact that the whole development is governed by a single plan. It is not known when Gillespie Graham made out his plan, but it was in existence early in July 1822, for a copy was then sent to the Trustees of Heriot's Hospital, Graham at the same time expressing the hope that the Trustees would agree 'that the Earl of Moray has done everything in his power, consistent with his own interest, to render the Plan ornamental. to the City, and convenient for the Inhabitants'.[18] It is indeed a splendid design. The opening of Randolph Crescent from Queensferry Street is perhaps not entirely well contrived, but the manner in which Moray Place succeeds Ainslie Place and in its turn leads on to Doune Terrace is admirable. As for Moray Place itself, it is, in the way of private building, the most splendid thing in Edinburgh. A little more ornamentation, just a little larger, and it would have been too magnificent, too grand, dwarfing its merely human inhabitants. But Graham has held his natural exuberance in check, and the result, although smaller than the great continental *places*, is yet not unworthy to be compared with, say, the Amalienborg in Copenhagen. Some may prefer the severer style of Robert Reid's Heriot Row, or the simpler and more elegant classicism of Charlotte Square; but no one can deny that Graham made splendid use of a difficult sloping site, giving to the New Town something quite unlike its customary straight streets and long vistas.

It is also noticeable that the Articles of Roup reflect concern not only for the streets and houses, but also for the stables, the pleasure grounds, and the views. The elevations of the stables were to be by Gillespie Graham just as much as the elevations of the houses themselves; the Earl is 'resolved to preserve the beauty of the bank on the south side of the river', and careful provision is made for its security and upkeep; and 'the view of the river and bank is not to be interrupted by stables, offices, or a boundary wall exceeding three feet in height'; all of which amenities, where expense is involved, are to be paid for not by the Earl but by the feuars themselves. This, indeed, is another remarkable aspect of these Articles of Roup. Except, presumably, for Gillespie Graham's fees and other unavoidable legal expenses, the Earl pays for nothing; the feuars, *per contra*, pay for everything – houses, streets, sewers, boundary walls, pleasure grounds, the lot; 'the purchasers', as the document bluntly and explicitly puts it, 'taking the whole burden thereof upon themselves'. In this the Earl of Moray was conspicuous only for taking to greater lengths than usual the common practice of private developers at that time. The City of Edinburgh, it is true, had paid a great deal for the provision of services in Craig's New Town; but Heriot's Trustees had not paid for much; and now the Earl proposed to pay for nothing. This raises an important question. If superiors did so little, development must have depended upon the actual takers of feus and builders of houses. Who were these people and where did they come from?[19]

Those who initiated building and carried it through fell, broadly speaking, into two categories: professional builders, and persons who had a house built in order to live in it. How the work was divided between these two sets of people is not quite clear. The evidence, such as it is, gives the impression that the finer and more fashionable streets were built more directly by people who intended to live in them than other streets less fine and less fashionable. Charlotte Square is the clearest case. Here, out of forty-seven original feuings, almost all of which were for single lots, only a minority were taken recognisably in the names of builders. Several builders took feus in 1782, but thereafter no builder's name appears before 1808, by which date almost one-third of the Square was built. Then appeared Edward Butterworth (1808), Robert Reid the architect (1811), Sibbald and Smith (1811), Peter Lorimer (1813), and (probably a builder) James Ritchie (1816). Of these, both Lorimer, and Sibbald and Smith, built on the south side. In short, three-fifths of Charlotte Square was feued to individuals who were to live there, and the only conclusion is that these people employed builders and paid for the houses as they went up. In the case of other 'fashionable' streets the evidence is not so clear. What seems to have happened in Moray Place is that a builder often built a house which he sold to a client at the same time that the client feued the ground from the Earl of Moray; but whether this client had to be found after the house was built or whether the client came in pretty well from the start, himself providing the money needed for building, is not clear. If the latter was the usual practice, then the situation from the economic point of view was the same as with the majority of Charlotte Square houses – that is to say, there was no 'speculative' building, the would-be house owner providing the capital. This is probably what usually happened. After all, these houses were expensive – Sir William Fettes bought his house in Charlotte Square in 1807 for £3,100; others in the Square cost more.[20] Few builders could afford to take the risk of building a £3,000 house on the chance of a sale – although we know that Butterworth seems to have been doing just that in 1808. In the Earl of Moray's lands as a whole only about one-seventh of the feus were taken by builders, and the maximum number taken in one name (that of Wilkie and Dobson) was four, all in Ainslie Place in 1825. Apart from this case, Adam and George Fowler feued three sites in Darnaway Street in 1826, Robert Watson feued three in Moray Place in the same year, Henderson and Currer took three in Ainslie Place in 1826, James and John Steedman took two in Forres Street and John Forsyth one feu in Great Stuart Street in 1828 and another in 1830. All these men were builders, and four other builders took one feu each. All other sites were feued to intending house-owners. This is in contrast to what happened in the eighteenth century, when fashionable areas – St Andrew's Square and St James's Square for example – were feued to a large extent to builders who appear to have carried out building operations even in the absence of an assured sale. The changed practice no doubt reflects the greater scale and expense of the better quality houses in Edinburgh in the nineteenth century.

The opposite case to that of the fashionable street, namely the side street or secondary street built largely and on their own initiative by builders, is easier to illustrate. The bulk of Gloucester Place, for example, was built between 1822 and 1824, and the fifteen feuings went to only three individuals, all builders. The same happened with

69. S E section of Moray Place.

224

nineteen feuings in Cumberland Street, mostly built between 1824 and 1828; again there were only three feuars, all builders. Elder Street, built earlier, between 1801 and 1804, is the extreme example; the entire street was feued to two builders, John Young (who took three feus) and John Reid (who took five). The only parallel to this sort of situation in the 'better' streets was the tendency for some builders to 'specialise', so to speak, in the building of certain streets. Thus William Wallace built at least eight houses in Heriot Row between 1806 and 1813, while Shennan and Walker seem to have built at least six houses in Moray Place between 1825 and 1827; the names of other builders are repeated frequently in connection with certain other streets. Lastly, it might be expected that the architects of the day would appear frequently as builders. This is not the case. William Wallace described himself as an architect, but was really a builder. Of the recognised architects, Gillespie Graham did a little building, and so did Robert Reid. Neither did much; and there is no evidence that Playfair, Hamilton, Elliot, Stark or Burn did anything. The architects' participation in the business of building must have been confined to comparatively unimportant private arrangements.

Probably the lawyers took a larger part than the architects in the work of building. There is some evidence to support the idea that lawyers sometimes provided builders with at least part of the capital required for house building. An example of the kind of evidence available is supplied by the history of David Stewart's lands (see p. 205/6) which came to be owned jointly by three 'architects' and two Writers to the Signet; moreover, one of the 'architects' was named Thomas Morison and one of the Writers John Morison. It is surely not fanciful to see in this partnership a provision of building skill on the one side and of capital and legal expertise on the other, nor to suggest that two of the men involved were brothers or perhaps cousins. In like fashion, two lots with houses in Charlotte Square were feued in 1818 and 1820 with the consent of James Ritchie, builder, and Henry Wylie, Writer.

The broad conclusion, that the building of the more important and more fashionable streets was financed by those who were first to live in them, drives us back to the question, who were these people? To some extent, the New Town grew as a result of movement out

70. Moray Place.

of the Old Town. The process was at first a gradual one, for the New Town was at first thought very inaccessible, the North Bridge, with its open balustrades, being described as 'all *in wind* that the Hellespont could be *in water*'.[21] Moreover, life in the New Town was more grand, and more costly than in the Old:

> A practice had long prevailed in Edinburgh, of keeping a great deal of society, and entertaining a vast circle of friends, for little expense, at tea and supper parties . . . But when a family, that had long indulged in good society in one of the *closes* of the High Street, and perhaps (if they are not belied) familiarly interchanged the civilities of tea drinking with their neighbours on the opposite side of the alley, without leaving their abode or putting themselves to any further trouble than merely opening their respective windows, removed to the genteel districts beyond the North Loch, their manner of life was materially altered. With their enlarged mansion, they were obliged to adopt more expensive habits – to give dinners instead of tea-parties, and routs instead of suppers, – and indeed to make such an extension of the whole domestic establishment as was felt seriously inconvenient . . .[22]

After the 1770s, however, movement out of the Old Town became increasingly rapid and more general. Nor was it simply a matter of movement out of the Old Town. The war was a stimulus to the growth of Edinburgh by immigration, for as long as hostilities lasted Edinburgh was 'the resort of many county families. The war which raged abroad prevented them going to the Continent. They therefore remained at home, and the Scotch families for the most part took up their residence in Edinburgh.'[23] By 1815 there were some two thousand houses[24] in the New Town, and the population must have been in the neighbourhood of fifteen or even sixteen thousand. By 1830 these figures had risen to something like five thousand and forty thousand. William Creech, the bookseller, whose shop at the east end of the Luckenbooths had once been occupied by Allan Ramsay and whose 'town house' was 'No. 3 George Street, north side', commented on the social eclipse of the Old Town as follows: 'In 1763 – People of quality and fashion lived in houses, which, in 1783, are inhabited by tradesmen, or by people in humble and ordinary life.

[70] *George Street about 1840, with statue commemorating King George* IV'*s visit to Edinburgh, 1824.*
EUL

The Lord Justice Clerk Tinwald's house was lately possessed by a French teacher – Lord President Craigie's house by a Rouping-wife or Saleswoman of old furniture – and Lord Drummore's house was lately left by a Chairman for want of accommodation.'[25] This may be a somewhat picturesque statement of the change which was taking place, but it is substantially correct. Using *Williamson's Directory,* second edition, 1775-76 (fuller and more accurate than the first edition, which refers to the years 1773-74) we can tell, for example, what were the addresses of Writers to the Signet at that time. Only one lived in the New Town, in St Andrew's Street. All the rest, and there were dozens of them, lived in the Old Town. They formed a very influential section of the population, their standing, socially, politically and in business life, higher even than it is today. Their addresses have a curious sound: *Carruber's close, Forrester's wynd, at Mrs Catanock's north bank close, above Balfour's coffee-house, back of fountain well, James's Court* (four Writers lived here), *Morocco's close* (an

227

unusually disreputable area), *baillie Fyfe's close, covenant close*. Of the advocates, only Hugo Arnot, lanky and asthmatic but famous above all his fellows for his *History of Edinburgh*, lived in the New Town, in 'Muse Lane'. The members of the Town Council were similarly domiciled in 1775-76. The Lord Provost lived on Castle Hill. Of the eighteen other full members of the Council, one lived in Princes Street, one in St Andrew's Street, one other gave his address as *new town*; the remainder lived, with the vast majority of the Writers to the Signet, in the wynds and closes of Old Edinburgh. It was much the same with the aristocracy. Lord Lauderdale's town address was *meal-market stairs*; Lady Gordon lived in *Duncan's close*, Lady Besbie in *Niddry's wynd*, Sir David Bruce, collector of excise, in *Charles's close, canongate*; Lady Duffus was content with *south back of canongate*. But the aristocracy did show a certain preference for some of the newer and more modern streets. Lady Agnew lived in Brown's Square, Lady Balcarras and the Earl of Selkirk in St John's Street.

Some fifteen years later, in the latter part of the 1780s, the picture was quite different. Advocates and Writers to the Signet no longer lived so commonly in the Old Town. Some were still there, in *Elliott's Court, Playhouse Close, High School Yards*, and so on; but the majority, about two-thirds of the total, now had addresses in the New Town. Titled persons had moved in much the same way. It is possible, admittedly, to trace a few who had not changed their addresses at all; Lady Duffus, for example, still lived at *south back of canongate* in 1790 just as she had done in 1776. And she was not alone in the Old Town – another two dozen or so titled people lived not far away; Lady Dalyell in *High School Yards*, Lady Dowager M'Leod in *shoemakers close, canongate*. But these were a minority. Titles were commoner in the New Town now, almost twice as common. The Earl of Selkirk and Lady Balcarras had abandoned St John's Street in favour of George Street. There were lords and ladies in Princes Street, Frederick Street, Thistle Street. Two places were especially popular, fashionable above all others, one in the New Town, the other neither in the New Town nor the Old. That in the New Town was St Andrew's Square. Fashionable from the very first, when sites in it had been taken by the Earl of Northesk, the Countess

Dowager of Leven, Sir Adam Ferguson, Sir William Forbes and (out-manoeuvring and out-shining them all, at least in conspicuous expenditure) Sir Laurence Dundas, the square in 1790 still housed a good number of notables, although it was not quite such a distinguished a place to live in as it had been. The other much-favoured location was George Square. The new areas to the south – Nicolson Square and St John's Street – had always been found attractive. George Square, also to the south, but more spacious, newer, half-rural, on its own, different, seemed to many wealthy families the ideal place to live. (The fact that it was outside the Royalty and therefore beyond the control of the Town Council may also have influenced them.) Here, in 1796, were to be found, among others, Lady Duff, Admiral Duncan, Sir William Jardine, Sir James Pringle and Lady Ruthven.

While it is thus easy to trace the Old Town provenance of many of the first inhabitants of new streets in the New Town, it is difficult to be very precise about the social groups involved. A study of the feu charters and vassalage books, however, gives us some information about the early residents. It is evident that the aristocracy played a part, but not a very great one even in the most fashionable areas. The lawyers were far more prominent. In Heriot Row, for example, Writers to the Signet took a third of the first twenty-seven feuings; in other prominent streets lawyers built a quarter or a fifth of the houses, seemingly for their own use. There were also a good number of country gentlemen, and a surprising number of widows, whose husbands must have been men of substance and most of whom seem to have come to Edinburgh from the country. There were a few merchants, such as Sir William Fettes, who had a house in Charlotte Square, or George Wauchope, described as 'wine merchant, Leith', who built a house in Moray Place in 1827. Also (an interesting source of capital, this) there were a few nabobs retired from the services of the East India Company – Colonel Cunningham in Moray Place, for example – and an occasional planter home from Jamaica. It is a very varied list. But it is weighted noticeably in the directions of the countryside and the law, of lawyers in Edinburgh and of minor aristocrats and country gentlemen from outside the city. These two sets of people were closely connected, for conveyancing was one of the Writer's chief lines of business. It is therefore a reasonable deduction that a main source of capital for the adornment, the improvement and the expansion of Edinburgh was provided by the profits of agriculture. The reward for successful estate development was a house in the New Town. And as the county families prospered, so the lawyers prospered, and as the city grew larger and wealthier, they too built town houses. And as the city grew wealthier it attracted fresh wealthy newcomers – such as James Hay, 'late of the West Indies' or 'of Bhaglepore' – by its vigorous social and intellectual life. The merchants and the small industrialists of Leith were likewise carried forward on the grand tide of industrial, commercial and agricultural expansion, and the service trades of Edinburgh could hardly keep pace with the demand. 'Everything is in a forward motion to better times.' And in Edinburgh the great architectural achievements of the age were the visible expression of the growing wealth of Scotland.

Not, of course, that Charlotte Square and Moray Place were Edinburgh. They were only a part of the New Town. Below them, in economic, social and artistic rank, came unnumbered the other streets of the New Town and the wynds and closes of the Old. If Charlotte Square and Moray Place were, in a sense, calm and still for a moment on their pinnacle of distinction, below them was continual change. The Old Town, as a place to live in, had become by 1800 an appendage to the New. But within the New Town itself some areas were already changing their character and some, in a social sense, already going downhill. Princes Street was one of the first to show signs of that social decay which has since overwhelmed it and turned it into little more than a shopkeepers' parade. In 1799, a quarter of a century after building began, it was still very largely a residential street. The non-residential intruders were comparatively few in number and confined almost entirely to the east end of the street, where the first twenty or so numbers (out of a total of ninety-two) were mostly of a non-residential character. (Numbers one to nine were on the south side of the street.) No. 1 Princes Street was Poole's Hotel, and No. 2 the Crown Hotel. Next door was a milliner, and a saddlery warehouse. Matthew Fortune kept his tavern (officially the Caledonian Coffee Room) at No. 5, No. 15 was a toy shop, and No. 16 was the scene of *Isbister's Ladies straw hat manufactory*.

71. Ainslie Place.

There was a bookseller at No. 17, a flesher and a dyer at No. 19, and another bookseller, David Walsh, at No. 22. Going further west than this the number of commercial addresses dwindled rapidly. Robert Cumming, Staymaker, worked and resided at No. 32, and further along, at No. 51, was James Monro, hairdresser, who a few years before had had his shop in the Luckenbooths. But the greater part of the street remained almost entirely residential in character. Writers to the Signet still lived in Princes Street in 1799 in full force. Starting from No. 12, there were twenty-two Writers to the Signet, and seven advocates. Nor was the law the only source of respectability. Apart from the usual collection of 'Esquires' and 'Mrs', Lady Clark lived at No. 37, Admiral Graham at No. 48, Dr T. C. Hope (in Charlotte Square ten years later) at No. 54, Wm. Fettes, Esq. (not yet knighted nor in his turn removed to Charlotte Square) at No. 57, Lady Dowager Elibank at No. 67 and Lady Mackenzie of Coul at No. 82. Princes Street was still on the whole a residential street, and a very respectable one. It is not difficult to think of reasons why deterioration should have begun at the east end. The east end, near the North Bridge, saw all the traffic passing between New Town and Old; it was also on a route to Leith; and it had on the south side the unattractive and rather squalid development about which there had been trouble in the early 1770s.[26] To make matters worse, the fleshers worked below the North Bridge, and, partly as a result, the semi-drained area which once had been the site of the North Loch was hereabouts at its most unwholesome.

Thirty years later the position was quite different. Instead of two hotels in Princes Street, there were six: Macqueen's Hotel (No. 8), Crown Hotel (No. 11), Campbell's Hotel (No. 21), Star Hotel (No. 36), Royal Hotel (No. 53) and the Albyn Hotel (No. 54). There were also numerous coach-offices, as well as the Aberdeen Smack and Steam Packet Office, several toy shops, tailors, furriers, booksellers, bootmakers, grocers, hairdressers, corset makers, staymakers, one bird stuffer, one cigar shop, and the Tax Office for Scotland. West of Hanover Street, polite residential use continued, and was dominant west of Frederick Street. Here a few aristocratic names were still to be found – Mary Lady Clark, Sir Henry Jardine,

72. Saxe-Coburg Place.

Lt. Gen. Sir James Hay. But they were far fewer than thirty years before, while the number of Writers to the Signet had shrunk from twenty-two to twelve. Polite society, fleeing before the advance of commercialism, had departed for the newer streets of the New Town, or, gathering its skirts about it, shrank back to the last blocks of what had been intended, only half a century before, as one of the finest residential streets in Europe.

In St Andrew's Square it was the same story. This, for thirty years before 1800, had been one of the most fashionable places to live in all Edinburgh, outclassed only by George Square, and rivalled only by Princes Street, George Street and Queen Street. In the square in 1799 lived Lady Betty Cunningham, Sir William Ramsay and the Countess Dowager Dalhousie. What was its fate by 1833? No. 1 housed Fraser and Anderson, clothiers, J. Crager, baby linen warehouse etc., and the London Hotel. No. 34 was another hotel. The Royal Bank occupied No. 35 (Sir Laurence Dundas's house), and the British Linen Company's Bank was next door, at No. 36. The Scottish Widows' Fund and Life Assurance Society was at No. 5, and at No. 41 G. Eckford, wine and spirit vaults, shared the house with five other occupants and a branch of the National Bank of Scotland. Besides these, other houses in the square were occupied by a miniature painter, two bootmakers, two people who kept lodgings, a baker, a druggist, a hairdresser and four booksellers. It was, in fact, very much the same as the east part of Princes Street. No wonder that Trotter in 1828 wanted to build new residential streets, finding 'the Principal Streets and Squares appropriated to shops and warehouses; which, but a few years ago, were places of residence for the principal Inhabitants'[27]; or that a Writer to the Signet who lived at the west end of Queen Street removed to Moray Place in 1825, giving his reasons as follows:

> I have changed my quarters, driven from my former by want of room, approach of building, shops etc. I am now 500 yards to the north-west of my former house; a new place formed in the fields to which we used to look with admiration, but now studded with houses. We are on the top of a bank above a ravine – which must exclude building for five or six hundred yards at least in rear.[28]

(Ironically enough, it was George Square, fully as old as Princes Street and not a part of the much vaunted New Town at all, which best maintained its social status. In 1833 the square was still entirely residential, and could boast among its residents Lord Balgray, Sir Hugh Purves Campbell and Lady Purves, as well as five Writers to the Signet, three surgeons and an advocate. On the other hand, it was becoming rather mixed. J. S. Brown, ironmonger and J. Chalmers, vinegar maker, did not add social tone. There was an auctioneer and even a dress-maker. Possibly worst of all, Mrs Shiells kept a boarding school at No. 25. George Square was respectable, certainly – no square with twenty-five 'esquires' could fail to be respectable – but it was going downhill. Lord Balgray and Sir Hugh Purves Campbell and Lady Purves must surely have been aware of the beckoning lights of Charlotte Square, Moray Place, Ainslie Place, and Heriot Row.)

These changes continually taking place and in some streets so noticeable by the 1830s added variety to the life of the New Town. Yet it remained grand, spacious, and altogether different from the Old. The neighbourliness of the closes was alien to it. No aristocratic little girls ever crossed George Street with the tea-kettle to get water from the nearest well, as the celebrated daughters of Lady Maxwell of Monreith used to cross the High Street.[29] Some visitors found the New Town a little sombre, even funereal. Blanqui, when he visited Edinburgh in 1823, formed such an impression:

> Malheureusement, la population semble fuir ces rues somp-
> tueuses, dont le pavé, tout en dalles immenses, paraît aussi
> intact qu'une statue sortant de l'atelier du sculpteur. On ne
> voit personne aux fenêtres de ces superbes palais, et les portes,
> qui en sont constamment fermées, pourraient faire croire que
> la ville vient d'être ravagée par un épidémie.[30]

The Old Town was different: 'Fidèles au respect dû à l'âge, nous avons traversé le pont du Lac, . . . Tout à coup la scène a changé. Au silence de la ville neuve ont succédé le bruit et le mouvement d'une cité populeuse.'[31]

[71] *Robert Adam. Original drawing of one of a pair of houses in St Andrew's Square. The drawing is in a volume of Craig's original drawings of Physicians' Hall, and appears to be by the same architectural draughtsman. (RCPE). For comparison, Plate 73 shows one of the houses today.*

VIII

Social Life

The society of Edinburgh has never been better, or indeed so good, since I knew it as it was about this time [1800]. It continued in a state of high animation till 1815, or perhaps till 1820. Its brilliancy was owing to a variety of peculiar circumstances which only operated during this period. The principal of these were – the survivance of several of the eminent men of the preceding age, and of curious old habits which the modern flood had not yet obliterated; the rise of a powerful community of young men of ability; the exclusion of the British from the Continent, which made this place, both for education and for residence, a favourite resort of strangers; the war, which maintained a constant excitement of military preparation, and of military idleness; the blaze of that popular literature which made this the second city in the empire for learning and science; and the extent, and the ease, with which literature and society embellished each other, without rivalry, and without pedantry.[1]

In this passage, Cockburn is thinking of the days of his young manhood (he became twenty-one in 1800), and his dating of the great days of Edinburgh society is to some extent a personal one. The intellectual and social life of Edinburgh was vigorous and fascinating long before 1800 and it was so still in the 1820s.

It is true, as Cockburn says, that the social scene was constantly changing. This was partly because the background changed. The increase in population, the growth of wealth, the spread of democratic feeling were all a part of this. In respect of its homeliness and neighbourliness, for example, Edinburgh in the 1760s was like a

74. Doorways in Broughton Street.

235

small market town of fifty years ago, but even more isolated, even more self-contained. People all knew each other by sight, and the presence of a stranger was the subject of general comment. There were great differences of wealth and clear distinctions of rank; but of the physical separation of social groups there was very little. Genteel places of residence such as Milne's Court and Blackfriar's Wynd were but a few hundred yards from disreputable areas like Morocco's Land or the closes at the foot of Candlemaker Row. The idlers and gossips who hung about the windows and stair-heads of the Lucken-booths, keeping an eye on the whole busy area round the Market Cross as well as on the entrances to the principal taverns in the vicinity, became as well-informed of the doings of the Lords of Session and their wives as those of the City Guard, the shop-keepers, the apprentices, the children and the beggars.

All this gradually changed. The better-off withdrew to George Square, or to the New Town. For a time, they or their servants had still to come to the markets in order to purchase their everyday requirements; and the lawyers, of course, had still to come to Parliament Close, or conduct at least some of their business, in the traditional manner, in convenient taverns in or near the High Street:

> O'er draughts of wine the writer penned the will,
> And Legal Wisdom counselled o'er a gill.

But after 1800 or a little later, shops became a not unfamiliar sight in the New Town, and some legal business began to be conducted there also. People now lived in Edinburgh who were rarely seen in the High Street – a thing unthinkable forty years before.

Everyday social behaviour also changed. There was in eighteenth-century Edinburgh a rough simplicity of feeling as well as an openness, not to say a coarseness, of manners which belonged entirely to that age. A typical celebration, for example, was the festive remembrance of the King's Birthday (before 1760 it had been the Restoration, 'the glorious twenty-ninth of May' which was thus honoured). This was one of the great holidays in Edinburgh, when the Town Council and some two hundred respectable citizens gathered in the Great Hall of Parliament House in the late afternoon to drink the King's health and other loyal toasts. The populace, which had spent the day in decorating the wells and lighting bonfires in the streets, assembled in and near Parliament Close, shouted, jeered, threw dead cats and cods-heads at unpopular guests and the Town Guard, and ended by taking possession of the town for more 'fun', minor outrages, and a general melée. This entertainment clearly could, and sometimes did, degenerate into a riot. But with the passage of the years society became less coarse, less boisterous, less drunken; and it is significant that the King's Birthday was celebrated in the traditional way for the last time in 1810. The rowdy ways of the eighteenth century thus gave place to the more colourless, the more restrained behaviour of the nineteenth. This was not all improvement, for the rough, ready kindliness of the eighteenth century tended also to disappear. Life became more institutional as communities grew larger. People helped one another perhaps more than ever before; but not in so personal a way; and individual lives were often more lonely.

Amidst these changes, which affected not only Edinburgh but the whole of Scotland, the upper ranks of society came together and organised a phase of Edinburgh's social life, from about 1780 to 1815 or perhaps 1820, which was peculiarly flourishing, exclusive and aristocratic. The hope expressed in the 1752 pamphlet, that city improvements might induce 'people of rank' to come and 'abide' in Edinburgh, was amply realised during these decades. Scarcely a close in the High Street failed to house at least one noble inhabitant by the late 1770s, while St Andrew's Square boasted over half a dozen, including the Earl of Buchan, the Earl of Haddington, and the Earl of Leven. Places of fashionable amusement multiplied without becoming in any sense 'common' and persons of rank continued to 'abide' in Edinburgh in large numbers until the end of the war, although, of course, the localities which they preferred were constantly changing – 'the tide of gentility' rolled from St Andrew's Square westward and northward. But soon after 1815, Edinburgh began to be less attractive to such people. It became fashionable (better transport making it much more convenient than ever before) to live in the country, and perhaps to have a town house in London. The literary and the legal sides of life were not much affected, and society still flourished; but its leaders were no longer aristocratic. In 1825 only two noblemen, the Earl of Wemyss and the Earl of Caithness, had houses in Edinburgh, and they did not live in them for more than a month in the year.

Within this 'aristocratic' phase the war was itself a phase. After 1803, invasion became a more common topic of discussion than Jacobinism – more common with the young than even chemistry or political economy – and Edinburgh, like every other town, took on a military aspect and became the scene of drilling by torchlight, of parades, reviews and mock battles on the Meadows or on Bruntsfield Links. Every able-bodied man was in some regiment or corps, and the sparkle and spectacle of uniform became a part of the life of the city. Brougham served with the same gun in a company of artillery as Playfair, and Francis Horner walked the streets with a musket, being a private in the Gentlemen Regiment. As for Sir Walter Scott, he became the life and soul of the Edinburgh troop of Midlothian Yeomanry Cavalry; with him, volunteering was not a duty or a pastime, 'but an absolute passion, indulgence in which gratified his feudal taste for war, and his jovial sociableness'.[2] But the war had its serious and tragic side. There was repeated dearness of food and other necessities; many a family shrank, and often with good reason, from reading the latest *Gazette* with its lists of killed and wounded; while the Castle was full of French prisoners of war, who whiled away the tedium of the years by making small handicrafts – toys, workboxes, brooches – out of bone or wood, and selling them for a few pence through the bars of the palisade which separated them from the passing citizens.

Yet despite all these changes, there was a certain unity in almost the whole of this period from 1760 to 1830. For these decades were the meeting point of two ages – of eighteenth-century Scotland with its poverty, its pawkiness, its wide differences of religious opinion and its very marked individualism, and the liberal, experimental, but always decorous and sometimes bigotted attitudes of the nineteenth century. It is that same meeting of cultures which makes Galt's *Annals of the Parish* so fascinating a novel, and which so readily turned Sir Walter Scott into an antiquarian, enthusiastic and tolerably well-informed, but at the same time self-conscious and incurably romantic. And the men were worthy of the occasion: Scott himself; Henry Mackenzie and Alexander Carlyle, survivors, old but shrewd, of an earlier age; Sir William Forbes; Principal Robertson; Joseph Black, founder of the theory of latent heat, and author, it has been said, of the most important graduation thesis ever written; Brougham, Jeffrey, Francis Horner and Sidney Smith, although for a few years only. And these were surrounded and supported by innumerable lesser men, architects, poets, scientists, as well as the greater part of the aristocracy of Scotland, the lawyers, the lairds 'in the height of their influence',[3] and the merchants, little regarded, but rising in the world.

As Edinburgh grew in size and importance, increasing attention had to be paid to the every-day organisation of life. It was all very well for Provost Drummond to have 'new-fangled notions about new towns',[4] but the problems of how to live comfortably and safely in the old ones had not yet been solved. Edinburgh, however, was fortunate in some respects, and its comforts, for the better-off at least, were always improving. In the first place, it was as a rule fairly orderly, at least by the standards of the time. 'An Englishman', wrote Topham in 1775,

> who has passed much of his life in London, and who has been entertained every morning with some dreadful account of Robbery or Outrage committed the evening before, would be much surprised, on coming in to this City, to find that he might go with the same security at midnight as at noonday. A man, in the course of his whole life, shall not have the fortune here to meet with an house-breaker, or even so much as a single foot-pad: and a woman shall walk along the streets at any hour in an evening, without being 'broke in upon', as Tristram Shandy says, 'by one tender salutation'. At eleven o'clock, all is quiet and silent; not so much as a watchman to disturb the general repose. Now and then at a late, or rather an early, hour in the morning, you hear a little party at the taverns amusing them-selves by breaking the bottles and glasses; but this is all in good humour, and what the constable has no business with.[5]

This state of affairs Topham attributed to 'the excellence of the Police', or City Guard. No doubt the Guard was better than nothing, but it seems that Topham's account is a somewhat flattering one. Even in the early nineteenth century it was unsafe to walk the streets of Edinburgh after dark, because of the numerous parties of young men who were to be met with, who had spent an evening in the taverns, and from whose ruffianly attentions the Town Guard offered, at best, very poor protection. More dangerous still, there were occasional outbreaks by the mob, that anonymous terror of urban life in the eighteenth and early nineteenth centuries. 'The Mob of Edinburgh', wrote Chambers, 'has ever been celebrated for its fierce and indomitable character.'[6] The Porteous riot of 1736 was no doubt the most famous example of mob violence in Edinburgh; but less serious riots, involving the destruction of property, were far from infrequent, and they continued, although with diminishing frequency, until 1832. Ringleaders were sometimes caught and hanged – this happened in 1812 – but it was not often that anyone was brought to justice on these occasions. Cockburn's reference to Edinburgh as a city 'long accustomed to undetected or irregularly detected crime'[7] is a reasonable one. Violent crime, however, seems to have been a good deal less common than in London and Glasgow, and it is probable that Edinburgh was better policed than most towns of the period. The Guard – 'this drunken burgher force'[8] – was disbanded in 1817 and its duties taken over by a civil police.

In the matter of cleanliness there was probably less to choose between Edinburgh and other cities. Topham, ever favourable, spoke well of the Old Town. He thought it amazing, having regard to the height of the houses and how they were crowded in one upon another, that decency was preserved, but declared that there was neatness and simplicity in the most obscure lodging. The worst feature of Edinburgh's sanitation he found to be 'the intolerable stench that is produced [at a stated time of the night] on the moving the tub of nastiness from each floor: such a concatenation of smells I never before was sensible of; it has been sometimes so powerful as to wake me, and prevent my sleeping till it was somewhat pacified'.[9] According to Topham, throwing rubbish from the windows was at this time subject to severe penalties. This was in 1775. The rapid growth of population in the next fifty years probably caused the situation to grow worse, and Chambers refers to the drum of the Town Guard being sounded at ten o'clock at night as 'a sort of licence for deluging the streets with nuisances and warning the inhabitants home to their beds.' In the New Town, of course, the density of population was in all decades far less, the streets themselves were far wider, and the general sanitary arrangements much superior.

In the matter of water supply, improvements were frequent and noteworthy, but it is doubtful whether they kept pace with the growth of population. An Act of Parliament passed in 1758 stated that 'this City of Edinburgh is not at present supplied with a sufficient quantity of good and wholesome water'; this still seems to have been true at least sixty years later. The original supply from outside the town was from Comiston, by means of lead pipes laid in 1681. This was supplemented in 1722. Steps were then taken in 1785 to extend the area of supply near Swanston in the Pentlands, and in 1787 a new iron-pipe was laid to the city. In 1790 a second seven-inch iron pipe was laid, also tapping the new sources of supply; and about the same time the old reservoir on Castle hill was supplemented by a new one, built near Heriot's Hospital in the 1780s. Nothing further was done during the war, and, population rising fast, the city was frequently 'thirsty and unwashed'.[10] There were acute shortages in 1810 and again in 1814. At last, in 1819, the Edinburgh Joint Stock Water Company was formed with a capital of £105,000, increased in 1826 to £223,000, and this company began to supply water from the well-known Crawley Springs. This improvement led to two results. First, it became worth-while to pipe water into the houses. This had been the usual practice in the New Town only, where the supply was more ample. The second result, a consequence of the first, was the disappearance in a few years of the water-caddies, those men and women whose business it had been, generation after generation, to carry water in little casks or kegs from the public wells dotted about the main streets of the Old Town into the private houses. It must have been an exhausting job, involving much stair-climbing, and hardly a rewarding one at a penny a cask; but every family had its favourite caddie, who knew the habits and wants of the household. One other custom is worth a mention. It seems once to have been the usual practice to flush down the High Street at frequent, sometimes even at daily intervals; but this depended on the state of the catchment area in the hills, and it was probably more commonly done in the eighteenth than in the early nineteenth century.

Much more marked was the improvement in the accommodation for visitors. Scottish inns in the eighteenth century varied from primitive to vile. Topham described his arrival in Edinburgh in the following words:

> On my first arrival, my companion and self, after the fatigue of a long day's journey, were landed at one of these stable-keepers (for they have modesty enough to give themselves no higher denomination) in a part of the town which is called the Pleasance; and on entering the house, we were conducted by a poor devil of a girl without any shoes or stockings, and with only a single linsey-woolsey petticoat, which just reached half-way to her ankles, into a room where about twenty Scotch drovers had been regaling themselves with whiskey and potatoes. You may guess our amazement, when we were informed, 'that this was the best inn in the metropolis – that we could have no beds, unless we had an inclination to sleep together, and in the same room with the company which a stage-coach had that moment discharged'.[11]

Declining this accommodation, the two travellers took apartments which 'had only two windows, which looked into an alley five foot wide, where the houses were at least ten stories high, and the alley itself was so sombre in the brightest sunshine, that it was impossible to see any object distinctly'.[12] The 'good dame by the name of Cross' who let these lodgings would have been one of the many 'room-setters', as they were called, who flourished in Edinburgh at this time. The town was full of them, some men, some women; it was one of the commonest Edinburgh occupations, and was not disdained by the most respectable citizens – a sister of Dr William Robertson, Principal of the University, kept a lodging house in the second flat of McLellan's land, Head of the Cowgate, looking up Candlemaker Row. But the dominance of the room-setters was ended by the rise of a superior type of 'tavern' and of hotels. This development began in the 1770s, although the most famous taverns and hotels date from somewhat later – Fortune's Tontine Tavern, for example, opened in 1796 at No. 5 Princes Street,[13] Barry's, the westmost house on the south side of Princes Street, opened in 1821, and the Waterloo Tavern and Hotel, in newly-built Waterloo Place, the property of a joint-stock company set up in 1818.

Food supply was not a serious problem. The Lothians were, as they still are, one of the granaries of Scotland, the sea was on Edinburgh's doorstep, and more distant parts of the country could and did supply the capital through the port of Leith. Dalkeith was a centre of the grain trade, and in the ordinary way of things the city was well supplied, although of course shortages occurred – Sir William Fettes noted in his diary in 1790 that oat meal had 'advanced to the enormous rate of 3/7 per peck of 8 lbs. Dutch weight, yet no riotous behaviour or discontent is visible'. With regard to vegetables, Topham thought that they were to be had in Edinburgh 'in greater plenty and perfection' than anywhere else. 'The soil seems peculiarly favourable to them' he wrote, 'and the whole country round Edinburgh is employed for that purpose. The great abundance of potatoes and carrots, which are excellent of their kind, makes it extremely comfortable to the poorer sort of people, who often can get nothing else to support their families during winter.'[14] Potatoes, according to Arnot,[15] were 'the chief article for the poor' in the 1780s, and sold at sixpence a peck. Haddock and cod were available from the Forth, and there was an abundant supply of shell-fish – 'no place supplied with such excellent variety of shell-fish as Edinburgh', wrote Arnot[16]; but he added, 'no fish is sold in Edinburgh so useful to the inhabitants as salmon. It is brought chiefly from Perth and Stirling.' Edinburgh was also famous for its strawberries, very large quantities of which were sold in the city during their brief season in July and August.

But if the food supply was varied and good, the manner in which it passed into the hands of the final consumer left a good deal to be desired. Cockburn thought that there were not half a dozen shops in the New Town, west of St Andrew's Street, in 1810. The markets were still supreme, the fish market and the flesh market being the most important, and to these markets housewives both rich and poor came in person, at least until about 1820. The former had been located in the eighteenth century in Fish Market Close, 'a steep, narrow, stinking ravine' where the fish 'were generally thrown out on the street at the head of the close, whence they were dragged down by dirty boys or dirtier women; and then sold unwashed – for there was not a drop of water in the place – from old, rickety, scaly, wooden tables, exposed to all the rain, dust, and filth'.[17] About 1800, this market became removed to below the North Bridge, where it was carried on in conditions little if any more sanitary than those of the eighteenth century, until about 1830. But prices were low: a good haddock or a crab for a penny, a dozen herring for twopence, lobsters threepence each. The flesh market was also below the North Bridge and was also offensive; it must, however, have presented a somewhat quieter scene than the fish market, for higgling over the price was not the custom, as with haddies, herrings and crabs. Vegetables were sold in a similar way. The trade was 'in the hands of a college of old gin-drinking women, who congregated with stools and tables round the Tron Church . . . Every table had its tallow candle and paper lantern at night. There was no water here either, except what flowed down the gutter, which, however, was plentifully used.'[18] But the business of marketing was at least often graced by the purchase of flowers, 'the floore', nothing rare and costly but an assortment of wallflowers, polyanthus, daffodils, or a bunch of lilacs, or a handful of the fragrant, old-fashioned moss rose.

Amid these rather primitive conditions the social life of Edinburgh flourished, in theatre, concert, supper-party, ball and club. Supper-parties were immensely popular – 'It is in these meetings that the pleasures of society and conversation reign . . . and you see people really as they are',[19] declared Topham in 1775; and Cockburn doubted if he had closed one day in the month, of all his married life beginning in 1811, when in town, 'at home and alone'.[20] Formal dinners, with interminable rounds of formal toasts, were for long the fashionable meal. But formality was declining throughout the period, and while dinners became later and later – by the time of Waterloo the usual hour was five o'clock – they also grew less popular. Supper, although not necessarily a light meal, was informal. Invitations were received up to the last minute, and friends might appear without any invitations at all. This was the custom in Cockburn's set, 'perhaps the merriest, the most intellectual, and not the most severely abstemious, in Edinburgh'.[21] The business of the day was over; its events were still fresh in everyone's mind; the approach of night enhanced the sociability of the hour. Similar customs prevailed in less fashionable circles. Friendship and neighbourliness at all levels of society were widespread, and they were freely expressed. Also the attachment of

75. The High Street with Tron Kirk.

relatives to one another, and their sense of duty towards one another, were much warmer, and extended far more widely than nowadays. The expression of friendship and relationship was an easy flow of informal hospitality. 'The visitor came in with his "Good e'en", and seated himself. The family went on with their work as before. The girls were usually busy with the needles, and others [the house is Nasmyth's] with pen and pencil.'[22] Supper followed, haddies, or a dish of oysters, with a glass of Edinburgh ale – nothing expensive or ostentatious. Many looked back in later life to such evenings as the ideal expression of a truly social existence.

Sociability had its ill effects, it is true, for the drunkenness to which sociability too often led was one of the greatest vices of the age. The margin between convivial meetings and drunken orgies was easily overstepped in a society which regarded intemperance as, at worst, a venial blemish. 'Every gentleman a drunkard and every drunkard a gentleman' was a well-known saying, and it was not a jest. No gentleman, of course, drank whisky; but the gentlemen drank enough port and claret, in the eighteenth century, to be commonly drunk on rejoining the ladies after dinner; while even in families which had a reputation for sobriety the circulation of the bottle was very likely, according to Somerville, to continue for many hours after the ladies had withdrawn.

As for getting drunk in a tavern, that was regarded as the almost inevitable consequence of going there. Tavern dissipation, as it was called, was fearfully common among all sections of the populace in the eighteenth century. It began to fall out of favour with respectable people after about 1780 or 1790, but others – labourers, journeymen, tradesmen, small tenant farmers on a visit to the city, bonnet lairds – continued the practice into the nineteenth century. This tavern dissipation, says Chambers (writing in the 1820s)

> formerly prevailed in Edinburgh to an incredible extent, and engrossed the leisure hours of all professional men, scarcely excepting even the most stern and dignified. No rank, class, or profession, indeed, formed an exception to this rule. Nothing was so common in the morning, as to meet a nobleman or two reeling home from a close in the High Street, where they had spent the whole night in drinking. Nor was it unusual to find

the half of his Majesty's most honourable Lords of Council and Session mounting the Bench, in the forenoon, in a state little removed from absolute civilation.[23]

And Chambers goes on to retail the story of the gentleman who one night stepped into Johnnie Dowie's,[24] opened a side-door, and discovered 'a sort of *agger* or heap of snoring drunkards upon the floor', lit by the gleams of an expiring candle. They turned out to be the clerks employed in Sir William Forbes' banking-house.

Resort to taverns was undoubtedly encouraged by the common eighteenth-century practice, already noticed, of doing business there. Taverns were also the meeting place of clubs, of which Edinburgh boasted an extraordinary number. A gentleman – most clubs, although not all, were for gentlemen – could be a member of the Wagering Club, the Friday Club, the Wig Club, the Poker Club, the Marrow-Bone Club, the Right and Wrong Club, the Easy Club, the Sweating Club, the Pious Club (so called because it met in a pie-house), the Spendthrift Club (where each member's nightly expenditure on food and drink was limited to the magnificent sum of fivepence), the Industrious Club, the Whin Bush Club, the Horn Order, the Assembly of Birds, the Antemanum Club, and others besides. Not all of these existed at the same time, and not all were chronically devoted to inebriation – at the Poker Club, for example, of which Hume, Smith and Henry Dundas were members, drunkenness was unknown. It was a different story at the Right and Wrong Club, of which an account is given in James Hogg's *Autobiography*. This club, according to Hogg was

> established one night (in 1814) in a frolic at a jovial dinner-party in the house of a young lawyer, now of some celebrity at the Bar. The chief principle was that whatever any member might assert, the whole were bound to support the same, whether right or wrong. We were so delighted with the novelty of the idea, that we agreed to meet next day at Oman's Hotel [in West Register Street] . . . We dined at five and separated at two in the morning before which time the Club had risen greatly in our estimation; so we agreed to meet the next day and every successive day for five or six weeks, and during all that time our hours of sitting continued the same.

No constitution on earth could stand this . . . The result was that several of the members got quite deranged, and I drank myself into an inflamatory fever. The madness of the members proved no bar to the hilarity of the society [but] an inflamatory fever . . . sounded rather strange in the ears of the joyous group, and threw a damper on their spirits. They continued their meetings for some days longer, and regularly sent a deputation at five o'clock to inquire for my health, and I was sometimes favoured with a call from one or more of the members at two or three in the morning when they separated. The morning after such visits I was almost sure to have to provide new knockers and bell handles for all the people on the stairs.[25]

Drunkenness on this scale could not go on, and the club's life was a very brief one.

A very different type of club, as long-lived as the Right and Wrong Club was ephemeral, was the Friday Club, established in 1803. This club met once a month in winter and spring, had no fines, no president, and no accounts, and its chief requirements for membership were agreeable manners and a taste for literature, along with the avoidance of party spirit, controversial exhibitionism and religious narrow-mindedness. The club first met in Boyle's Tavern, on the east side of Shakespeare Square, then at Fortune's in Princes Street, and by the later 1820s at Barry's. The staple drink was rum punch, made in the early days by Brougham – 'a very pleasant but somewhat dangerous beverage'[26] – and latterly claret. Never abstemious, the members after 1814 'soared above prejudice, and ate and drank everything that was rare and dear',[27] with the result that dinner in the 1820s cost over two pounds a head. To this club belonged some of the most distinguished citizens of the day, including Dugald Stewart, Professor John Playfair, Sydney Smith, Sir Walter Scott, Henry Brougham, Henry Mackenzie, Cockburn himself, Francis Home, Professor John Robinson and the Earl of Selkirk.

Finally, an older club of a very different type was the Wig Club, founded in 1775. Membership was limited to twenty-five, and in its early days the club was remarkable for its devotion to Twopenny, the cheap but strong native ale. This was not its only peculiarity. The ballot-box represented the naked figure of a man, some two feet high from knees to waist, and – as one historian primly but ominously observes – 'unnecessarily proportioned'.[28] There was also 'a glass of offensive shape' from which new members had to drink a bumper of claret, and a seal 'which could not nowadays be exhibited in decent society'. To this club belonged Henry Dundas, first Lord Melville, the eighth Earl of Moray, the Duke of Buccleuch, and, in its latter days in 1823, the Earl of Lauderdale. This club at various times patronised Fortune's Tavern in Old Stamp Office Close, Fortune's Tavern in Princes Street, and the Royal Exchange Coffee House.[29]

In all this array of clubs, the ladies, needless to say, never appeared. In the 1770s, according to Topham, ladies were often to be met in the oyster-cellars, where, 'as the evening begins to grow late' parties of 'the First People in Edinburgh'[30] repaired to eat oysters, drink pots of porter and brandy-punch, and dance reels. The freedom of manners of the Edinburgh ladies never ceased to amaze Topham:

> The women, who, to do them justice, are much more enter-
> taining than their neighbours in England, discovered a great
> deal of vivacity and fondness for repartee. A thousand things
> were hazarded, and met with applause; to which the oddity of
> the scene gave propriety, and which could have been produced
> in no other place. The general ease, with which they conducted
> themselves, the innocent freedom of their manners, and their
> unaffected good-nature, all conspired to make us forget that we
> were regaling in a cellar; and was convincing proof, that, let
> local customs operate as they may, a truly polite woman is
> every where the same.[31]

But this sort of behaviour cannot have continued for long after 1775. More 'civilised' entertainments were coming into fashion. The concert, for example, was becoming a more important item in the social scene. The Musical Society was created in 1728, and, from a social point of view, was an extremely exclusive body. Although its membership in 1752 was limited to 130, it was able to collect 'a considerable Subscription'[32] for the building of a new concert hall to relieve it of dependence on St Mary's Chapel in Niddry's Wynd. Under the guidance of Provost Drummond, the new hall, designed by Robert Mylne[33] for a fee of ten guineas in 1760, was sited near the foot of Niddry's Wynd, and completed in 1762 at a cost of £1,328 exclusive of the site. The situation of the hall was unfortunately ruined by the building of the South Bridge, some twenty-five years later, the foundations of which stand on the site of Niddry's Wynd, so that the projecting buildings on each side of the hall had to be partially demolished, and the hall itself, now dark and overhung, looks straight into the back of the South Bridge buildings only a few feet away. Happily, the internal beauty of the hall remains. It is oval in shape, designed for about five hundred persons, with a concave elliptical ceiling, lit by a single lantern. It had, originally, no gallery. This was 'the most selectly fashionable place of amusement'[34] in Edinburgh in the 1760s and 1770s, where society, and nothing but society, came to hear the best musicians in Scotland, many expressly brought over from Italy, perform works by contemporary composers, especially by Handel. The Society fell upon evil days financially in the 1770s, however; and with the move of fashionable society to the New Town and the opening of the Assembly Rooms in George Street in 1787, where concerts could conveniently be given and much more conveniently be attended, the hall just off the Cowgate began to be deserted, and the Musical Society was wound up in 1801.

Two other scenes of fashionable amusement were the theatre and the series of assembly rooms, of which the last-built, in George Street, has just been mentioned. Theatrical performances in Edinburgh began, according to Somerville,[35] early in the eighteenth century, and caused great offence to a large body of the inhabitants. Plays continued to be given, nevertheless, in what must have been a very small theatre in Old Playhouse Close off the Canongate, where it was customary in the 1760s to camouflage the performance by advertising and selling it as an interlude's entertainment in the midst of a 'concert of music'; but everyone knew that the concert was perfunctory and that the interlude was the real business of the evening. Plays given included *Venice Preserved*, *The Beggar's Opera* and – little calculated to assuage the passions of presbyterian divines – items of Restoration drama such as *The Provoked Husband* and *A Journey to London*. Offence was no doubt taken, but drama was popular enough for a new theatre to be opened just north of the

North Bridge, in Shakespeare Square, in 1769. This was a small and rather barn-like building, later known as the Old Theatre Royal. Its success, to begin with, was in serious doubt, for the collapse of the bridge in 1769

> cut off the only tolerable communication with the city; so there stood the theatre on the lonely slope, no New Town whatever beside it; only a straggling house or two at wide intervals; and the ladies and gentlemen obliged to come from the High Street by the way of Leith Wynd, or by Halkerston's Wynd, which, in the slippery nights of winter, had to be thickly strewn with ashes, for the bearers of sedan chairs. Moreover, the house was often so indifferently lighted, that when a box was engaged by a gentleman he usually sent a pound or so of additional candles.[36]

By the middle of the 1770s, however, the building, which could hold seven or eight hundred people, was sometimes 'very crowded'.[37] Its interior, according to Topham, was 'in an unaffected plain style' but on the whole 'very elegant'. The company of actors Topham thought 'very small as well as very bad',[38] but he believed that Digges, who was manager in the 1770s, was in some respects and some parts the superior of Garrick. Among Digges's successors on this stage was Mrs Siddons, who played to extremely crowded audiences in the 1780s. Scott's *Rob Roy*, suitably dramatised, was performed in 1819, and such was its success that when George IV visited Edinburgh in 1822 he ordered this play to be put on for the special performance given in his honour.

The popularity of the theatre was almost certainly outdistanced by the popularity of dancing. This – as a later age would have thought it – unpresbyterian diversion was carried on in the form of public assemblies in the Old Assembly Room in the West Bow as early, perhaps, as 1710. In 1723 there was set up a new Assembly in what came to be called Old Assembly Close, its establishment hailed by a later writer as a 'symptom of the gradual softening away of the sombre habits of the people'.[39] The Assembly was reconstituted in 1746, and for the rest of its existence met in New Assembly Hall, a little to the east of the first building. This Assembly, like the earlier one, was intended not only to provide entertainment for the wealthy, but also, incidentally, to raise funds for the support of the poor.

[72] *Old Assembly Room, West Bow, looking towards the Grassmarket.*
Grant

These eighteenth-century assemblies were exclusive and formal. Ball-room discipline was maintained by the Directors, and still more by the Lady Directresses, who were in charge of the proceedings. Nothing could be done without their sanction or contrary to their wishes. 'The ladies who from 1746 to 1776 directed the Assemblies all belonged to well-known Scottish families'[40]; they included the Countess of Leven, Lady Elliot, Mrs Grant of Prestongrange, and the Hon. Miss Murray, sister of the Earl of Mansfield. The assemblies could secure the services of ladies of high birth partly because the company was select, and partly because the aim was 'polishing the youth and providing the poor'.[41] In the latter aim much success was achieved; between 1746 and 1776 £2,495 was donated to the Royal

251

Infirmary, the same amount to the Charity Workhouse, and £1,439 went to the Directresses for their private charities.

As time passed, the Assembly in the High Street faced increasing competition. First, in 1777, a new Assembly appeared in Buccleuch Street, to serve the wishes of the fashionable inhabitants of the new southern areas; in 1783-84 this Assembly moved to the 'George's Square Assembly Rooms', newly-built in Buccleuch Place. Here, says Cockburn, was to be found

> in my youth the whole fashionable dancing, as indeed the fashionable everything . . . here were the last remains of the ball-room discipline of the preceeding age. Martinet dowagers and venerable beaux acted as masters and mistresses of ceremonies, and made all the preliminary arrangements. No couple could dance unless each party was provided with a ticket prescribing the precise place in the precise dance. If there was no ticket, the gentleman, or the lady, was dealt with as an intruder, and turned out of the dance . . . Woe on the poor girl who with ticket 2.7, was found opposite a youth marked 5.9! It was flirting without a licence, and looked very ill, and would probably be reported by the ticket director of that dance to the mother. Of course parties, or parents, who wished to secure dancing for themselves or those they had charge of, provided themselves with correct and corresponding vouchers before the ball day arrived. This could only be accomplished through a director; and the election of a pope sometimes required less jobbing.[42]

Restraints and difficulties such as these, the cramped conditions in the hall in Old Assembly Close, where the onset of supper marked the termination of dancing (because there was not room for both), and the shift of society to the New Town combined to produce the eclipse of these older assemblies. In the 1780s enterprising hotel-keepers such as John Dunn and Matthew Fortune advertised assemblies to be held at their elegant rooms, and in 1781 it was resolved, at a meeting presided over by the Earl of Moray (the same earl who was a member of the Wig Club!) that new assembly rooms should be built in the New Town. The Town Council gave a site in George Street, and the foundation stone of the existing assembly rooms there was laid in 1783. The building was opened in 1787.

76. Interior, Assembly Rooms, George Street.

Theatrical performances and dancing do not sound like welcome bed-fellows for a Presbyterian Church. To some extent this is correct. The performance upon the Edinburgh stage in 1756 of Home's *Douglas*, for example, written by a clergyman, became the occasion of a *cause célèbre*, and led to the passing of an Act in the General Assembly forbidding the clergy to countenance the theatre. But the Scottish Church, divided at this time into the 'High-Flying' party and the 'Moderate' party, was far from unanimous, and twenty years later, when Mrs Siddons first appeared in Edinburgh during the sitting of the General Assembly, 'that court was obliged to fix all its important business for the alternate days when she did not act, as all the younger members, clergy as well as laity, took their stations in the theatre on those days by three in the afternoon'.[43] There was a variety of religious opinion about theatres, dances, or other social activities, and different views predominated at different times. But undoubtedly the attitude of the Church to merry-making of all kinds

[73] The New Assembly Rooms, George Street. The portico was added in 1818. shepherd

253

became more severe in the nineteenth century, and Sabbath observance became correspondingly more strict. A change such as this is never easy to account for. It may have had something to do with the war, with the economic difficulties which followed the war, and with the rapid influx of Highlanders and Irish into the Lowlands, and the multiplication of sects. It is tempting, too, to think that the decline in the intellectual level and capacity for moral leadership of the ministers of the Church, of which Cockburn complained, was a reality in the early nineteenth century, and a contributory factor in the hardening of attitudes.

Nevertheless, in spite of all its difficulties, the Church remained an active, unifying, and powerful force in Scottish life. Church-going was common to almost all sections of society and was extremely popular – a good preacher could fill a church to the doors Sunday after Sunday and send the income from seat rents soaring – and not to attend church was generally regarded as disreputable. The Church thus united country and town, rich and poor, noble and common. This was an important function, for the gay, fashionable, artistic, intellectual life of Edinburgh, of which so much is written, had little enough to do with the lives of ordinary people. And Edinburgh was full of ordinary people, engaged in an extraordinary variety of employments: there were shop-keepers of every kind, tailors, carpenters, cobblers, carriage makers, apothecaries, all sorts of builders, brewers, tanners, hotel-keepers, lawyers' clerks, wheelwrights, dustmen and dancing masters. Also, there were many families in the middle ranks of life in which grew to manhood such distinguished Scots as James Nasmyth, Sir J. Y. Simpson, and Robert Louis Stevenson. Edinburgh, at least by the time that its expansion was well under way in the 1780s, was a good place to live for people like these. There was a growing demand for professional, artistic and craft services. The facilities for education were perhaps unrivalled anywhere in Britain. Servants were plentiful and good – 'for the most part country-bred – daughters of farm-servants or small farmers'[44] – and were treated as one of the family and kept in touch with for many years after marriage separated them from the household. Maidservants used to take the smaller children up Calton Hill to sit with them or play about while the 'claes' bleached in the sunshine. There were 'promenades' and walks, for the country was easily accessible. And for everyone there was golf on the Links at Leith or (after about 1750) on Bruntsfield Links, horse-racing at Musselburgh (supported by the Town Council) and the ancient pastime of bowls, in which women as well as men took part.

Finally, there were the poor. Many of them were very poor. 'No people in the World', wrote Topham, 'undergo greater hardships, or live in a worse degree of wretchedness and poverty, than the lower classes here.'[45] There were those who had a settled trade or occupation, and who lived lives of friendship and hope, unless dragged down by the abominable housing standards to which they were condemned, by sickness or by old age. There were thousands who eked out an existence they scarcely could tell how, but who found sufficient employment to lead humble, meagre, insecure and yet not completely wretched lives, withstanding at least the worst examples and most miserable temptations. There were others, many of them – 'single, unconnected phenomena, owning no relation apparently to any other human being'[46] – whose physical wretchedness was surpassed only by their intellectual and moral degradation: 'It is little to say they are scarcely covered'.[47] The Old Town was a grand repository of history; a deep pool of struggling, jostling humanity; but as the years moved on from 1800 to 1850 it became more and more a scene of wretchedness and vice. Miserable at all times, the condition of the poorest people – and often of others too – was desperate in years of bad harvest or trade depression, and their numbers were then greatly augmented. In the spring of 1795, according to Cockburn, about eleven thousand people, or one-seventh of the population, depended on charity for enough to eat. This was quite simply referred to as a famine. Distress was again widespread and severe in the winter of 1816-17, when, according to Cockburn, the number of destitute in Edinburgh was larger than at any previous time.

But although poverty was an apparently ineradicable evil in the nineteenth century just as it had been in the eighteenth century, and although in the large cities like Edinburgh it was in a sense worse because it affected more people as population grew, it was at least an evil not looked on with hopelessness or indifference. Employment,

albeit on too small a scale and of a makeshift character, was sometimes arranged by local people. During the depression which
followed the close of the Napoleonic War,

> a large number of the starving weavers came [mostly from the
> West of Scotland] to Edinburgh. A committee was formed and
> contributions were collected, for the purpose of giving them
> temporary employment. They were set to work to make roads
> and walks round the Calton Hill and Salisbury Crags. The walk
> immediately under the precipitous crags, which opens out such perfect
> panoramic views of Edinburgh, was made by these poor fellows.[48]

At the same time and in the same way, 'Bruntsfield Links were cleared
of whins and of old quarries'.[49] On such occasions all classes of the
community stood ready to help, although in varying degrees and in
different ways at different times. 'My experience has indicated',
wrote Thomas Somerville towards the end of a very long life,

> not only an increase, but a growing increase of attention to the
> sufferings of the poor, even within the period in which I have
> seen it put to the test.[50]

Likewise in nearby Edinburgh the unity of society, the feeling of
neighbourliness and of mutual responsibility lived on and in some
ways even increased, at any rate until the end of the eighteenth
century. After 1800 the physical organisation of existence, and with
it the social atmosphere, subtly changed. There were now two
Edinburghs, not one. The lawyers might continue to work in the
Old Town, but they no longer belonged to it. They lived, along
with other rich folk who were never seen in the High Street, in the
spacious streets and squares of Craig, Adam and Gillespie Graham.
It was said in the 1850s that the Princes Street gardens had this
advantage, that they 'tend to keep from the too close view of the
New Town gentry the poor population of the Old Town'.[51] The poor
knew something of the lives of the rich because they worked for
them as servants. But what the rich knew of the lives of the poor
became less and less. Comparative ignorance did not breed indifference, but charity took the place of neighbourliness and true
sympathy. Unity of social feeling was one of the most valuable
heritages of old Edinburgh, and its disappearance was widely and
properly lamented.

77. A Hanoverian tombstone in Greyfriar's Churchyard, with the old Edinburgh rising behind.

IX

After 1830

That the financial affairs of the City of Edinburgh were in an uncertain and probably in an insecure state was first seriously suggested
by a member of the Town Council in 1799. Thomas Smith, one of
the Old Baillies, addressed the Council on the subject of its finances
in September 1799, and his remarks were subsequently printed. He
said:

> At the period when Mr. Hay[1] came into office, I met him by
> accident in North Frederick Street and talked a little of his
> appointment. He said he was sorry to acquaint me the town's
> affairs appeared to him to be in very bad order. I answered I
> was sorry to hear it, inquiring how they stood. He replied he
> did not know their actual situation. I asked who knew then,
> receiving nothing in answer but a very significant shrug of his
> shoulders. 'What!' said I, 'does the Lord Provost not know?'
> 'He does not.' 'The Town Clerk?' 'He does not.' 'Then Mr.
> Buchan [Chamberlain from 1766 to 1796] must surely know?'
> 'Mr. Buchan knows nothing of the matter.' I was thunderstruck
> at the information that a gentleman who had been for thirty
> years Chamberlain of the city, having the whole revenue and
> expenditure passing through his hands, was unable to give
> satisfactory information on the state of the town's affairs. I
> never afterwards thought it surprising that the same thing
> should appear in any member of the Council.

According to Baillie Smith, the city debt in 1798 amounted to
£168,982, an increase in ten years of no less than £63,781. He
alleged that the collection of revenue showed increasing arrears, that
there were no sinking funds of any kind, and that interest on the

78. Gothic revival in
York Road, Newhaven.

debt was paid by resort to further borrowing. He ended by warning the Town Council that unless the city's finances were completely overhauled and 'economy . . . in every department . . . rigidly enforced' then before long 'the administration of the city's affairs will go from under the Magistrates and be placed in the hands of Trustees'.

It is hardly possible to check the accuracy of the Baillie's figures; but the drift of his argument was entirely correct and his last words were prophetic. He made, however, no practical impression on his contemporaries – except that they took care to remove him from the Town Council – and far from embarking on courses of economy, public works of a far grander and more ambitious character than those of the eighteenth century became the order of the day. The city debt rose further – according to a pamphlet entirely favourable to the Town Council published in 1819[2], it rose from £52,000 in 1798 to £141,000 in 1818 – and apprehensions about the state of the city's finances increased. In 1819, a Committee of the House of Commons extracted statements and returns from both the Chamberlain and the City Accountant, and took evidence from the Lord Provost and other members of the Town Council. The witnesses were not disposed to be helpful. They all tended to confirm Baillie Smith's statement made twenty years earlier that members of the Town Council did not understand the financial affairs of the city. Indeed, they went further; for most of them made it clear that they had no wish to enquire into these affairs: 'It appears from the Lord Provost's evidence that during the last 18 months a series of motions and protests in succession were made by Deacon Paterson and others, but no statement was laid before the Council; for which the Lord Provost has in evidence assigned as a reason that he did not consider it his duty merely to gratify Deacon Paterson.' The conclusions reached by the Committee were that between 1807 and 1816 the amount borrowed by the city and raised by annuities, plus money received for property sold, had exceeded the amount of debts paid off and money given for property purchased by just over £90,000; and that the excess of expenditure over income in 1817 and 1818 was £16,000 and £18,000 respectively.

Still the magistrates went on their way. They were borrowing to

build the Royal High School in the mid-1820s, and much larger sums for the western approach a few years later. But what finally landed them in trouble was their enlargement of Leith Docks.

Leith was not a separate burgh in those days, and the docks at Leith were a source of revenue for the Edinburgh Town Council. The size of the revenue, however, substantially depended on the state of the docks, and the Town Council was well aware that its interest lay in investing money for their improvement. Accordingly, power was secured in 1799 to borrow up to £80,000 for this purpose; in 1805, power for another £80,000 was taken; and in 1813 for another £80,000. These were enormous sums although their careful expenditure might have been justified. But the downfall of the Corporation – or at least the timing of its downfall – lay in its acceptance in

[74] *Leith Harbour from pier, 1820.* shepherd

259

1805 of a loan of £25,000 from the Lords of the Treasury upon an assignment of the rates of the harbour and docks along with 'all the estate, right, title and interest of the said Lord Provost, Magistrates and Council in and to the same, and all quays, houses, lands or other property purchased for the purposes of the said harbour, basins, docks and other works.' This, from the magistrates' point of view, was a fatal mistake, for it brought the Government upon the scene – as a creditor.

For some years, however, matters continued in the same way, with a debt on the harbour and docks of £240,000 due to individuals, and of £25,000 due to the Government. Extensive improvements were carried out. A new dock was opened in 1806, designed by Rennie, and another, the Queen's Dock, begun in 1810, was completed in 1817. Whether these improvements were as satisfactory from a commercial and economic point of view as they were showy and grand is not clear. There were many complaints. It was alleged, for example, that cargoes of wood were landed at Grangemouth and brought to Edinburgh by the Union Canal in order to save excessive port charges at Leith, and that streets near the docks were so ill-lighted that theft on a large scale was the perpetual accompaniment of commercial activity. There was probably a good deal of truth in these charges. Certainly it is significant that in 1825 the Town Council attempted to get rid of its responsibilities by transferring the docks to a Joint Stock Company. This failed. And instead, the Council made a second agreement with the Government whereby the latter obtained the use of certain parts of the docks – notably of the new Queen's Dock – for the Navy, and in return took over the whole of the existing dock debt by means of an advance of £240,000. The harbour and the docks, with all the rates and duties derived from them, were transferred as security for the loan to the Barons of Exchequer.

The city's financial position was now growing worse. It was in debt to the Government; its debts to private individuals were multiplying; and it had lost a valuable asset from which much revenue might have been obtained. Moreover, at the very time that the financial position was deteriorating, the political supremacy of the Town Council was undermined by Reform. The Commissioners on

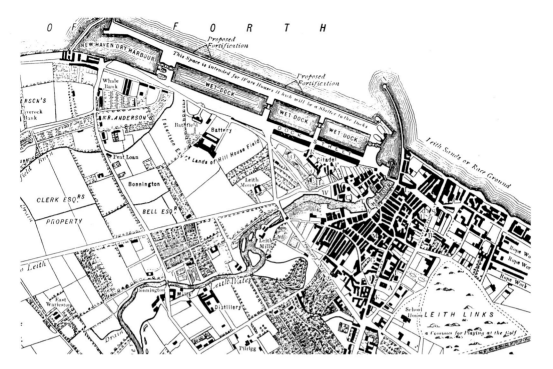

Municipal Corporations, who had been appointed by the Government, examined the affairs of Edinburgh, and their Report in 1833 was far from favourable, financially, administratively or even morally.

We have not found sufficient evidence to entitle us to report that the disastrous state of the city affairs has been caused by actual embezzlement or fraudulent malversation. Exaggerated expectations of the continued and indefinite increase of the city in prosperity and size may have led the Managers of the Corporation into an increase of expense far disproportioned to the really considerable growth of the revenue; officers were multiplied and salaries raised; a spirit of litigation prevailed, great profusion took place in the expenses of civic parade and entertainments, and extravagant sums were expended on public buildings and other works, as ill adapted in general to their object of embellishing the city as they invariably were disproportioned to its expenses. The expense of law proceedings for the city for the period from 1819 to 1832 was £24,162; for the year 1819 the cost of city entertainments was £782; in 1820, £1,066; and the election dinner of the Magistrates that year cost £533 . . . The closeness and irresponsibility of the Corporation could not alone account for the continuance of such a system; the studied concealment of the affairs of the community for a long period, and the partial and confused statement of them which was afterwards periodically made, probably kept the respectable members of the Corporation in ignorance of their financial embarrassment, and it is that ignorance and reckless confidence in the future improvement of their finances which can alone save the city managers from a charge of fraud both as regards the community and their creditors.

Thus did the new broom of the nineteenth century, full of Benthamite principles and conscious rectitude, come to sweep away the cobwebs from the dark places of the world before Reform.

What the situation of the city was at this point is extremely hard to determine. It was bankrupt, certainly. The Burgh Reform Act became law on 28 August 1833, and on the following day an Act was passed appointing Trustees for the creditors of the City of Edinburgh. But what had made the city bankrupt? In what proportions was bankruptcy a consequence of fraud, of incompetent book-keeping, of poor financial administration and arrangement, of over-optimism, and of extravagance? A prolonged study of the Chamberlain's account books over a number of years might yield answers to these questions. But it is doubtful whether such a study would be rewarding, precisely because the book-keeping was so bad. A petty tradesman operating on a small scale might have kept track of his affairs by the methods used by successive City Chamberlains; for a city with an income derived from many sources, some of it ear-marked, and engaged in operations of a speculative character in both the best and the worst senses of that phrase, operations, moreover, which were carried on with borrowed money, the Chamberlain's methods produced only obscurity and confusion.

The city debt was authoritatively and impartially reckoned at £402,000.[3] This had been rising, according to the best available evidence, at the absolutely ruinous rate of over £15,000 per annum during the six years from 1827-28 to 1832-33.[4] The free and regular revenue of the city was at this time in the region of £24,000 or £25,000 per annum. The principal items in this revenue were the Common Good[5] (£12,700 p.a. during the years referred to, of which £7,600 came from feu-duties) and seat rents from the city churches (£7,000 p.a.). The revenue from Leith harbour and docks was of course no longer available, having been assigned to the Government; and the ale duty (two pence Scots on each pint of ale and beer sold in the city), first imposed in the seventeenth century, had dropped greatly in value, due, it was said, to the spread of tea and whisky drinking. But the Town Council had continued to the end its established courses, including the ancient practice of engaging in what were called 'Casual Transactions' and of treating money obtained in this way as income. These transactions included the mortgaging of city property, the selling of property nominally feued out for elusory feu-duties, the total alienation of city property by the sale of superiorities, and other devices of doubtful legality all of which, in general, tended to amount to the consumption of capital.

Expenditure was as follows.

CITY EXPENDITURE[6]

Annual Average for six years, 1827/8–1832/3

I	Feu-duties	£2,696
II	Expenditure on causeways	£1,965
III	Ministers' stipends and schoolmasters' salaries	£10,969
IV	Expenses of local government	£6,746
V	Dean of Guild Account (mostly church expenses)	£1,520
VI	College expenses	£1,732
VII	Criminal department	£896
VIII	Charity workhouse	£200
IX	Property purchased (main item, Canal Stock at £2,160)	£665
X	New buildings and repairs (main items, St Stephen's Church, £16,687 Royal High School, £19,252 St Giles, £8,254)	£8,163
XI	Loan for unemployed workmen, advanced to Improvements Commissioners, 1830	£83
XII	Legal and parliamentary expenses	£2,490
XIII	Miscellaneous payments	£3,826
XIV	Liferent annuities and interest paid	£15,008
XV	Payments on account of Leith Harbour	£6,260
XVI	Advanced on account of deficiencies in Leith West Dock revenue	£4,007
XVII	Arrears	£4,545

[76] *View of Leith Walk.*
ᴇwbank

What strikes one is the enormous volume of expenditure – just over £69,000 p.a. on the average – especially having regard to the fact that by 1833 the city's unpaid arrears amounted to no less than £27,271. For a city which was clearly approaching bankruptcy at a rapid rate, an average expenditure on new buildings and repairs (item X) of over £8,000 p.a., or about one-third of regular free income, was sheer lunacy. The city was also purchasing property (item IX) and making miscellaneous payments (item XIII) as if economy was no object: these miscellaneous payments included 'Race prizes and expenses at [horse] races' to the tune of £668 p.a., and 'Tavern expenses and convenary dinners' at £1,993 p.a.! The Lord Provost received an annual salary, to the bitter end, of £500 (no small sum in 1830), and various scraps of evidence appearing throughout the period suggest that local government could have been managed for a good deal less than just under £7,000 p.a.

All things considered, the major part in the debacle was played by financial incompetence on a very large scale. The Town Council could plead ill luck in that it borrowed a lot of money between 1795 and 1815 when prices were high, and then had to pay interest after 1815 when prices were lower and the real burden of the debt was therefore greater. But already in 1799, in Baillie Smith's time, there was much debt and much muddle; and after 1815, when borrowing on a very large scale took place, prices were not, on the whole, falling. It is clear that the basis of the financial policy of the Town Council throughout this period was, to an increasing extent, a careless optimism about the future rise of revenue; that this optimism was fostered by the almost total obscurity which surrounded the current financial position; and that in these circumstances schemes of improvement were embarked upon which could not, properly speaking, be afforded. Beside these major factors, fraud and the simpler kinds of extravagance played a small part; though no doubt it should not be forgotten that much city expenditure came, in various roundabout ways, to benefit the pockets of members of the Town Council and of their relatives and friends.

Four years were spent on deciding the terms of a settlement with the city's creditors. The debts themselves were not disputed; the difficulties were to decide how much revenue the Town Council genuinely required, which assets of the city could be treated as legally liable for the debts, and what revenue, if any, could in future be expected to accrue to the city from the Port of Leith. These difficulties were discussed at length, but the basis of the settlement was Labouchère's very able *Report to the Chancellor of the Exchequer*, published in 1836, along with the proposal, made by a Select Committee of the House of Commons in 1835, that the Government should partially abandon or suspend the debt due to it from the City of Edinburgh. Labouchère's Report, which would have given the creditors a $2\frac{1}{4}$ per cent return on their claims, was not accepted, but arrangements similar in character to those which he had proposed, giving the creditors 3 per cent, were agreed in 1838, and embodied in the so-called Agreement Act of that year. Thus ended the palmy days of lavish, uninhibited expenditure.

To say that nothing could ever be the same again is almost an understatement. A new chapter, almost a new book, began in 1833. In terms of population the city continued to expand; but it grew far more slowly than before. The population in 1831 was 136,000. This represented an increase of some 69,000, or over 100 per cent, in the thirty years between 1801 and 1831. But in the forty years between 1831 and 1871 the population rose by only 61,000, or less than 50 per cent. In other words, whereas population increased by rather over 2·5 per cent per annum between 1801 and 1831, it increased by only about 1·0 per cent per annum between 1831 and 1871. These rates of growth were consistently below the rates for Glasgow, where population far more than doubled between 1801 and 1831 and then considerably more than doubled again between 1831 and 1871. As a result, Edinburgh had less than half the population of Glasgow by 1871, and indeed at that date had fewer people than Glasgow had had in 1831. The reason, of course, was the prodigious increase in the manufacturing capacity and commercial activity of Glasgow and indeed of Lanarkshire as a whole. Iron and coal mining, textile manufacture, and the production of machines and implements were occupations which employed about 150,000 people in Lanarkshire in the 1870s; in Midlothian, except for coal-mining, they hardly figured at all; and coal-mining employed only some 14,000. Edinburgh was not a manufacturing town, and Midlothian was not a manufacturing county, to anything like the extent of Glasgow and Lanarkshire. Edinburgh was still, as it always had been, a city of government, of the law; of learning, of society and of art. The census of 1881 expressed the same thing in a different way, in figures and occupational classifications. It recorded that of the occupied population of Lanarkshire, thirteen per cent were in professional employment or domestic service; for Edinburgh the corresponding figure was twenty-nine per cent.[7]

An inevitable consequence of Edinburgh's less rapid growth of population after 1831 was a slowing down in the rate of building. The hectic activity of the 1820s no doubt anticipated many needs, and was bound to be followed by a pause; but the revival of house building, when it came, was gradual, limited, and indeed inadequate. For thirty years after 1831 almost the sole development was that more houses were built in existing streets of the New Town.

The result was that the density of population increased, and in the Old Town, where almost no new houses were built at all, increased alarmingly. The Old Town was almost the only place where the

poorer sections of the community could live, for not until 1851 was
the first block of houses for ordinary working people built in Edinburgh.[8] As a result, the tenements of the Old Town, greatly reduced
in value, were rapidly subdivided into smaller 'houses', each now
consisting sometimes of no more than a single apartment; moreover,
many rooms opened into other rooms, and were themselves divided
by partitions, so as to allow still more people to be packed into the
available space. According to Littlejohn,[9] the population of the wynds
and closes of the Old Town was by this process of division and sub-
division 'quadrupled by a class notorious for its neglect of the most
ordinary sanitary precautions'. That the population quadrupled is
perhaps doubtful – Littlejohn's use of the word may be picturesque
rather than mathematical – but making all reasonable allowance for
the growth of the New Town, it seems certain that between 1800
and 1870 population in the Old Town more than doubled, scarcely

*[77] View of the Pleasance
shepherd*

267

any additional houses being built in this period. And of the dirt and overcrowding there can be no doubt either. The pavements of the closes, upon which all the rubbish and filth of the place was deposited, were broken and uneven, harbouring dirt and defying efforts at proper cleansing; and the common stairs of the tenements, unlighted and dark, were kept now in a far worse condition than in the eighteenth century: 'I have personally examined the stairs in the High Street and Old Town generally, and found them almost universally in a disgraceful state.'[10] The overcrowding, which in the Old Town was universal, was carried to an almost incredible extent. A wide range of the most sordid and the least productive occupations might be carried on by the inhabitants of a single room, let alone of a single tenement – shebeening, out-of-door apple selling or dram selling, match-hawking, speech-crying, organ-grinding, thieving, prostitution, or 'subletting for an hour to vagrant couples not intent upon singing psalms'.[11]

Words cannot do justice to the living conditions, and a single quotation must suffice:

> Ascending to the third storey of the same land, by means of a dilapidated wooden stair, we came upon what is falsely called a lodging-house, kept by an Irishman. It has two rooms, but one of them is sublet to a third party, concerning whom he studiously maintained a profound silence. His own place was in a shocking state. When we opened the door, the confined air rushed out and nearly upset us with its loaded foetor. The cause was soon explained. Within one small apartment, not more than fifteen feet in length by nine in breadth, we found no fewer than eleven persons, all of them grown-up men and women. Four of the inmates, young girls, were in bed, of which there were three. Others sat crouching round a miserable fire, in a state of half-nudity, and with a shawl or petticoat thrown carelessly over the shoulders. The male portion of the company, big hulking fellows, stood with their backs to the fire, or leaned on the edges of the beds. The furniture consisted of a deal table, a few chairs, and a press. The beds were covered with dirty rags of a brown colour, and the effluvia was sickening.[12]

Quotations like this one could be repeated *ad nauseam*. Figures – authoritative, careful figures – tell the same story.

MIDDLE MEALMARKET STAIR

	Rooms	Families	Children under 5	Adults	Total	Sinks	Water Closets
First Flat	12	12	10	39	49	—	—
Second Flat	11	11	14	40	54	—	—
Third Flat	12	12	10	45	55	—	—
Fourth Flat	12	12	11	45	56	—	—
Fifth Flat	12	9	6	28	34	—	—
Total	59	56	51	197	248	—	—

ELPHINSTON'S LAND, CARUBBER'S CLOSE

	Rooms	Families	Children under 5	Adults	Total	Sinks	Water Closets
Ground Flat	4	4	5	15	20	2	—
First Flat	6	2	4	9	13	—	—
Second Flat	—	—	—	—	—	—	—
Third Flat	8	7	4	20	24	1	1
Fourth Flat	10	8	7	21	28	2	2
Fifth Flat	10	8	4	23	27	2	2
Sixth Flat	7	6	4	19	23	2	2
Total	45	35	28	107	135	9	7

These figures – by no means the worst which could be quoted from Littlejohn's Report of 1865 – require no comment.

To make matters worse, the Old Town continued to be the main scene of such manufacturing industry as the city possessed. In such districts as Canongate, Tron, Grassmarket and St Giles were printing works, breweries, tanneries, foundries, tobacco manufactories and 'such trades as prepare cat-gut from the intestines of animals'.[13] Many gave off obnoxious smells, and all polluted the air with their smoke, causing people in rooms already overcrowded to keep the windows almost permanently closed. There were also, in all parts of the city but especially in the poorer quarters, byres – byres which housed, in 1865, rather over 2,000 cows. These byres, part of an important trade, were intermingled with the houses and in some cases were actually below occupied dwellings.

The New Town was comparatively free of such nuisances, although on the slope below Queen Street there was a large number of printing establishments and small metal workshops. The situation worsened, however, when the city Gas Works was established in the Canongate, so low down that 'the fumes of the manufacture rendered almost un-inhabitable the houses which skirt the Calton Hill'; to overcome the difficulty 'a chimney-stalk had to be erected, of such gigantic pro-portions as to form a landmark and eyesore from what quarter soever the city is approached'.[14] The very large Caledonian Distillery also came to disfigure the West End. Its refuse was a serious problem; Littlejohn complained that it 'finds its way westwards for a distance of 300 yards, polluting the atmosphere of the western districts of the city until it reaches the Water of Leith, flowing eastwards through the city for a distance of three miles, and thus the in-habitants are again subjected to the annoyance'.[15]

In the New Town as a whole, nevertheless, living conditions were very much better than in the Old. Yet here also a contribution was made towards Edinburgh's notorious reputation in the first half of the nineteenth century for epidemics of fever. A few streets, such as St James's Street, had already succumbed to the process of degrada-tion carried to such lengths in the Cowgate.[16] Others, such as Rose Street, Thistle Street and Jamaica Street, originally planned for 'the better class of artisans', were becoming considerably overcrowded and, devoid of water-closets and sewers, a source of possibly serious infection. Even the finest streets and houses were far from perfect. Their drains, 'porous as a sieve',[17] were liable to be connected with internal sanitary arrangements which were inadequate, inconvenient, often unhealthy and quite often positively offensive.

> The domestic use of baths [in 1825] was apparently unknown, and the conveniences were few in number and awkwardly placed, either so as to deprive a principal room of its amenity, or in such a confined space as to be entirely without ventilation. Princes Street, George Street, Queen Street, York Place and Heriot Row can still furnish specimens of such faulty arrange-ment. When unhealthy competition prevails in the building trade, and houses are erected with undue haste, many points of essential importance to their sanitary conditions are very apt to be overlooked, while others which bulk largely in the eye of intending purchasers, such as external decoration, receive an undue amount of attention. This, I have no doubt, was the case during our building mania in 1825.[18]

Also, New Town houses of the best class were frequently damp on the ground floor and generally musty, due to imperfect drainage. Most surprising of all, they were also liable to overcrowding, because sleeping accommodation was limited by the undue amount of space taken up by dining-rooms and drawing-rooms, and the servants, of course, were crowded together in odd rooms and closets, with the man-servant frequently huddled under the staircase.

As new houses were built, many of these defects were no doubt increasingly avoided. But improvement can only have been gradual because of the slow rate of house-building. Building went on in a moderate way in the later 1830s, but very few houses indeed seem to have been built between the depression at the end of the '30s and the revival of general economic activity towards the middle of the 1850s. A definite acceleration then took place, however, and such streets as Royal Terrace and Melville Street, both on the outskirts of the New Town, filled up with houses and were virtually completed.

What really struck observers in the 1850s, however, and what was still more noteworthy in the 1860s and early 1870s, was the growth of outlying districts. This expansion of what were Edinburgh's earliest suburbs was very gradual. The nearest and earliest development was that by Raeburn at Stockbridge, reached from the city by a steep brae and a narrow stone bridge probably built in the 1780s. But the steepness of the brae and the narrowness of the bridge were a serious inconvenience. The Water of Leith was indeed something of a barrier to northward expansion. In 1824 Lord Provost Learmonth began to put forward proposals for a new bridge. Learmonth had purchased the estate of Dean, mostly north of the river, but near the west end of town, and he wished to make an easy access to his property with a view to its development for housing. Most of the money required he appears to have provided himself, but financial support was given by the Cramond Road Trustees, who stipulated that there should be no toll on the Bridge, and that it should be designed by Telford. From an engineering and civic point of view the result was entirely a success. Begun late in 1829 and open for traffic at the end of 1831, Telford's Dean Bridge is a very fine construction, and provides a convenient route from the centre of town towards Queensferry. Its four arches carry the roadway more than 100 feet above the rocky river bed, and the passer-by can look down on the little, old-fashioned, confused looking village of Dean, and on the old Bell's Mills Bridge, which used to carry the main road to the north. From Learmonth's own point of view the result was not so satisfactory. The 1830s and 1840s were a dead time for building in Edinburgh, and twenty years elapsed before the Dean feus began to be taken up and the first houses to appear in Clarendon Crescent in the early 1850s. It is remarkable that the principal bridge across the Water of Leith – and from the city's point of view a not inconvenient one – should thus have been provided by a private developer in the pursuit of his own interest.

Expansion to the south was easier, and here were built Edinburgh's first detached suburban houses,[19] realising the desire for a house like a country gentleman's, but more modest and closer to the life of the town. A feuing plan for the lands of Newington was engraved in 1795 for Bell and Reid. James Reid was a member of the Scottish Exchequer. Bell was a highly successful surgeon, a farmer, and an astute property developer. The essential feature of the feuing plan is an 'intended new road' to join the Newington area to Nicolson Street and thence to the New Town via the North Bridge. (This road, emerging from St Patrick's Square, appears as the 'Intended Road to London' in Ainslie's map of 1806.) In 1805 Bell gathered the whole estate of Newington into his own hands, and from that date the residential character of the Newington area was settled for a hundred years. Feuing began in 1806. At that time, the area – except for a few odd houses at Mayfield, Echo Bank and the Powburn – was all open fields, through which the London Mail passed after leaving the city by East Cross Causeway. But by the time of Waterloo there were numerous 'tenements of houses' strung along Clerk Street, and further south 'finely situated villas, each with its garden plot in front and at the back, dotted the uplands between Salisbury Road and Mayfield Loan'.[20] It was a fashionable area and a significant point of development in the 1820s. Blacket Place, guarded by gates which were shut at nightfall so that the houses within the gates should have 'all the privacy and convenience of country residences',[21] was forming in the later 1820s. Also in the 1820s detached houses, mostly Grecian in style, began to be built in Salisbury Road and

79. Dean Bridge.

Minto Street. After a pause in the 1830s and '40s, Newington grew rapidly in the 1850s, and by 1865 was recognised as 'the most densely-peopled'[22] of the suburban districts. Just to the west of it, Grange began to grow in the 1850s, and shortly became 'a township of villas . . . thinly peopled',[23] with Grange Road, Dick Place, Grange Loan, and a sprinkling of houses also on the intersecting streets. Morningside, 'a secluded village, consisting of little more than a row of thatched cottages, a line of trees, and a blacksmith's forge',[24] still slumbered in rural solitude in 1850. There were a few large villas, some old, like East Morningside House and the White House, some comparatively new, like Falcon Hall, but they and the nearby cottages were all in the country, separated by fields of oats and barley from both Edinburgh and Newington, until building began seriously in the 1850s. In that decade the street geography of the area was for the first time mapped out, and streets – or country roads as they then were – such as Churchill, Colinton Road, Hope Terrace and Blackford Road were created, each furnished with at least a few villas, and every villa with its coach-house. An extremely rapid development then took place in the '60s and '70s, and by 1880 almost the whole area lying between the Meadows and Bruntsfield Links on the one hand and the Jordan Burn on the other was covered with houses; only the streets between Warrender Park Terrace and Thirlestane Road – the Warrender Park feu – were not built up. Simultaneously – although with a very different type of house – the area west of Fountainbridge and around the Haymarket became occupied, and large numbers of dwellings, many of them of a very unpretentious character, were also built along the Water of Leith, particularly near Canonmills where there was a large distillery, and also along and on streets branching off Leith Walk.

This expansion of the town, particularly noticeable on the gentle slope rising from the Meadows and then, from the line of Grange Road and Strathearn Road, falling away southward to give a charming prospect of the fertile country towards the still distant villages of Liberton and Colinton, towards Blackford Hill and the Braids and the paler, more distant heights of the Pentlands, demanded, inevitably, a greatly improved system of urban and suburban transport. The mid-decades of the nineteenth century were the age of the

80. *Good planning was still known in the 1860's, as in this housing development on the banks of the Water of Leith, carried out by the Edinburgh Co-operative Building Society.*

hackney carriage and the horse bus – the number of horses stabled in town in the mid-nineteenth century may have exceeded even the number of cows. Later, in 1871, came the horse-drawn tramcar. By 1880 the system of tramcars and tramlines had been enlarged to eighteen miles and eleven hundred horses, and this was an important factor in the development of suburban housing.[25]

The great transport innovation was of course the railway. It is true that in a sense railways made less difference to Edinburgh than to most towns of any importance. Their introduction did not lead in Edinburgh's case to a great expansion of manufacturing activity nor did it put the city on a newly created trade route. The general development of railways around and into Edinburgh was gradual and the results unspectacular, but the railways did have an important and obvious effect on the economic geography of the centre of the town.

The earliest line which affected Edinburgh was the Edinburgh and Dalkeith, originally planned by Robert Stevenson in a survey addressed to 'His Grace the Duke of Buccleuch and Queensferry and other noblemen and gentlemen, subscribers for a survey of a railway from the coalfield of Midlothian to the City of Edinburgh and port of Leith'. An Act was obtained in 1826, and the line was opened in 1831 from St Leonard's, on the south-eastern outskirts of the city, to Dalkeith; the extension from Niddrie to Leith was completed in 1838. Horses provided the motive power for this line, except for a short section from Duddingston to St Leonard's which was too steep for horses and which was worked by a stationary engine. This was the line which was called 'The Innocent Railway' – some said because it had never killed anyone,[26] some because of its easy-going and carefree ways, the horses quiet and unhurrying as they ambled along through the countryside, being whoa-ed to a halt by their driver wherever and whenever it suited those who used the line. Yet the Edinburgh and Dalkeith was not devoid of either enterprise or success. Passenger services were introduced in 1834, and in the early 1840s the railway was carrying some 300,000 passengers per annum.

This line, connecting the coalfields with Edinburgh and the sea, could scarcely be said to enter the town at all. No railway, indeed, entered Edinburgh until after 1840. But in the middle of the 1830s, in the 'little railway mania', the inevitable suggestion was put forward that a line be built to connect Edinburgh with Glasgow, and that it should enter Edinburgh via Haymarket and then run through the low-lying ground between Princes Street and the Castle as far east as the North Bridge.

This proposal aroused very strong opposition, not from the Town Council, but from a private body called the Princes Street Proprietors.[27] This body, consisting of those who had feued houses in Princes Street between Hanover Street and Hope Street, seems to have come into existence informally about 1811, when plans were discussed for draining and improving the area once occupied by the North Loch. Nothing came of this. But the proprietors retained their interest in what happened on the south side of the Street, for in 1816, when the building of St John's Church was under consideration, they began negotiations with the Town Council regarding future building in that area, negotiations which resulted in an Act of 1816. By this Act, the erection of any additional buildings on the south side of Princes Street was prohibited, the feuars obtained authority to erect a parapet and railings on the south side of the street, and the Corporation undertook to lease or feu the ground on the south side to the feuars 'for the purpose of laying out the same in whole or in part as a garden, nursery for trees, or pleasure ground or under grass or otherwise embellishing and enclosing the same'. To carry out this project, the feuars obtained powers to levy assessments of up to twenty per cent of their rentals, and to borrow up to £5,000. No time was lost in carrying the project into execution. The parapet and rail were completed in 1817 at a cost of almost £1,500, the street being widened a little, as its edge seems to have lain originally along the line of the kerb bounding the present south pavement. Simultaneously, Robert Stevenson was drawing up a scheme of drainage, and on the basis of his Report the Committee of the Proprietors opened a cash credit for £3,000 with Sir William Forbes' bank (what would the improvers have done without that bank?), work was put in hand, and completed – not too satisfactorily as it turned out – by the end of 1820. During 1821 and 1822 a large part of the ground was laid out in walks and planted extensively with trees – 34,000 of them, it was said, most of which died – and what was not so laid out and planted was leased as a nursery garden. These expensive operations resulted in a debt of almost £3,000, but against this the proprietors had exclusive access to agreeable walks which at one time, before Johnstone Terrace was completed, included an upper walk around the south side of the Castle at an elevation 'affording an extensive view of the Pentland Hills'. This exclusive amenity soon attracted public attention, and in 1821 the system of selling an annual right of access to suitable individuals was introduced.[28] Among the first purchasers were the Lord Justice-Clerk, Baron Hume, Carlyle Bell, T. W. Brougham and George Wauchope. 'Within a few years it came to be a mark of fashion to possess a key to the gardens.'[29] The standard payment for a key was three guineas, and in 1830 the revenue from keys was no less than £300.

Into this situation there irrupted the idea that a railway – a steam railway – might conveniently be driven right through the feuars' fashionable and carefully tended gardens. The railway directors could hardly expect this proposal to be greeted with universal enthusiasm, and, knowing what to expect, they prepared a circular signed by John Learmonth, Chairman of the Edinburgh and Glasgow Railway Company and a recent Lord Provost of Edinburgh. In this circular it was boldly stated that the fears of objectors to the railway plan were groundless. The railway would occupy only the lowest-lying land, and would be enclosed on each side by a wall, if necessary also by an embankment planted with trees and shrubs 'which would entirely conceal every part of the railway . . .' As to smoke, the idea that smoke would be a nuisance 'proceeds upon a mistake, for owing to the improved construction of the furnaces the smoke is now scarcely seen. Besides, when it is considered that the engines will not occupy more than a minute in passing through the gardens, it is almost impossible that they should create a nuisance with all the smoke which they can possibly send forth in so short a space.' Thus do men delude themselves through optimism and self interest. The proprietors were not deceived. They replied that they had spent £7,000 in turning the North Loch area 'from its original condition of a filthy and offensive bog' into a garden of privacy, quiet and comfort, enjoyed by all who saw it as well as by those who walked in it. 'These are objects of importance . . . It is accordingly vain to suppose that any consideration could compensate for such a loss . . . It is inconceivable how a railway, in whatever manner masked or enclosed, along the line of which numerous steam carriages will be constantly passing (and steam engines do not generally pass without a certain degree of noise, smoke and disturbance), can prove otherwise than a most serious annoyance.'

Nor did the proprietors stop at argument and remonstrance. They were, after all, wealthy and influential men. At a meeting late in 1836, presided over by Lord Meadowbank, they resolved to resist the railway bill in the House of Commons. A case was prepared, forceful and accurate, complaining that by carrying the railway through the gardens 'the vested interests of a numerous body of citizens are gratuitously assailed for the sole benefit of a private speculation in which they have no share, and they are threatened to be deprived of the proper use and enjoyment of a property embellished at so great an expense . . . Public utility does not require any such sacrifice, and the railway could terminate with much more propriety on the west side of Lothian Road, in a situation detached from the new town and equally convenient.'

This skilful appeal to the rights of property, well calculated to enlist parliamentary sympathies in the 1830s, and supported by, among others, General Ramsay, the Board of Trustees and the Society of Antiquaries, had its effect, and the railway promoters did not obtain the permission which they sought. The railway itself was built, but rather slowly; and the line was not open for traffic until 1842. The Edinburgh terminus was at Haymarket.

But of course the railway interests were not satisfied. Hardly was the line open when, encouraged doubtless by the trade revival of the early 1840s, the railway directors proposed to bring a bill into Parliament to allow trains through to Waverley. Opposition again arose; but this time it was not so vigorous and not so effective. Partly, no doubt, this was due to the success of the early lines throughout the country and to the strength which this gave to the greatly increased and extended 'railway mania' of the 1840s. Another consideration was the existence of the Edinburgh, Leith and Newhaven Railway Company, incorporated in 1836, which opened a line from Scotland Street to Trinity in 1842 and which had

[78] The terminus building, Haymarket railway station.

plans to extend its line southward to the site of the present Waverley Station. This would mean a railway station east of the Princes Street gardens, as well as Haymarket to the west. And a station east of the gardens would, of course, be the natural terminus for a line from Berwick, also projected in the early 1840s. Surrounded, seemingly, by planned railway lines and proposed stations, and with more and more feuars now the owners of shops and hotels and accordingly less enthusiastic in opposition, the Committee of Proprietors weakened and began to talk less of prevention and more of compensation. Agreement was reached in 1844, Playfair being given the task of hemming the railway in with a stone wall and embankment, high enough to conceal the locomotives and rolling stock from the draw-ing-room windows of the houses in Princes Street. On 1 August 1846 trains began to run from Haymarket to Waverley, and three years later work on the gardens was completed, the Proprietors receiving, in addition, compensation which fell only a little short of £2,000.[30] Once again, a radical change had taken place.

Of distinguished or important new building in this so quickly changing physical and political environment of the 1830s and 1840s there was a fair amount. Some of it, moreover, was visually important, for it included several structures which are still of the greatest prominence.

The first of these to be completed, in 1832, was Surgeon's Hall, erected almost opposite the University at a cost of some £20,000. It was designed by Playfair, and has been described as the culmination of his Greek period, only to be equalled by his final masterpiece, the National Gallery. It has a Hexastyle portico, with the front row of columns mounted on a broad screen wall. A large and ingenious building, somewhat massive and severe in its proportions, it is decorated with scroll work as fine as that of the Royal Institution. Unfortunately, Surgeons' Hall is today almost ruined by the press of mean buildings which surrounds it, and by the ceaseless flow of modern traffic within a few yards of its massive front door.

The Scott Monument, most prominent of all these later buildings, has fared better. Sited in the eastern Princes Street gardens (after the Proprietors had refused to allow it to be built in the west gardens) it was designed by a Mr George Kemp 'an humble artist, not far removed from the position of an ordinary workman, residing in Canning Place, a somewhat obscure street in the southern suburbs of the city'.[31] The foundation stone of the monument was laid in 1840, only eight years after Scott's death. One hundred and eighty feet in height, it is, after the Castle and the deplorable North British Hotel (built just before 1900) the most dominating and inescapable single structure in the centre of the city. Without it and the Castle, Princes Street would be unrecognisable. It is a gothic fantasy in a style of romantic nostalgia not unsuited for its purpose, crowded with arches, pillars, pilasters, niches and pinnacles in the utmost profusion, details said to be copied from the ruins of Melrose Abbey which Sir Walter so ardently admired. Nothing could be more alien to classical Edinburgh than this monument. Its completion, in 1846, wrote finis to an architectural era. Yet, mellowed a little by the passage of time, it makes a unique and not altogether unpleasing contribution, gay, irresponsible, fantastic, to the tremendously varied spectacle of Princes Street.

Next in time came the new hall for the Royal College of Physicians in Queen Street. This was designed by Thomas Hamilton in

1843. The contract for building was signed in 1844, and occupation began in 1846. The contract price was £4,838, but, as usual, expense increased. The estimate was shortly revised to £5,415; the contractor's account as rendered turned out to be £5,898; subsequent additional work, including most of the furnishing, raised the bill to £7,194, in addition to which the College paid £2,750 for the original building on the site, which was demolished. But it can hardly be denied that the money was well spent. The exterior is somewhat square and severe in its proportions, but is relieved by a portico which frames the central window of the upper floor; mounted on each side of the lower portico is a large classical figure, and a third figure, equally large, is poised on top of the pediment of the upper portico. The effect is extraordinary but not unpleasing, although it might be better if the building were somewhat wider. The interior is in a similar style. The entrance hall and stairway are severe and yet grand, while the main hall is a magnificent apartment in the construction of which expense has clearly not been spared. Slightly longer than it is broad, and high in proportion to its size, it is surrounded by eighteen free-standing marble columns, above each of which, along the frieze, stands a life-size classical figure. The effect is spectacular, although it is perhaps not unfair to say that it is more Victorian than Roman.[32]

The Free Church College and Assembly Hall is very different. This too marks a break with the past. The Disruption rent the fabric of Scotland's religious and therefore social life, bringing widespread dissension and spiritual suffering. After it, too, nothing could be the same. The Assembly Hall is hardly an expression of this; but it is a reminder of it. The design of the hall was the subject of a competition which was won by Playfair, and the building was erected between 1846 and 1850. It occupies a site on which stood previously the sixteenth-century Palace of Mary of Guise, along with some other less interesting buildings, all on the property of Tod's Trustees, and its completion led to the clearing away of what was called 'the trash of temporary buildings' which disfigured the Mound, and also, indirectly, to the construction of the steps leading from the Royal Institution to the foot of Bank Street. The College itself is an undistinguished building, not in Playfair's classical style but in a kind

81. Physicians' Hall, Queen Street.

280

of gothic. Its chief fault seems to be that it is on a scale too small for either its architectural pretentions or for the splendid site which it occupies at the head of the Mound. It can, indeed, be seen from almost any point on Princes Street. Its main recommendation is, perhaps, that it is not too prominent, and that it makes a little less violent the transition from the tall, plain flat-faced lands fronting Bank Street to the romantic red-roofed constructions in Ramsay Gardens, which stand in close proximity to the severe and massive proportions of the Castle.

The College was not Playfair's first essay in a non-classical style, and his lack of success on this occasion makes all the more remarkable his triumphant performance in the design of Donaldson's Hospital. This building lies almost two miles west of Princes Street, and can hardly be said to have anything to do with the New Town. It is, however, one of the largest public buildings erected in Edinburgh in the nineteenth century, visible from a great number of different points; and the nineteenth century tended to regard it as Playfair's masterpiece. The money for its construction and endowment was left by James Donaldson of Broughton Hall, a printer, who had his business at one time at the foot of the West Bow. The building was erected between 1842 and 1851 at a cost of almost £100,000. It encloses on all sides a very large quadrangle, has four square towers of four storeys at each corner, and, in the centre of the south front, a set of four octagonal five-storeyed towers, each 120 feet high. The whole structure is much decorated with buttresses and tall, mullioned windows, and is reminiscent of the style which English architects created, late in the sixteenth and early in the seventeenth century, in the wake of the impact upon them of the Renaissance, a style in its heyday when Inigo Jones was a young man. In this sense, Donaldson's Hospital is almost exactly two hundred and fifty years out of date. It reminds us of Hatfield House, in Hertfordshire, built in the early seventeenth century, or of Burghley House (which, indeed, it quite closely resembles, both in general plan and in detail) built near Stamford in the sixteenth century. It echoes also the style of Heriot's Hospital; but Heriot's is plainer and more sensible, less frivolously ornamented and better proportioned; and Heriot's, of course, was designed in Inigo Jones's own lifetime, although probably

82. Playfair's National Gallery of Scotland, the Mound, with the same architect's New College behind.

281

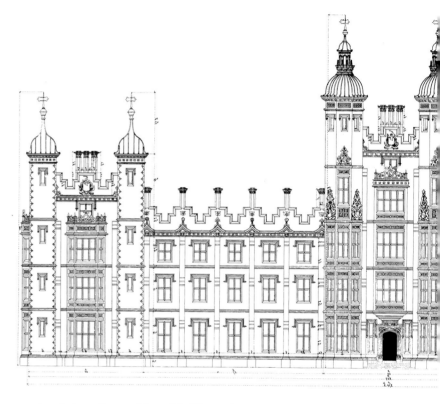

not by Inigo Jones himself. Nevertheless, Playfair's building has merit, and like the Scott monument it adds a light-hearted and fanciful touch (or so we see it now) to Edinburgh's skyline.

Lastly – and surely it is right that we should end with Playfair, to whom Edinburgh owes so much – there is the National Gallery of Scotland, begun in 1850 but not completed until 1857, the year in which Playfair died. The building of a National Gallery evolved out of the work of the Board of Trustees, which in 1760 had set up the Scottish School of Design. As time passed, the Trustees were given increasingly wide discretion in the application of their funds, which had originally been earmarked for the encouragement of trade and manufacture. In 1847 an Act was passed which permitted the Treasury in London to provide money for education in the fine arts generally, and as a result of this new liberty, negotiations were begun

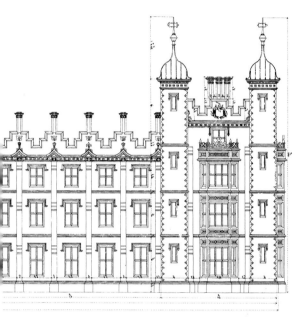

between the Trustees and the Treasury with a view to erecting a
National Gallery in Edinburgh. The Treasury agreed to provide
£30,000, the Board of Trustees £20,000, and the city a large part
of the site at a nominal rate. Playfair provided the plans, returning
not only to the classical style but to a pure and simplified form of it
which makes his Royal Institution appear fussy and over-ornate.
The gallery is a long low building, its length intercepted by a broad
and high transept. The main lengths of wall are unornamented save
by a series of flat Ionic pilasters, and there are splendid Ionic porticos
on the wings. This dignified and magnificently proportioned building,
seen against the mighty background of the Castle, full of variety and,
on a summer's day, even of colour, is not unworthy of its setting,
and has a good claim to be considered one of the two or three finest
classical buildings in Edinburgh.

When Playfair died in 1857 the golden age had been over for twenty years. In those twenty years some important building had been done, and as a result of the additions then made, the centre of Edinburgh had assumed very much the appearance which it has today, the appearance which has done so much to make Edinburgh one of the famous and beautiful cities of the world. This was the achievement of a brief, and not in all respects glorious, seventy or eighty years. But it was by and large a conscious and deliberate achievement, the result of imagination, co-operation, and hard work.

THE ROYAL INSTITUTION BUILDINGS.

There were forces which worked against it, and which began to destroy it even before it was complete. Such forces still exist. But those who worked for the creation of beauty and harmony prevailed, because they were expressing the best aspects of the life of a vigorous and on the whole healthy society. No vigorous and healthy society today will neglect or impair what was done then. It is for those who inherit the achievement of Edinburgh's classical age to understand it, to adapt it, to use it, and to enjoy it.

[80] Playfair. The National Gallery of Scotland, with the Royal Institution (RSA) *to the right.*
EUL

Appendix

One profession with which this study is a good deal concerned is that of architecture. Yet it can hardly be said that there was an architectural profession in Scotland before the foundation of the Institute of the Architects of Scotland in 1840 (the Institute of British Architects was founded in London in 1834). Prior to the 1830s the training of architects and the practice of architecture were in no way standardised. Broadly speaking, men who belonged to three different social groups might become architects in the eighteenth and early nineteenth centuries. There were, first, the well-born and talented amateurs. Many noblemen and gentlemen of the eighteenth century had some knowledge of the principles of architecture, especially of Palladian architecture, and many of them visited and made sketches of famous classical buildings while on the Grand Tour. Not a few put their knowledge to use, and, aided by the ability of first-class masons who could erect structurally sound buildings from rough plans, designed houses as a hobby, both for themselves and their friends. Occasionally, as in the case of Lord Burlington, the most famous of these amateurs, architecture became a full-time occupation. Secondly, the masons themselves might aspire to rise from the construction of buildings and the occasional modification of plans to the actual business of design. Their technical qualifications for the 'minute and mechanical' parts of the work were unquestionable, but their taste, their sense of proportion, was another matter. Frequently the difficulty was got over by co-operation between the talented amateur who had taste and imagination but no knowledge of building, and the mason who knew how to build and who could restrain the wilder flights of fancy of his 'patron'. Masons who thus acquired some knowledge of design might later launch out as 'architects'. Lastly, there were young men who could not afford to be without an occupation, but who aimed higher than to start life as masons. These were the men, gentlemen's sons, sometimes the sons of architects, who went into an architect's office as pupils or apprentices to learn arithmetic and geometry, mechanical drawing and perspective, as well as something of the history of architecture. This training seems to have lasted anything from two to six years. Of the twenty-four architects selected by Briggs[1] as representative of the eighteenth century, only nine were trained in an office. 'Many of the rest stepped into architecture from the position of a clerk-of-works, a mason, or a carpenter; while others approached it from painting or sculpture . . .'[2] But towards the close of the eighteenth century it became increasingly common for architects to have received some sort of office training.

It is significant that all the architects, except one, who were important in Edinburgh between 1760 and 1830 have one thing in common, and one thing only; and that is, that not much is known about them. This is particularly true of the man who gave the New Town its original shape and form and who thus determined, to a large extent, its subsequent development: James Craig. Craig is reputed to have been born in 1740.[3] He was a son of William Craig, merchant, of Edinburgh, and Mary, younger daughter of the Rev. Thomas Thomson of Ednam in Roxburghshire, a sister of the poet Thomson who wrote 'The Seasons'. There are some grounds for believing that Craig's grandfather was Robert Craig, College Treasurer in 1702, Merchant Councillor from 1704 to 1705, Commissioner of Royal Burghs in 1714 and Dean of Guild in 1714 and 1715. If these facts are correct, Craig belonged to a family of some standing in the city. Virtually nothing is known about his education. It is sometimes said that he was a pupil of Sir Robert Taylor,[4] but this seems to rest on a statement in Redgrave's *Dictionary of British Artists*, a book which was not published until eighty years after Craig's death. The fact is that Craig suddenly leapt into prominence in 1767 when his plan for the New Town was accepted. He was young; overnight, almost, he became comparatively famous; and for a few years he seems to have been well employed. His most considerable architectural work in Edinburgh was the Physicians' Hall in George Street (which no longer exists), of which the foundation stone was laid in 1775. He also designed the first observatory on Calton Hill, likewise begun in 1775, and about 1780 he was employed by the Town Council in various projects, including work on St Giles Church and the Battery at Leith. He also was engaged in building work in Glasgow. But from about 1780 until his death in 1795 little is heard of him; and the important proposal which he put forward in this period, his 'Plan for Improving the City of Edinburgh' (1786) was rejected by the magistrates. His death aroused almost no interest; and only the *Scottish Register* did more than merely note the fact that he had died. In these circumstances this sole contemporary comment is of particular interest. A man, according to the *Register*, of great abilities,

> he was unfortunate, owing chiefly, perhaps, to some visionary ideas of consequence which he fancied he was entitled to indulge on account of his relationship to Thomson the Poet, a connection which he vainly flattered himself was to procure him consideration and employment, and to supersede in him the necessity of prosecuting those sober plans for success in life which prudence requires of other men.

> This ingenious and accomplished architect in the latter part of his life was not successful, his remuneration being but slender. He appears to have died in rather poor circumstances.[5]

All the available evidence corroborates this final paragraph. After 1781 Craig was constantly borrowing money, and he died in debt. It is sad to think that a man who has probably as good a claim as anyone to be the founder of modern Edinburgh, who met Boswell at Prestonfield and dined with him at Lord Kames's, should have sunk in middle age into obscurity, disappointment, and comparative poverty.[6]

The obvious comparison with Craig, in point of both material success and posthumous fame, is Robert Adam. About Adam much is known, and therefore much need not be said here.[7] His father, William Adam, was one of the leading Scots architects of the day, Master Mason to the Ordnance in North Britain, designer and builder of many important country houses such as Hopetoun House, Duff House and House of Dun. Robert was educated at Edinburgh

High School and the University – where he is said to have been friendly with Adam Ferguson – and he then became absorbed in his father's business. First with his father, and then with his elder brother John, Robert Adam was able 'to complete his architectural studies, to arrange his ideas and acquire his first rudiments in the practical construction of buildings'.[8] In 1754 he went to Italy, where he did a vast amount of work and at the same time lost no opportunity to cultivate the friendship of travelling English noblemen who might later be his patrons.[9] Gay, affectionate and personable, he was, like many an ambitious young Scot, at the same time enthusiastic and calculating. It was his conscious ambition to become the leading architect, not merely in Scotland, but in Great Britain: 'Scotland is but a narrow place. [I need] a greater a more extensive and more honourable scene I mean an English Life.'[10] With his usual shrewdness he recognised that Sir William Chambers was his principal rival, and he analysed Sir William's qualifications with coolness and skill:

> All the English who have travelled for these 5 Years are much prepossest in his favours, and imagine him a prodigy for Genius, for Sense and good taste. My own opinion is that he in great measure deserves their encomium. Though his taste is more Architectonick than Picturesque . . . His Sense is midling, but his appearance is genteel and his person good which are most material circumstances . . . [his manner] slow and dignify'd . . . conveying an Idea of great Wisdom, which is no less useful than all his other endowments, and I find sways much with every English man.[11]

During his three years abroad, Adam spent, according to his own reckoning, between eight and nine hundred pounds a year.[12] This was a very large investment, but it was worth it. He set up in London on his return, and thanks to his ability, his knowledge, his acquaintance in aristocratic circles and the publication in 1764 of his magnificent *Ruins of the Palace of the Emperor Diocletian at Spalatro*, he was soon the most sought-after architect in Britain. He led British taste out of the house of bondage designed for it by Lord Burlington according to the dictates of Vitruvius and Palladio, and established his own version of classical elegance, ornament, and 'movement'. For many years even his prodigious capacity for work was strained to the utmost. And when he died in 1792 he was accorded a funeral which was the measure of his success: his pall-bearers were the Duke of Buccleuch, the Earl of Coventry, the Earl of Lauderdale, Viscount Stormont, Lord Frederick Campbell, and Mr Pulteney.

Born in Kirkcaldy and buried in Westminster Abbey, Adam is a figure of distinction not only in the history of Scotland but in the whole history of architecture. His interiors especially – the proportions of his rooms, the furniture friezes and ceilings – are superb. Much of his work was done in England. All or large parts of Syon House and Osterley House in Middlesex, of Compton Verney in Warwickshire and of Kedleston Hall in Derbyshire are among his finest achievements, and rank with the masterpieces of British architecture. But it was in Scotland, in that 'narrow place', that he was given the opportunity to design great public buildings. Much of Edinburgh University is his, although it is not the original design in full; Register House is largely an Adam building; he also did the elevation of Charlotte Square, a specimen of eighteenth-century architecture and town planning which is still, in spite of some deficiencies and mutilations, one of the finest squares in Europe. Adam's contribution to the architecture of the New Town is substantial, and no one studying his work can afford to neglect what he did in Edinburgh.

The third architect who left a prominent mark on the Edinburgh scene was William Playfair. Playfair belonged to a later generation. He was born in London in 1789, the son of a Scots architect or builder of whom little is known except that he worked in London and wrote a treatise on 'A Method of Constructing Vapour Baths'. His father dying in 1793, young Playfair came north to join his uncle, Professor John Playfair, professor of mathematics and later of natural philosophy in the University of Edinburgh from 1785 to 1819. For a time he was a pupil of William Starke, an architect who had spent most of his life in the west of Scotland and who enjoyed a high reputation – seemingly well deserved – in his day.[13] Subsequently he went to London and worked in the office of Smirke and Wyatt, and in 1816 he visited France. Returning to Scotland in that year, he won the competition for a design for the completion of the University buildings, and at the age of twenty-seven found himself on the high road to fame and fortune. In the very centre of the city he has left his mark in the shape of two prominent and distinguished buildings, the Royal Institution (now the Royal Scottish Academy) and the National Gallery. His largest work is Donaldson's Hospital, built in the 1840s in what was then open country to the west of Edinburgh. Besides these, there are Playfair buildings all over central Edinburgh, both public buildings and private houses, and in addition Playfair was responsible for the lay-out of part of the city. In terms of the amount of building which he planned and supervised, Edinburgh owes more to Playfair than to any other architect. He was well trained and competent, meticulous in his plans, a devotee of the classical style (except in his country houses), a style which he interpreted in a manner which is sometimes a little heavy, but which, at its best, produced some of the finest classical buildings in Scotland. His masterpieces are probably the National Gallery, the Royal College of Surgeons, and the interior of the University Library. Dogged by ill health from the early 1840s, Playfair died, after a long illness, in 1857.

After these three men come a number of architects whose contributions to the building of Edinburgh, although not so important, were significant nevertheless. Probably the best known of these is William Burn. The son of a successful Edinburgh builder who designed the Nelson Monument on Calton Hill, Burn, like Playfair, worked for a time in Smirke's office in London. Returning to Edinburgh, he came second to Playfair in the design for the completion of the University, built St John's Episcopal Church in admirable imitation Gothic, and designed the Merchant Maidens' Hospital in 1816. The Melville Monument, which rises almost one hundred and fifty feet above St Andrew's Square and dominates any view of George Street looking east, is also by Burn. So is the Edinburgh Academy, built between 1823 and 1836, and so is John Watson's Hospital, at Belford. This latter is a long low building with a Doric portico, so simple and severe and with so much window space as to seem almost modern. It is hard to believe that the same architect designed the equally admirable but very different St John's Church.

Burn must have been nothing if not versatile. Perhaps this explains why, by the 1820s, he had already embarked on a career of un-interrupted professional success. After about 1830 he did little in Edinburgh, because his country houses, in which he departed from classical norms, came to occupy more and more of his time. By the 1840s he was probably the principal designer in Scotland of large houses for the nobility and gentry. In England too his popularity became very great, so much so that in 1844 he went to London and settled there. Genial, independent, frank and plain-spoken, he worked untiringly in his profession. It is said that in some years a million pounds worth of business passed through his office. Scottish baronial, it is to be feared, was as much his creation as anyone's; but the few public buildings in Edinburgh which he designed in the early part of his career are dignified and meritorious.

Four other men deserve to be remembered. Thomas Hamilton, born in 1784, was, like Burn, Playfair and Adam, the son of an architect or builder. He served, in his own words, 'a regular ap-prenticeship as an operative carpenter with my father, and after-wards acted as my father's assistant'.[14] In 1816, like Burn, he com-peted unsuccessfully against Playfair for the completion of the University buildings, but in 1825 he was given the contract for what is possibly his greatest work, the design of the Royal High School on Calton Hill. Another prominent building for which he was responsible was the Orphan Hospital (now the Dean Orphanage), erected in 1833 in what were then the outskirts of the town, and in the 1840s he designed the Physicians' Hall in Queen Street. He also provided a plan for the so-called 'western approach' south and west of the Castle. Hamilton did not make quite the same impact on his contemporaries as Burn or Playfair,[15] but he seems to have been a highly competent classical architect and an imaginative planner, besides which he was a founder member of the Royal Scottish Academy and an ardent early supporter of the National Gallery. He died in 1858. The others were born slightly earlier. Robert Reid (1776-1856) was the last King's Architect in Scotland. He designed the Bank of Scotland building on the Mound, and his re-facing of Parliament Square has called down upon his head much later oppro-brium. His design for St George's Church was also, unfortunately, preferred to a much superior design by Robert Adam. But, along with William Sibbald, of whom very little is known except that he worked for the city as a surveyor and built a house in Charlotte Square which was later owned by Sir William Fettes, Reid produced the plan for the streets of the New Town lying north of Queen Street. He also produced the altogether admirable elevation of Heriot Row. These are no mean achievements, and although Reid made mistakes and seems to have been somewhat touchy and difficult to get on with, Edinburgh owes him a great deal. Finally, there was Gillespie Graham (1777-1855). Born in Dunblane of poor parents, his architectural training is a mystery, and one of the few facts known about his personal life is that he married an heiress and added her name of Graham to his own name of James Gillespie. His first important commissions seem to have been for the designing or remodelling of country houses in central and south Scotland, and he continued to do such work throughout his life; Brodick Castle is probably his most notable achievement in this direction. His work in Edinburgh seems to have been less extensive than that of the other architects in this group, and his principal commission was to lay out and design houses in the Earl of Moray's property at Drumsheugh. But what he did here was superb. In and around Moray Place there are probably, from an architectural point of view, the most magnificent private dwelling houses in Edinburgh, combined into arrangements of streets and circuses which set this part of the New Town – always excepting Charlotte Square – in a class by itself. In later life Graham became a friend of Pugin, with whom he sometimes worked. He competed in the competition of 1836 to design new Houses of Parliament, but his design was not chosen. It is gratifying to know, however, that Graham, like Adam, Burn and Playfair, had his full share of material success in life.

Except for Robert Adam, the lives and personalities of these men remain somewhat obscure. Even the names of some of them are not widely known. There is no monument to any one of them in Edinburgh. But it is not necessary. The New Town is itself their memorial.

Appendix

1. M. S. Briggs, *The Architect in History* (Oxford, 1927).
2. Briggs, *op. cit.*, p. 303.
3. But if this is correct, it seems odd that he should have possessed at the time of his death a folio register of the baptisms in Edinburgh for the years 1732 to 1737.
4. Sir Robert Taylor was one of the most successful architects of the eighteenth century – in Hardwicke's well-known words, he and James Paine the elder 'nearly divided the practice of the profession between them, for they had few competitors till Mr Robert Adam entered the lists'. Taylor's experience was very varied. He built a house for the Duke of Grafton in Piccadilly; was architect to the Bank of England for several years; built Heaveningham Hall in Suffolk; the bridge at Maidenhead in 1780; and laid out the Foundling Hospital. Born in 1714, he began his career penniless and on his death in 1788 left £180,000.
5. Scottish Register, Vol. VI 1796, pp. 361-362.
6. From Craig's Executry and Testament, dated 11 November 1795, a complete list of the books in his library can be extracted. The principal architectural works are as follows:

    Adam: *Plans of Public Buildings and Gentlemen's Seats in Scotland.*
    Alberti: *On Painting and Statuary.*
    Campbell: *Vitruvius Britannicus* (including supplements by Wolfe and Gandon).
    Chambers: *Treatise on Civil Architecture. Plans Elevations and views of the Buildings etc. at Kew.*
    Gibbs: *Description of the Radcliffe Library. Rules for Drawing the Several Parts of Architecture. A Book of Architecture, containing Designs of Buildings and Ornaments.*
    Gwynn: *London and Westminster Improved.*
    Langley: *The Builder's Compleat Assistant.*
    Le Clerc: *Architecture.*
    Palladio: *On the Five Orders of Architecture.*
    Richardson: *Collection of Emblematical Figures.*
    Ware: *Designs of Inigo Jones and others.*
    Wood: *The Origin of Building.*

    Besides books on architecture, Craig's library contained numerous volumes of English poetry, works by Smollet, Swift and Sterne, and a substantial collection of miscellaneous items. He also possessed two violins, a collection of statuary, and a large number of paintings.
7. The reader is referred to the admirable biography, *Robert Adam and his Circle in Edinburgh and Rome* (London 1962) by John Fleming.

8. John Clerk of Eldin, quoted in Fleming, *op. cit.*, p. 86.
9. Referring to the Duke of Bridgewater he wrote, with no small satisfaction, 'we are as familiar as two Lap dogs' (letter dated 9 August 1755). After meeting the Earl of Chesterfield he remarked, 'This is the man I want for a patron' (letter dated 18 December 1755).
10. Letter dated 18 April 1755.
11. Letter dated 18 April 1755.
12. See letter dated 4 September 1756.
13. Starke died in 1813, apparently while still fairly young. He was, according to Cockburn, 'the best modern architect that Scotland had produced' (*Memorials*, p. 278). His ideas on town planning are set out in a small pamphlet entitled *Report . . . on the Plans for laying out the Grounds for Building between Edinburgh and Leith*, which shows an unusual blend of good sense and imagination. This small piece of writing brings Starke nearer to us as a personality than are many of his better-known contemporaries.
14. Letter to the Lord Provost, 1819.
15. According to a contemporary, this was largely due to 'taciturnity and bashfulness, the result in great measure of a constitutional deafness'.

I: The 'Proposals' of 1752

1. The Flodden wall was built in the sixteenth century. Traditionally, it is supposed to have been built immediately after and as a response to the disaster at Flodden in 1513. But in fact it was building from 1514, possibly earlier, to at least 1560. Where the wall crossed existing roads or streets, fortified gates were built, and these gates or ports, such as the West Port or Bristo Port, continued in use until the eighteenth century. A few fragments of the wall still remain. These fragments, and the general course of the wall, are described in the volume *City of Edinburgh* in the series prepared by the Royal Commission on Ancient Monuments (Scotland).
2. H. Arnot, *The History of Edinburgh* (Edinburgh 1788), pp. 233-234.
3. The Royalty consisted originally of those lands received in gift from the Crown and held under a series of Royal Charters conferring exclusive rights and priviliges in connection with markets, customs and other dues – powers which became, in effect, those of local government. Such powers could be extended geographically only by extension of the Royalty, and this required an Act of Parliament.
4. J. Grant, *Old and New Edinburgh* (London 1882), Vol. 1, p. 2.
5. That is, a room where the Convention of Royal Burghs might meet.
6. Letter to the Town Council, dated 12 October 1688. The Town obtained a Charter from James VII, but this was never ratified in Parliament.
7. Quoted in OSA, Vol. VIII, pp. 648-649.
8. *The Gentleman's Magazine*, 1745, p. 687.
9. The site of Argyle Square is now occupied by the Royal Scottish Museum. Adam Square was near the north-east corner of Chambers Street.
10. Drummond's Diary, 13 October 1738 (Manuscript, University of Edinburgh Library).
11. *Miscellanies in Prose and Verse* by Claudero (James Wilson) (Edinburgh 1766), p. 57.
12. T. Somerville, *My Own Life and Times, 1741-1814* (Edinburgh 1861), pp. 47-48.

II: Economic Background and Local Government

1. 'The Canongate was the greatest sufferer by the loss of our members of Parliament (which London now enjoys), many of them having their houses there, being the suburbs of Edinburgh, nearest to the King's Palace.' *Lucky Wood's Elegy* (1717).
2. D. Defoe, *History of the Union* (1786 edition), p. 415.

3. *Scottish Diaries and Memoirs, 1746-1843*, ed. J. G. Fyfe (Stirling 1948), p. 78. See also *ibid.*, pp. 234-235.
4. R. Chambers, *Traditions of Edinburgh* (Edinburgh 1825), Vol. I, pp. 20-21.
5. *ibid.*, Vol. II, p. 203.
6. H. Arnot, *The History of Edinburgh* (Edinburgh 1788), p. 379.
7. R. Chambers, *op. cit.*, vol I, p. 22.
8. 'Proposals for carrying on certain public works in the city of Edinburgh', *Scots Magazine* (1752), pp. 371, 375.
9. R. Somerville, *General View of the Agriculture of East Lothian* (1805), p. 215.
10. J. Hendrick, *General View of the Agriculture of Forfarshire* (1805), p. 517.
11. Sir James Steuart, *Works*, Vol. V (1805 ed. London), p. 321.
12. OSA, Vol. XVIII, p. 547.
13. OSA, Vol. XVIII, p. 547.
14. See Sir James Steuart, *op. cit.*, Vol. V, pp. 317-319.
15. NSA, Vol. I, p. 755.
16. H. Hamilton, *The Industrial Revolution in Scotland* (Oxford 1932), p. 241.
17. G. Robertson, *General View of the Agriculture of Kincardineshire* (London 1813), p. 325.
18. OSA, Vol. XI, p. 108.
19. OSA, Vol. VIII, p. 10.
20. OSA, Vol. XVIII, p. 177.
21. NSA, Vol. IX, p. 957.
22. OSA, Vol. XVI, p. 473.
23. OSA, Vol. VII, p. 341.
24. OSA, Vol. II, p. 308.
25. Hand-loom Weavers, *Reports from Assistant Commissioners (South of Scotland)*, pp. 2-5.
26. R. Bald, *General View of the Coal Trade of Scotland* (Edinburgh 1812), Chapter VII.
27. Of a mine in Old Monkland it was said in 1793, 'could colliers be placed in the pit to keep her constantly employed, she would turn out about 200 tons per day. The present output is 35,000 tons per year.' (OSA, Vol. VII, p. 389. Also Bald, *op. cit.*, pp. 73-74.)
28. See A. J. Youngson, 'Alexander Webster and his Account of the Number of People in Scotland in the Year 1755', in *Population Studies*, Vol. XV.
29. The statements in this paragraph are based on information about wages and prices scattered through the OSA and the NSA, and in the Reports on Agriculture. The following are a few of the many references used. OSA, Vol. V, pp. 59, 129, 162-163, 505-506; Vol. XVIII, pp. 287-291; Vol. XIX, pp. 84-85; Vol. XX, pp. 329, 442-444; NSA, Vol. II, pp. 45 and 222; Vol. X, pp. 511-512, 667-670; Vol. XI, pp. 229-230. See also Keith's *General View of the Agriculture of Aberdeenshire*, p. 526.
30. In this case the Government helped consumers by removing the tax on coal in 1794.
31. D. Bremner, *The Industries of Scotland* (Edinburgh 1869), p. 279.
32. D. Macpherson, *Annals of Commerce*, Year 1785.
33. NSA, Vol. XIII (Elgin), p. 53.
34. NSA, Vol. VI, p. 326.
35. NSA, Vol. VI, p. 233.
36. NSA, Vol. XV, p. 7.
37. OSA, Vol. IX, p. 210.

38. Reports of 200 illicit stills in Glenlivet alone need not, perhaps, be taken too literally; but for interesting and authentic details about the trade see *Scottish Diaries and Memoirs, 1746-1843* (ed. J. G. Fyfe, Stirling 1942), pp. 320 and 522-523.
39. NSA, Vol. I, p. 27 (parish of Liberton).
40. NSA, Vol. XIII (Banff), p. 36.
41. Around 1750, if Alexander Webster's *Enumeration* is to be trusted (as it probably is) Edinburgh was only twelve times the size of Haddington, and Glasgow only eight times as big as Ayr: by 1831 Edinburgh was twenty-three times the size of Haddington and Glasgow twenty-five times as big as Ayr. Webster's figures for the six largest towns are as follows: Edinburgh 48,815; Glasgow 23,546; Aberdeen 15,730; Dundee 12,477; Leith 9,405; Perth 9,019.
42. The figures were as follows: *Town population, 1801*, Glasgow 77,421; Edinburgh 66,544; Aberdeen 27,508; Dundee 26,804; Leith 15,272; Perth 14,878; TOTAL 228,427.
43. The figures were as follows: *Town population, 1831*, Glasgow 202,426; Edinburgh 136,301; Aberdeen 58,019; Dundee 45,355; Leith 25,855; Perth 20,016; TOTAL 487,972.
44. G. Robertson, *General View of the Agriculture of Midlothian* (1793), p. 26.
45. OSA, Vol. VI, p. 547.
46. NSA, Vol. II, p. 193.
47. OSA, Vol. X, p. 139.
48. The Census of 1841 is the first to contain detailed information about the occupations of the people.
49. These clerks, according to Littlejohn, were 'universally acknowledged to be the hardest worked (so far as mere time is concerned) of the labouring class'. H. D. Littlejohn, *Report on the Sanitary Condition of the City of Edinburgh* (Edinburgh 1865), p. 105.
50. Cockburn, *Memorials of his Time* (1910 ed.), p. 137.
51. During his subsequent career he was also, at different times, Home Secretary, Secretary at War, First Lord of the Admiralty, and, for all practical purposes, Secretary of State for India.
52. G. W. T. Omond, *The Lord Advocates of Scotland* (Edinburgh 1883), Vol. II, pp. 157-161.
53. Cockburn, *op. cit.*, p. 73. Cockburn also says: 'if the ladies and gentlemen who formed the society of my father's house believed all that they said about the horrors of French bloodshed, and of the anxiety of people here to imitate them, they must have been wretched indeed. Their talk sent me [a small boy] to bed shuddering.' (p. 39.)
54. Omond, *op. cit.*, Vol. II, pp. 313-314.
55. 'He was dragged to the parapet of the bridge, and was on the point of being thrown over, when he seized one of his assailants, exclaiming, "If I go, sir, you go with me!" He was then pulled back into the middle of the roadway, and, managing to escape, took refuge in a shop in one of the adjoining streets.' Omond, *op. cit.*, Vol. II, pp. 316-317.
56. Omond, *op. cit.*, Vol. II, p. 338.
57. D. Robertson and M. Wood, *Castle and Town* (Edinburgh 1928), pp. 188-189.
58. Cockburn, *op. cit.*, p. 87.
59. Sir William Forbes was born in 1739. His family was ancient but impoverished. Educated in Edinburgh, he was apprenticed in the famous Banking house of Messrs Coutts, where he became a partner in 1761. The

business was reconstructed in 1763, and in 1773 it became Forbes Hunter and Co. In this form it continued into the nineteenth century with Sir William as leading partner, and was notable for its sound management. Sir William, who inherited the family estate at Pitsligo in 1781, always took a prominent share in charitable and other public work in Edinburgh. He was closely associated with the Merchant Company, the Royal Society of Edinburgh, the Society of Antiquaries and the Royal Infirmary. He died, a rich man, in 1806.

60. A. R. B. Haldane, *New Ways through the Glens* (Edinburgh 1962), pp 41-42.

III: Public Buildings before 1784

1. Defoe, *A Tour of Great Britain* (1927 ed. Vol. II), p. 708.
2. A. Topham, *Letters from Edinburgh* (London 1776), pp. 8-9.
3. *The Gentleman's Magazine*, 1745, p. 685.
4. These buildings ran along the north side of St Giles and were separated from the Church by a narrow, gloomy foot-path only a few feet in width. Their position is clearly shown on Edgar's maps of 1742 and 1756.
5. James Grant, *Old and New Edinburgh*, Vol. I, p. 156.
6. Smollett, *Humphry Clinker* (ed. Saintsbury, Vol. II), p. 54.
7. Quoted in Grant, *op. cit.*, p. 155.
8. An Exchange had been privately built in Edinburgh in 1680, in Parliament Close. It was never used for the purpose intended, and was severely damaged in the Great Fire of 1700.
9. TCM, 6 May 1752.
10. TCM, 6 May 1752.
11. TCM, 1 July 1752.
12. TCM, 1 July 1752.
13. *ibid*.
14. *ibid*.
15. Where agreement could not be reached, the price was determined by a jury of fifteen 'substantial and disinterested persons' with power to examine documents and to call witnesses.
16. The price was kept down in some cases by understandings that sellers of property would have the first refusal of space in the new building. Not all vendors were obliging: 'It is not to be expected that among so many proprietors as the area of the Exchange belongs to, some wrong-headed covitous man would not be found who will insist on an extravagant price.'
17. Now the site of Charlotte Square and nearby streets.
18. Quoted in OEC, Vol. XXII, p. 190.
19. *The Caledonian Mercury*, 2 July 1763.
20. TCM, 22 October 1763.
21. *ibid*., 7 November 1764.
22. TCM, 16 January 1765.
23. *ibid*., 20 February 1765.
24. William Mylne was a member of the well known family which held the hereditary office of master-mason to the kings of Scotland, conferred by James III. His father was a magistrate, and he himself was a member of the Edinburgh town council in 1761-62 and 1764-65. He was a brother of Robert Mylne, one of the better known architects of the eighteenth century.

25. TCM, 1 May 1765.
26. *ibid.*, 17 July 1765.
27. This accident seems to have been due to a failure by Mylne to appreciate how high the southern part of the bridge would have to be built in order to meet the road from the High Street without that road having to fall very steeply to the level of the bridge. The Town stipulated that the road should have only a gentle slope. When Mylne found that the initial height of the bridge did not answer, he raised the height by piling earth on top of the arches. The additional weight, coupled with inadequate foundations, caused the collapse.
28. TCM, 24 August 1770.
29. According to Arnot, writing in 1778, the bridge at that date had already cost £17,354. (H. Arnot, *The History of Edinburgh*, 1788 ed., p. 315.)
30. Quoted in 'The General Register House' by H. M. Paton in OEC, Vol. XVII, p. 149.
31. Register of Reports to Exchequer, Vol. VI.
32. Seven in number, these Trustees were the principal judicial officials of Scotland.
33. It had been proposed in 1722 that the records might be lodged in one of the towers of Heriot's Hospital.
34. Act of the Town Council, 13 September 1769.
35. Minutes of the Trustees, 30 July 1772.
36. *ibid.*, 12 October 1773.
37. Reference in OEC, Vol. XVII, p. 163.
38. See Chapter VI.
39. 'Before the erection of the South Bridge', says Chambers, 'the Horse Wynd was the best access to the City from the southern districts, and was then a place of fashionable resort. Many respectable people and even noblemen had their residences in it, as most of the houses, which are spacious and well built, testify to this day, though the place is now completely degraded by the intrusion of the vulgar.' (Chambers, *op. cit.*, Vol. I, p. 189.) Horse Wynd entered the Cowgate from the south, a little to the east of Parliament Square, being a continuation of Potter Row.
40. Grant, *op. cit.*, Vol. II, p. 269.
41. *ibid.*, Vol. I, p. 379. This area is clearly shown on Edgar's map of 1765, where it appears as 'Mr Adams New Building'.
42. Chambers, *op. cit.*, Vol. I, p. 38.
43. The familiar comment, which appears in Chambers' *Traditions of Edinburgh*, is apposite: 'It was formerly considered a great affair to go out to George's Square to dinner; and on such an occasion a gentleman would stand half an hour at the Cross, in his full dress, with powdered and bagged hair, sword and cane, in order to tell his friends *with whom* and *where* he was going to dine.' (Chambers, *op. cit.*, Vol. I, p. 38.)

IV: The New Town: Craig's Plan

1. The Town Council agreed to put forward a new request for extension in August 1765. The Act extending the royalty was finally passed in 1767 (Geo. III an. 7. c. 27).
2. We do know that some street names were changed in the course of 1767. Thus Forth Street became Queen Street and St Giles Street became Princes Street. This latter alteration was made on the personal suggestion of George III, to whom Craig dedicated his plan. The dedication made no

mention of the Magistrates, who apparently were not consulted. This high-handed action on Craig's part caused the Town Council some justifiable irritation, and it is possible that bad feeling over this had an adverse effect on Craig's subsequent career.

3. In the Clerk of Penicuik papers in Register House, however, there are 'Notes on a plan for the New Town' dated 1776 and bearing the initials M.T. The notes unfortunately give no indication of the nature of the plan to which they refer.

4. Arnot, *op. cit.*, p. 319.

5. S. E. Rasmussen, *London, The Unique City* (1934). For an altogether admirable account of the development of the London squares and of London in general, see Sir John Summerson, *Georgian London* (London 1945).

6. The Royal Crescent, the masterpiece of the Wood's, both father and son, was not begun until after 1766.

7. Leon Battista Alberti (1404-72), author of *De re aedificatoria*.

8. Antonio Averlino, pseud. Filarete (*c.* 1400 - *c.* 1469), author of *Trattato d'Architettura*.

9. S. E. Rasmussen, *Towns and Buildings* (Liverpool 1951), p. 114.

10. John Gwynn, *London and Westminster Improved* (London 1766), p. 77.

11. *ibid.*, p. 80.

12. Even the proposed canal was far from a new idea, for similar proposals were current in the fifteenth century.

13. The architect seems to have regretted this omission, for in 1774 he published an amended plan showing a very large circus indeed.

14. TCM, 14 October 1767.

15. In November 1767 a committee was appointed to advise with John and William Adam regarding sewers for the New Town.

16. TCM, 31 January 1781. The implication seems to be that the inhabitants of the New Town, 'inconvenienced' by the distance from church, solved the problem, at least to some extent, by staying at home.

17. The house was begun in 1772. The master mason was William Jamieson, who was also employed in the building of Register House. It is a curious point that Dundas's house was the only one in the New Town with no kind of basement or sunk floor. In 1795 the house became the headquarters of the Office of Excise for Scotland, and then in 1825 was purchased by the Royal Bank for £35,300. It still serves as the head office of the bank.

18. TCM, 7 March 1781.

19. *ibid.*

20. TCM, 5 September 1781.

21. TCM, 25 March 1795. This cost includes a model of the church and spire, priced at £63 0 4d.

22. Approximately the present site of the North British Hotel.

23. Sir William Forbes lived on the south-west corner of St Andrew's Street; Hume on the east side of South St David's Street.

24. Mr David Rae, advocate, afterwards Lord Eskgrove.

25. Quoted in OEC, Vol. I, p. 150.

26. According to Chambers (*op. cit.*, Vol. I, p. 62) Young had already, in 1766, built the first house in the area of the New Town, a tenement near the site of St Andrew's Church, 'quite different, in appearance, from the surrounding buildings, [it] rather resembled the comfortable country-houses of the period. When it was erected, the New Town was hanging *in dubio*, and it was uncertain if it would ever be more than a retired rural villa; wherefore the interest excited on its foundation was very

great, and an immense concourse of people was gathered to witness the ceremony.'

27. Chambers, *op. cit.*, Vol. I, p. 67.
28. As is well known, David Hume lived latterly in South St David's Street. His name appears in a somewhat obscure entry in the Town Council Minutes for 22 December 1773. According to this entry, William Jameson, mason, bought two lots of land in St Andrew's Square in 1767 and another, lying near to his previous purchases, in South St David's Street in 1770. He built three houses, and sold them to Mr Hunter, Patrick Crawford of Auchinames and David Hume Esq. In July 1771, Mr Hume feued a lot fronting South St David's Street next to his own, 'and gave part of the said lot to Mr. Hunter, and Mr. Crawford', making them liable for the feu duty on that lot. What advantage Hume obtained from this transaction is not clear; perhaps he kept a small piece of garden ground in the new lot.
29. TCM, 8 October 1788. The boundary line appears not to have cut through the open space of Charlotte Square itself. But if no building could be erected within 90 feet of the line, even a line well clear of the square itself would have made building an impossibility.
30. *ibid.*, 28 March 1792.
31. The garden walls to the north of Charlotte Square still provide evidence of where the boundary ran. It is shown very clearly in Ainslie's map of 1804.
32. TCM, 24 August 1791.
33. J. Farington, Notebook No. 3, unprinted MS. in the Edinburgh Room, Edinburgh Public Library.
34. J. Farington, *ibid.*
35. Arnot, *op. cit.*, p. 371 (1788 ed.).
36. Grant, *op. cit.*, Vol. I, p. 343.
37. *Historic Sketch of the Royal College of Physicians* (Edinburgh 1925), p. 41.
38. The college had already had experience of the too grand ideas which architects might entertain. Planning in 1760 to build a new hall on the site of the old one in the Cowgate, the College sent plans for a hall costing £800 to Robert Adam, for his comments. Adam, after inspecting the plan, 'gave it as his opinion that it was unsuitable, and quite unworthy of the Body for whom it was intended; – and with great liberality, Mr. Adam gave, spontaneously and gratuitously, a plan of his own, the execution of which was estimated to cost between £5,000 and £6,000, exclusive of the statues, bustos, and bas-reliefs, which he recommended as appropriate and almost necessary. This plan, after being handed about and admired was laid aside as unsuitable to the finances of the College.' (*Historic Sketch of the Royal College of Physicians*, p. 41.)
39. Letter dated 10 November 1779, in archives of the Royal College of Physicians.
40. The Royal College of Physicians' Library contains some of Craig's original elevations. The College also possesses the large model of the Hall which was made to accompany the plans.
41. Farington, notebook number 3, in Edinburgh Public Library, Edinburgh Room, manuscripts.
42. Letter to Robert Adam dated 23 March 1791. In the possession of Dr D. C. Simpson.
43. *The City of Edinburgh* (Royal Commission on Ancient Monuments, Scotland; Edinburgh 1951), p. 207.
44. TCM, 31 January 1781.

45. TCM, 22 February 1792.
46. TCM, 21 June 1797.
47. TCM, 3 March 1784.
48. For further details, see T. Hunter and R. Paton, *Report on the Common Good of the City of Edinburgh* (Edinburgh 1905), pp. 25-29.
49. Arnot, *op. cit.*, p. 521.
50. D. Robertson, *The Princes Street Proprietors* (Edinburgh 1935), p. 269.
51. TCM, 3 March 1784.
52. TCM, 23 November 1791.
53. TCM, 26 October 1791.
54. The sum of £2,308 appears in the accounts for 1791-92, spent on a new water supply for the city. Seven-inch cast-iron pipes were laid between Swanston and Edinburgh, and distribution throughout the city included a conduit over the North Bridge. Over £2,000 had been spent a few years before, in 1787-88, on laying cast-iron pipes from Comiston Reservoir to Heriot's Garden.
55. Feuars in the Ancient Royalty do not seem to have been prompt in payment; their arrears in 1797 amounted to no less than £1,436, or about two years' payment!

V: Extensions Southward

1. The area in question lay outside the Royalty, and had been divided into six districts by an Act of 1771. This Act appointed five Commissioners for each of the districts, with powers to arrange cleaning, lighting, and watching, and to assess occupiers of houses and shops for these purposes. The system was extended throughout Edinburgh in 1785, and made uniform in its working in 1805.
2. TCM, 16 February 1785.
3. It was laid down that this cess did not 'give any right whatever or found any claim' to any other extension of the authority of the city over the southern districts.
4. Act of Council, 16 February 1785. Brown was one of the Commissioners, and Wm. Jameson, who had acted as clerk of works on behalf of the town while the North Bridge was building, was another.
5. The town guard-house, 'long, low and ugly', stood about thirty yards further up the High Street from the Tron, towards St Giles.
6. Disposition by John Adam, dated 21 March 1786, in Edinburgh Town Council archives.
7. TCM, 14 September 1785.
8. Chambers, *op. cit.*, Vol. I, p. 187.
9. J. Stark, *Picture of Edinburgh* (Edinburgh 1825), p. 80.
10. TCM, 22 August 1792. The muddle of the city's finances is discussed in Chapter IX.
11. The general lay-out of the University building, which is relatively modest in scale, is traditional in conception; it is very similar, for example, to Queen's College in Oxford. There is no date on the University frontage plans, but the design for the building to face the University is dated 1791. This plan carries the following explanation:
    Elevation of a new Design for a building proposed to front the new College of Edinburgh, containing in the center a Concert room, Retiring rooms, Tea rooms, Kitchen Offices and other conveniences. In the

South Wing a Bookseller or Stationers Shop and also an apartment for the Highland Society. . . . In the North Wing a commodious Coffee or Eating house with ten front and back shops under Colonades in the intermediate spaces with Kitchens below and Bed rooms above for the Shop keeper.

12. Most of the surviving criticisms are contained in letters and papers, the majority seemingly written by Robert Adam, in the Penicuik Collection in Register House, Edinburgh (Box 189).

13. Letter in the *Morning Chronicle*, dated 30 July 1786.

14. There are two copies of this rare pamphlet in the Edinburgh Room of the Edinburgh Public Library.

15. These were west of the approach from the High Street to the North Bridge – approximately behind the present-day *Scotsman* offices.

16. TCM, 10 May 1786.

17. On Ainslie's map of 1780 Lower Baxter's Close has disappeared and there is shown a road which joins the 'Earthen Bridge' with the Lawn-market, more or less following the route of the existing Bank Street. This no doubt depicts what was in the minds of the Town Council in the 1780s.

18. There is, however, an 'Account for the Lawn Market Communication' in the City Chamberlain's books which covers the period May 1786 to November 1795. This account covers expenditures of over £12,000. Most of them, however, are for the purchase of the properties mentioned above, and for their upkeep.

19. The figure hazarded by Stark is 1,800 cartloads a day. Supposing each cart to be unloaded in only five minutes, and ten carts to be unloaded at a time, this would have required a working day of 15 hours.

20. Arnot, *op. cit.*, p. 300.

21. *Scots Magazine* (1785), p 632.

22. Quoted in Grant, *op. cit.*, Vol. III, p. 20.

23. Minutes of the Senatus Academicus, 14 December 1767.

24. Report of the Joint Committee relative to the intended plan of Rebuilding the College, in TCM, 23 December 1767.

25. City Treasurer's Accounts, 1767-68, p. 72.

26. According to one visitor, William Robertson, then Principal, considered 'this method more advantageous to youth than keeping them shut up in colleges, as at Oxford and Cambridge. He says that when young men are not kept from intercourse with society, besides that they do not acquire that rude and savage air which retired study gives, the continual examples which they meet with in the world, of honour and riches acquired by learning and merit, stimulate them more strongly to the attainment of these; and that they acquire, besides, easy and insinuating manners, which render them better fitted in the sequel for public employments.' Quoted in Grant, *op. cit.*, Vol. III, p. 20.

27. Minutes of the Senatus Academicus, 19 October 1789.

28. Proceedings of the Trustees, University of Edinburgh manuscript collection.

29. *The City of Edinburgh*, p. 115. (Royal Commission on the Ancient Monuments of Scotland, HMSO, 1951.)

30. Details of the squabbles which went on are to be found in a series of letters written by John Paterson to Robert Adam, now in the possession of Dr D. C. Simpson. I am much obliged to Dr Simpson for allowing me to draw on these letters, and to make a small quotation from one of them.

31. Letter to the Lord Provost, dated 30 August 1791, University of Edinburgh manuscript collection.
32. A rough draft says 'upwards of £3,000', so £5,000 may have been an exaggeration.

VI: Public Works

1. OEC, Vol. III, p. 237.
2. On the east side of the Square had stood a tenement reputed to be the highest building in Edinburgh. It had seven storeys towards Parliament Close and fifteen towards the Cowgate. It was seriously damaged in the Great Fire of 1700, and rebuilt to a height of eleven storeys.
3. Cockburn, *op. cit.*, p. 98.
4. Hot air circulated through the legs of small cast-iron tables. These tables are still in place.
5. Grant, *op. cit.*, Vol. II, p. 107.
6. Report by William Rae Esq., Sheriff-Depute of the County of Edinburgh; to the Commissioners for Erecting a New Jail, etc. in the City of Edinburgh. (Edinburgh 1813.)
7. Cockburn, *op. cit.*, p. 228.
8. Cockburn, *op. cit.*, p. 228.
9. To be precise, estimated total cost rose from £37,433 to £76,923. This was due partly to early underestimating of the main items, partly to the adoption of more ambitious plans, chiefly to the virtual omission in early estimates of allowance for 'sundries' – legal expenses, compensation for damage, interest payments, drains, retaining walls etc.
10. Minute Book, Calton Bridge Commissioners, 30 July 1816.
11. *ibid.*, 6 December 1815.
12. Cockburn, *op. cit.*, p. 328.
13. Minute Book, Calton Bridge Commissioners, letter dated 21 April 1818.
14. *ibid.*, 6 February 1818.
15. Minute Book, Calton Bridge Commissioners, 13 October 1818.
16. *ibid.*, 20 January 1820.
17. Minute Book, Calton Bridge Commissioners, Vol. II, 24 January 1822.
18. The triumphal arch was agreed to immediately after Lorimer's first offer of £25,000 for feuing areas had been received.
19. Why less was repaid to the Royal Bank and to Sir William Forbes & Co. than was originally borrowed is not explained.
20. The main item in Elliot's remuneration was £889, or 5 per cent of the cost of the bridge, stated for this purpose at £17,785. But in the accounts themselves the cost of the bridge is given as £12,329.
21. Minutes of Committees for feuing Calton Hill Grounds, etc. July 1812.
22. George Heriot (1563-1623) was an Edinburgh jeweller who became goldsmith to Anne of Denmark ('never, truly, did tradesman get a better customer' – W. Steven, *History of George Heriot's Hospital*, p. 5), then to her husband James VI, and finally to large numbers of the Scottish and English nobility and gentry. Almost all his estate, some £24,000, went to the establishment of a trust to found and administer a 'Hospital' for poor children. Provision was made for the funds being invested in land, in as close proximity to Edinburgh as was expedient, and the Trustees pursued this policy with energy and success. By the middle of the eighteenth century the Trust possessed the greater part of the lands

on which Edinburgh now stands. Heriot's Hospital was largely built between 1628 and 1659. There is no evidence that it was designed by Inigo Jones. The attractive north gateway was designed and the grounds were laid out by Playfair on the 200th anniversary of the foundation, in 1828.

23. James Clerk of Craighall (latterly Clerk-Rattray), advocate, Sheriff Depute of Edinburgh, Baron of Exchequer from 1809. Died 1831.
24. Gilbert Innes of Stow, Director of the Royal Bank 1787-93, Depute Governor, 1794-1837. He was reputed to be one of the wealthiest men in Edinburgh in his day.
25. Minutes, Calton Hill Grounds etc., p. 54.
26. Minutes, Calton Hill Grounds etc., p. 55.
27. Cockburn, *Memorials*, p. 278.
28. *loc. cit.*, p. 16.
29. *loc. cit.*, p. 7.
30. *loc. cit.*, pp. 7-8.
31. *loc. cit.*, p. 8.
32. *loc. cit.*, p. 10.
33. *loc. cit.*, p. 7.
34. *loc. cit.*, pp. 11-12.
35. Minutes, Calton Hill Grounds etc., 1 July 1815.
36. The actual figure was £877. This included the first prize of three hundred guineas, divided between William Reid of Glasgow, Alexander Nasmyth of York Place, Edinburgh (the landscape painter) and Richard Crichton, of James's Street, Edinburgh.
37. Minutes, Calton Hill Grounds etc., 5 February 1818.
38. *Playfair's Report*, 1819.
39. Appeal was made to the example of Queen Street: 'Who would not regret if the gardens below Queen Street were to be swept away, and their place occupied by an insipid and monotonous pile of buildings?' *loc. cit.*
40. TCM, 3 July 1822.
41. *ibid.*
42. *ibid.*, 26 February 1823.
43. TCM, 9 April 1823.
44. *ibid.*
45. Cockburn, who attended the school, had a different opinion. He describes it as 'notorious for its severity and riotousness. . . . I was driven stupid.' Cockburn, *op. cit.*, pp. 3-4.
46. TCM, 9 April 1823.
47. *ibid.*
48. TCM, 7 June 1825.
49. TCM, 6 July 1825.
50. Sir James Summerson, *Architecture in Britain, 1530-1830* (London 1953), p. 311.
51. It is so referred to in a letter by Playfair of 1829.
52. Notice of 1822, in National Library for Scotland, MS. Collection.
53. William Burn to R. E. Cockerell, letter dated 9 July 1824. According to Burn, Cockerell's suggestions for his own remuneration were misrepresented, by the secretary, to a meeting of the Committee to which some members were not even invited. Playfair then offered to do the work for less, and so secured the appointment. The truth of this cannot be checked.
54. Playfair to Cockerell, letter dated 30 June 1829.

55. Playfair to Cockerell, letter dated 27 May 1825.
56. Playfair to Cockerell, letter dated 3 June 1829.
57. A. Malcolm, *History of the Bank of Scotland* (Edinburgh, 1948), p. 205.
58. TCM, 24 July 1822.
59. In the Library of the University of Edinburgh there is an elevation of the Royal Institution dated 26.9.1822.
60. Manufactures in Scotland: Fine Arts, Minute Book, 14 January 1823.
61. Board of Manufactures, Minutes, 18 May 1824.
62. Of the pillars, only the northern part of the west colonnade is Culallo stone.
63. Board of Manufactures, Minutes, 2 April 1832.
64. In 1835 the building naturally did not have the statue of Queen Victoria over the main pediments, nor did it have the two sphinxes above the side pediments. These three items were added in 1844.
65. TCM, 18 March 1824.
66. TCM, 8 April 1824.
67. TCM, 1 June 1824.
68. This report also put an end to plans by Archibald Elliot for 'improving' St Giles, having 'for their object a complete and entire demolition of its external form . . . with the exception of the tower'. Instead, Burn and Hamilton suggested that repairs be carried out at a cost of £13,000. Unfortunately, what Elliot proposed to do to the exterior was subsequently done to the interior, more or less, by Burn himself.
69. Report of a Committee of the Faculty of Advocates accompanying a letter to the Town Council dated 9 March 1825.
70. Letter to the Town Council dated 1 March 1825.
71. *Report on the Improvements of the City of Edinburgh* (Edinburgh 1827), Section I.
72. *loc. cit.*, p. 7.
73. *ibid.*, p. 2.
74. *loc. cit.*, p. 4.
75. *loc. cit.*, p. 4.
76. *loc. cit.*, p. 8.
77. TCM, 14 March 1832.
78. Letter from Tod's Trustees to the Town Council, dated 30 March 1831.
79. *Statement relative to the Improvements on the City of Edinburgh by a New Approach from the West* (Edinburgh 1826), p. iii.
80. *ibid.* The quotations which follow are likewise from this Report.
81. *Report on the Improvements of the City of Edinburgh by a Committee to consider and prepare the Heads of a Bill* (Edinburgh 1827).
82. This was to be Tolbooth St John's, built in 1843 as a meeting place for the General Assembly.
83. The Committee also mentioned that the desirability of draining the High Street had been 'urged upon their notice', but they did not include this among their proposals because a drain there would not serve 'the inhabitants of the wynds and closes, who are to those of the front street in the proportion of at least ten to one, [and who] would continue, after the drain as much as now, to discharge their filth into the street'. To drain the closes would be enormously costly, although 'the Committee do not say that these objections should for ever stop the project of making drains in the High Street'.
84. *loc. cit.*, p. 13.
85. *loc. cit.*, p. 22.

86. This ridiculous number was reached largely by including 30 Commissioners of Police and 28 private citizens.
87. *loc. cit.*, p. 15.
88. *loc. cit.*, p. 25.
89. *loc. cit.*, p. 51.
90. Reports to the Commissioners, Minute Book, Vol. II, 17 August 1834.
91. John Grindlay and Grindlay's Trustees promised £75 each. Other prominent guarantors were Ramsay Bonar and Co. (£100), Sir William Forbes Hunter and Co. (£100) and Sir John Sinclair (£50).
92. The task of preparing plans and elevations for Castle Terrace, however, was separately reserved for Burn and Hamilton.
93. Expenditure to date plus the estimated £26,568 still needed to complete totalled £155,177. This was, of course, much less than the estimated £270,000 which the far more grandiose original scheme had been calculated to cost in the 1820s. But even the more modest burden kept proving too heavy for the plans made to meet it.
94. TCM, 10 April 1811.
95. TCM, 10 April 1811.
96. *ibid.*, 3 March 1813.
97. According to Adam Black, the ultimate cost was £35,627. See *View of the Financial Affairs of the City of Edinburgh* by Adam Black (Edinburgh 1835).
98. *The Scots Magazine*, Vol. 76, p. 166.
99. I. G. Lindsay, *Georgian Edinburgh*, p. 33 (Edinburgh 1948).
100. The screen within the church was erected as late as 1912. It is a masterpiece of modern Scottish woodwork.
101. Quoted in Grant, *op. cit.*, Vol. II, p. 134. Grant himself describes St Cuthbert's, after its rebuilding in 1774 and 1789, as 'completed in the hideous taste and nameless style peculiar to Scottish ecclesiastical architecture during the times of the first three Georges' (Vol. II, p. 134). The appearance of St Cuthbert's has been considerably altered since these words were written.
102. Sederunt Book, Register House Trustees, 1827.
103. TCM, 15 March 1815.
104. *ibid.*
105. Communication from the Committee, quoted in TCM, 7 June 1815.
106. In 1812 the Town Council had paid Reid no less than £571 15/- for 'plans and elevations to complete the University on a reduced plan and for drawings and designs for St. George's Church'. TCM, 4 March 1812.
107. *Reports etc. relative to the Completion of the College Buildings* (1816), Appendix I, p. 19.
108. *ibid.*, Appendix II, p. 48.
109. *ibid.*, p. 43.
110. *ibid.*, p. 61.
111. *ibid.*, p. 31.
112. Playfair's *Report*, p. 10.
113. *ibid.*, p. 7.
114. Professor Leslie, Professor of Mathematics, in Reports of the Senatus etc. Appendix II, p. 38.
115. The north face of the north range was left plain because it overlooked nothing but a narrow lane. It now overlooks Chambers Street, and is unfortunately the most easily seen of all the external elevations.
116. Hamilton treated his chair as a complete sinecure, and never lectured. But

to do him justice, his predecessor, who had tried hard had never succeeded in attracting an audience.

117. *Report*, Appendix II, p. 53.
118. Parliamentary Papers, 1826, Vol. XX. Estimates and Miscellaneous Services, Paper 135.
119. The existing dome was added in 1887 to a design by Sir R. Rowand Anderson.
120. *ibid.*, 1831-32, Vol. XXVII, Miscellaneous Estimates I, item No. 9, p. 14.

VII: Private Development after 1800

1. Cockburn, *op. cit.*, pp. 347-348.
2. Heriot Trustees, Minutes, 18 April 1791.
3. *ibid.*, 7 June 1790.
4. *ibid.*, 13 December 1792.
5. *ibid.*, 8 October 1792.
6. *ibid.*, 31 December 1801.
7. *ibid.*, 22 August 1796.
8. *ibid.*, 15 February 1802
9. 'Reminiscences of a Town Clerk', being the diary of James Laurie, quoted in OEC, Vol. XIV, p. 156.
10. These last few words are a little mysterious, as it is clear from the Register of Feus that lots in Heriot Row were feued as early as 1803, and it seems unlikely that no building was completed on any of these lots before 1806.
11. Heriot Trustees, Minutes, 21 January 1814.
12. *ibid.*, 16 April 1821.
13. Heriot Trustees, Minutes, 15 December 1812.
14. *Miscellanies in Prose and Verse by Claudero* (James Wilson) (Edinburgh), 'On Laying the Foundation Stone of St Bernard's Mineral Well, 15 September 1760'.
15. Quoted in Grant, *op. cit.*, Vol. III, p. 75.
16. Cumberland Hill, *Historic Memorials and Reminiscences of Stockbridge* (Edinburgh 1887), pp. 59-60.
17. Heriot Trustees, Minutes, 21 August 1829.
18. *ibid.*, 4 July 1822.
    While there is no doubt that Gillespie Graham was responsible for the ground plan, there is one piece of evidence which suggests that William Burn may have at least had a hand in the design of the buildings. This is a letter, now in the muniment room at Darnaway Castle, from Burn to the Earl of Moray, which includes the following words: 'I asked Mr. Gillespie [Graham] to call and showed him my sketches . . . I have been most anxious to produce something that shall be extremely productive of advantageous speculation, and totally different from the monotony of our present Streets and Squares.' (Letter dated 15 April 1822). There is no trace of a reply to this letter, and Burn may not in the end have been employed. But the obvious inference is that Burn and Graham were collaborating.
19. The Earl of Moray built only one house, No. 28 Moray Place. Heriot's Trustees completed four houses in Lynedoch Place, but the circumstances, as explained above, were peculiar. The City of Edinburgh, as far as is known, built no private houses in the New Town.

20. Fettes' house was No. 13. Sir William records in his diary, with satisfaction, that Sir John Marjoribanks paid £3,420 for No. 12, that No. 23 changed hands at £3,700, and that in 1815 No. 7 fetched no less than £5,005. Houses in the Square were frequently the security for loans of between £3,000 and £4,000. Good houses elsewhere cost far less.
21. Chambers, *op. cit.*, Vol. I, p. 51.
22. *ibid.*, pp. 52-53.
23. Nasmyth, *op. cit.*, p. 55. Compare Chambers: 'Towards the end of the century, an unexpected impulse was given to the whole [expansion of the town] by the French Revolutionary war, which threw immense accessions of genteel inhabitants into the capital.' (Chambers, *op. cit.*, Vol. I, p. 76.)
24. That is to say, two thousand dwellings; many of these dwellings were flats, only parts of a house. The number of actual buildings was therefore much less than two thousand.
25. Creech in OSA, Vol. VI, p. 583.
26. See above, p. 86.
27. A. Trotter, *A Plan of Communication between the New and the Old Town of Edinburgh* (Edinburgh 1829), p. 1. See also p. 170 ff. above.
28. Letter from James Hope, W.S., quoted in Haldane, *op. cit.*, p. 202.
29. Chambers, *op. cit.*, Vol. I, p. 239. Chambers adds: 'An old gentleman, who was their relation, told us that the first time he ever saw these beautiful girls, was in the High Street. Miss Jane, afterwards Duchess of Gordon, was riding upon a sow, which Miss Betty thumped lustily behind with a stick.'
30. A. Blanqui, *Voyage d'un Jeune Français en Angleterre et en Ecosse* (Paris 1824), p. 237.
31. *ibid.*, p. 227.

VIII: Social Life

1. Cockburn, *op. cit.*, p. 197.
2. Cockburn, *op. cit.*, pp. 181-182.
3. Cockburn, *op. cit.*, p. 164.
4. The reference is in Chambers, to an 'ancient inhabitant . . . who has seen Provost Drummond's coach mobbed in the High Street for his new-fangled notions about new towns'. (Chambers, *op. cit.*, Vol. I, p. 35.)
5. Topham, *op. cit.*, pp. 355-356.
6. Chambers, *op. cit.*, Vol. II, p. 141.
7. Cockburn, *op. cit.*, p. 183.
8. Cockburn, *op. cit.*, p. 184.
9. Topham, *op. cit.*, p. 152.
10. Cockburn, *op. cit.*, p. 333.
11. Topham, *op. cit.*, pp. 18-19.
12. *ibid.*, pp. 19-20.
13. The original Fortune's Tavern, so popular in the 1760s and '70s was in Old Stamp Office Close. It was kept by Matthew Fortune senior. The building had earlier been the town house of the Earl and Countess of Eglinton.
14. Topham, *op. cit.*, pp. 227-228.
15. Arnot, *op. cit.*, p. 347. The peck of potatoes contained 24 lbs. Arnot also observes that early peas 'are sold for about half a guinea, if the general assembly [of the Church of Scotland] be sitting; but, if that court be risen, about five shillings per peck'.

16. *ibid.*, p. 346. In 1778, according to the OSA (Vol. VI, p. 604) 8,400 barrels of oysters were exported from Edinburgh.
17. Cockburn, *op. cit.*, pp. 405–406.
18. Cockburn, *op. cit.*, p. 406.
19. Topham, *op. cit.*, p. 67.
20. Cockburn, *op. cit.*, p. 37.
21. *ibid.*
22. Nasmyth, *op. cit.*, p. 52.
23. Chambers, *op. cit.*, Vol. II, pp. 237-238.
24. Johnnie Dowie's tavern was in Liberton's Wynd. It was a favourite resort of Robert Burns during his time in Edinburgh.
25. James Hogg, quoted in OEC, Vol. III, pp. 166-167.
26. Cockburn, quoted in the OEC, Vol. III. The above description is based on Cockburn's short history of the club, quoted *in extenso* in OEC, Vol. III, pp. 108-125.
27. *ibid.*
28. OEC, Vol. III, p. 138.
29. The most complete and interesting record of a club's place of meeting relates to the Wagering Club, founded in 1775 'to keep up acquaintance and promote mirth and good-fellowship'. From 1776 to 1779 this club met in Fortune's Tavern, Old Post Office Close. Between 1780 and 1803 it met in a variety of taverns in, for example, Don's Close, Fish Mercat Close, and the Cowgate. Its first meeting in the New Town was in 1804, in Fortune's Tontine Tavern. Thereafter it met only three times in the Old Town, except for two meetings in the Royal Exchange.
30. Topham, *op. cit.*, p. 128.
31. *ibid.*, pp. 130-131.
32. Minutes of the Musical Society, 10 June 1752. No fewer than twenty one earls subscribed to the building of St Cecilia's Hall, along with the Duke of Queensferry and lesser mortals like Sir Laurence Dundas, Sir William Dundas, Sir William Forbes and Principal Robertson.
33. Brother of William Mylne, who designed the North Bridge. Robert Mylne studied on the Continent as a young man, and sprang into public notice with his design for Blackfriar's Bridge over the Thames, begun in 1760.
34. Cockburn, *op. cit.*, p. 26.
35. T. Somerville, *op. cit.*, p. 115.
36. Grant, *op. cit.*, Vol. I, p. 342.
37. Topham, *op. cit.*, p. 106.
38. *ibid.*, p. 111.
39. Chambers, *Domestic Annals of Scotland*, Vol. III, p. 480.
40. J. H. Jamieson, 'Social Assemblies of the 18th century' in OEC, Vol. XIX, p. 53.
41. Assembly Minute Book No. 1, 16 December 1746.
42. Cockburn, *op. cit.*, pp. 27-28.
43. A. Carlyle, *Autobiography* (Edinburgh 1860), pp. 322-323.
44. Nasmyth, *op. cit.*, p. 72.
45. Topham, *op. cit.*, p. 361.
46. J. Heiton, *The Castes of Edinburgh* (Edinburgh 1860), p. 253.
47. *ibid.*
48. Nasmyth, *op. cit.*, p. 103. Some of those relieved were unemployed weavers suspected of radical political opinions; hence the name for the road round the Crags, 'The Radical Road'.

49. Cockburn, *op. cit.*, p. 264.
50. T. Somerville, *op. cit.*, p. 384.
51. Heiton, *op. cit.*, p. 240.

IX: After 1830

1. Mr Thomas Hay became City Chamberlain in 1796. The City Chamberlain kept the accounts for the City, and was the official directly responsible for all receipts and expenditure.
2. *Statements respecting the Affairs of the City of Edinburgh as at Martinmas 1818* (Edinburgh 1819).
3. H. Labouchère, *Report to the Chancellor of the Exchequer regarding the Affairs of the City of Edinburgh and Port of Leith*, p. 11 (Edinburgh 1836).
4. *Report of the Committee of the Trustees for the Creditors of the City* (Edinburgh 1835), Appendix I, p. 8, quoting figures supplied by the City Accountant.
5. The Common Good consisted of feu duties, casualties and rents, customs of trades and markets (affecting the sale of meat, fish, vegetables, etc.), harbour dues and fines of Court.
6. *Report of the Committee of the Trustees for the Creditors of the City*, Appendix I. The expenditure here stated did not all have to be met by the regular revenue plus borrowing, as there was also a special revenue item of £9,000 p.a. 'belonging to the Ministers of Edinburgh' which largely met Item III in the list.
7. So-called 'industrial' employment in Edinburgh was not only on a smaller scale than in Glasgow, it was of a different and more old-fashioned kind. The principal 'industrial' classifications recorded for Edinburgh in 1841 were 'Houses, furniture and decoration', 'Dress-making' and 'Food and lodging' – all what we should describe to-day as service trades, appropriate to a city dominated by professional people of comfortable means.
8. This was named the Ashley Buildings, after Lord Ashley, and was situated near the foot of the High Street.
9. H. D. Littlejohn, *Report on the Sanitary Condition of the City of Edinburgh* (Edinburgh 1865), p. 108.
10. *ibid.*, p. 109.
11. Heiton, *op. cit.*, p. 248.
12. Quoted in Heiton, *op. cit.*, p. 248.
13. Littlejohn, *op. cit.*, p. 48.
14. *ibid.*, p. 46.
15. *ibid.*, p. 46.
16. No. 23 St James's Street, according to Littlejohn, had 70 rooms, 220 inhabitants, 11 sinks and 1 water closet.
17. Littlejohn, *op. cit.*, p. 102.
18. *ibid.*, p. 102.
19. The villas strung along the west side of Inverleith Row date from the mid-1820s, and were thus two or three years later than the earliest houses in Minto Street and Salisbury Road. The Inverleith development depended on the old bridge across the Water of Leith at Canonmills.
20. OEC, Vol. XXIV, 'The Lands of Newington' by W. Forbes Gray.
21. Announcement in the *Edinburgh Evening Courant*, 10 October 1825
22. Littlejohn, *op. cit.*, p. 18.
23. *ibid.*
24. Grant, *op. cit.*, Vol. III, p. 38.

25. The steep gradients of some Edinburgh streets, notably between Hanover Street and Goldenacre and between Frederick Street and Comely Bank, told against horse-drawn transport, and led to the introduction of a cable-tram system by a private company in the 1880s. The Hanover Street route was opened in 1888 and the Frederick Street route in 1890, power for the cable being delivered from a power-station in Henderson Row. By 1898 the cable system had been extended to cover almost the whole of Edinburgh.

26. At least it never killed any *passengers*. There were, however, several fatalities involving trespassers on the line.

27. For a fuller account of the genesis and activities of this body the reader should consult D. Robertson, *The Princes Street Proprietors* (Edinburgh 1935), on which what follows above is largely based.

28. A key was presented to Sir Walter Scott, who still had his house in Castle Street, in 1827. Scott dedicated the fourth canto of *Marmion* to James Skene, who, as a member of the Proprietors Committee, planned the gardens and later, in the 1830s, led the opposition to the introduction of the railway.

29. D. Robertson, *op. cit.*, p. 27.

30. The line from Berwick was opened on 22 June 1846. Its terminus was Waverley Station, originally called the North Bridge Station. The Caledonian Railway, from Carlisle, reached Edinburgh in 1848, but used a small passenger station in Lothian Road, near the site of the present goods station. The city was thus spared 'a massive station in the Italian style', which, according to the chairman of the line, was to have been 'on a scale that wd. do no discredit to the magnificence of the City of Edinburgh'.

31. J. Colston, *History of the Scott Monument, Edinburgh* (Edinburgh 1881), p. 64.

32. The Physicians also occupy the adjacent house, No 8, which was the first to be built in Queen Street. It was erected in 1770 to the plans of Robert Adam, and is an excellent example of the best domestic architecture of the day.

Index

Where references are given to notes, the page number is that *on* which the note is printed, not *from* which the reference emanates

Abercromby Place 207, 208, 210
Aberdeen 30, 50
Act, Acts
    for building New Town 80, 81-2
    for Burgh Reform 262
    for conversion of Parliament Building 133
    for education in Fine Arts 282
    for erecting Public Buildings 55
    for extension of Royalty 59, 301n1
    for narrowing loch and building street to north 13
    for new buildings in city 135, 138
    for prohibiting building on s of Princes Street 87-8
    for purchase of Calton Hill 13
    for railway line from Edinburgh to Dalkeith 274
    for raising money for Calton Bridge Scheme 145
    for Register House 192
    for s and w approach Schemes 180-2, 186
    for South Bridge 111
Adam, James 66
Adam, John
    co-judge on New Town plans 71
    plan for: Exchange 53; North Bridge 62-4; Register House 67
Adam, Robert
    appointed joint architect to the Crown 20
    architect for new Bridewell 123, 135
    dispute with Town Council 113, 116-17
    life of 289-91
    plan for Register House with James 66
    plan for s approach 111
    plan for University 125

Adam, William 194-5
Adam Square 14, 68, 112, 297n9
Advocates, Faculty of
    preservation of Mound 168
    purchase of Library by Writers to the Signet 135
    subscription to the University 125, 128
    Upper Library in Parliament Building 134
afforestation, beginning of 23
agriculture 23, 31-3
Ainslie Place
    Articles of roup 221
    builders taking feus in 223-4
Albany Street 110
ale duty 102-3, 263
Allan of Hillside, feuar for Calton Hill Scheme 148, 155
Allan's Parks 104, 300n17
Anderson, Sir Rowand 310n119
Ann Street 214, 215
architects
    lives of: Adam 289-91; Burn 292-3; Craig 288-9; Gillespie Graham 294; Hamilton 293; Playfair 291-2; Robert Reid 293-4
    training of 287-8
Argyle Square 14, 297n9
Arnot, H.
    on cost of North Bridge 301n29
    on musical society 24
    on price of vegetables 311n15
    on situation of Edinburgh 1-2
    on Theatre Royal 94
    on Tolbooth 305n20
    residence of 228
Arthur's Seat 1

Assemblies
  in Buccleuch Place 252
  in George Street 252
  in High Street 252
  in Old Assembly Close 250
Assembly Hall, Free Church College and, 280-1
Assembly Rooms 95
Atholl Crescent 215

Bald, Robert 36
Bank of Scotland
  building of 161-2
  lends money for Calton Bridge Scheme 139,140
  lends money for s and w approaches 182
  previous building 161
Banks, *see* Bank of Scotland; British Linen Bank; Commercial Bank; Coutts's Bank; Messrs Ramsay, Bonar and Co.; Royal Bank; William Forbes and Co.
Bank Street 161-2, 174, 187
Bath 74, 79-80
Baxter, John 63, 149
Bearford's Parks 17, 60, 103
Bell, Benjamin 272
Bellevue Crescent 210
Bill
  of Suspension and Interdict (ground southward of Princes Street) 86, 87, 90
  Improvements 169-70
  2nd Improvements 176-7
Blacket Place 272
Blanqui, J.A. 233
Board of Manufacturers (Trustees)
  and building of National Gallery 282
  and extensions to Royal Institution 164
  as feuars on Mound 162
Bremner, David 38
Bridewell 122, 135
bridge, bridges
  early building of 27-9
  Dean 271-2
  King George IV 182
  King's 182
  over north loch (North b) 60-5
  South 111-12
  Waterloo 139-45
Briggs, M.S., *The Architect in History* 288
Bristo Port 176

Bristo Street 111, 176
British Linen Bank 139, 140
Brough, John 101
Brougham, Lord 247
Brown, James 49
Brown, Robert 149
Brown Square 14, 68
Bruntsfield Links
  building forbidden on 181
  cleared 256
  development south of 272-3
  golf on 255
  parades and reviews on 238
Buchan's Feu 104
burgh reform
  Commissioners on Municipal Corporations report on Edinburgh 261-2
  election system 43-6
Burn, Robert 149, 159
Burn, William
  and National Monument 160
  and Royal Institution 164
  commissioner for s and w approaches 181
  connection with Drumsheugh development 310n18
  country house 293
  designs: John Watson's Hospital 292; Melville Monument 292; Merchant Maiden's Hospital 292; St John's Church 191-2
  life of 292-3
  prepares plans for: school on site of Edinburgh Academy 156; University building 194, 195
  proposals for Western approach project 166-7
  reports on Calton Hill Scheme 149
  views on developments on Mound 173
Burns Monument 159
Burns, Robert 21, 52, 98, 312n23
Butter, William 140
Butterworth, Edward 100, 223, 224

Caledonian Canal 29
Caledonian Mercury, The
  on bridge over North Loch 60
Calton Bridge Scheme
  borrowing for 139, 140-1
  Commissioners for 139
  contract for 142
  difficulty over North Bridge Buildings 142-3

Calton Bridge Scheme (*contd*)
  Elliot as architect for 142
  feuing by Lorimer 144, 145
  finances for 139-40
  state of roadway 144-5
  Stevenson as engineer 139
  total costs of 139
Calton Hill
  as open space 254
  buildings on 158-60
  pollution of air by gas works 269-70
  walks on 256
Calton Hill Scheme
  advertisement for submission of plans
    148
  competition prizewinners 307n36
  cost of road building 155
  Playfair, architect for 152, 154-5
  principal feuars 148
  Royal High School 156-9
  slow development of area 155-6
  Stark's Report on 149-52
Calton Place 155
Canal Building 30
Canongate
  decay of 22, 297n1
  gas works in 269-70
  lighting, cleansing and police in 48-9
  manufactures in 269
Canonmills 273
Carron ironworks 35
Castle, French prisoners in 238
Castle Street 92
Castle Terrace 188, 215, 309n92
Chambers, R.
  on Cowgate 301n39
  on effects of the Union 24
  on first house in New Town 302n26
  on George Square 301n43
  on Society in New Town 226
  on Society in Old Town 311n29
  on tavern dissipation 245-6
Chambers, Sir William 20, 84, 290
Charlotte Square
  circus or crescent 93
  Earl of Moray and 93
  elevations by Robert Adam 93, 95-6
  feuars of 223
  feus in 97
  land not owned by town 92-3, 303n29
  later building in 217
  letter from builder 101-2
  payment to Robert Adam for 96

Charlotte Square (*contd*)
  price of houses in 224, 311n20
  rural nature of 204
  style of 96-7
Church attendance 254
Claudero (James Wilson)
  on Drummond 213, 297n11
Clerk, Baron 149, 307n23
Clerk Street 272
clubs 246, 248, 312n29
coal and other fuels
  in Lanarkshire 266
  Monkland Canal 30
  Old and New Monkland Colliery 30
  output and consumption 36
  scarcity of 32
  Union Canal 30
Coates Crescent 215
Cockburn, Henry
  Commissioner for s w approaches 181
  member of Friday Club 247
  on assemblies 252
  on destitution 256
  on Henry Dundas 43
  on High School 307n45
  on protest over North Bridge
    Buildings 142-3
  on public relief 130
  on Reid's conversion of Parliament
    Square 134
  on rural surroundings of Charlotte
    Square 204
  on social life 244
  on society 235
  on Stark 150
  Solicitor General 45
  subscriber to Edinburgh Academy 158
  subscriber to National Monument 159
Cockerell, C.R. 160
Commercial Bank 182, 189
common good 102, 263, 313n5
Cope, General and army 16
Cornwallis Place 210
cotton industry
  costs of yarn 38
  expansion of 35
  first mill 35
  labour force 35, 41
Coutts's Bank 24
Cowgate
  desirability of bridge 68-9
  route for s Bridge 69, 113
  situation of 2

Craig, James
  alterations to: Battery at Leith 289; St
    Giles 289
  designs Old Observatory 159
  designs Physicians' Hall 95
  designs St James's Square 98
  Earl of Mar as forerunner of 13-14
  Executry and Testament 295n6
  life of 288-9
  plan for Improving City of Edinburgh,
    1786 117-19
  plan for New Town 71, 77-9, 80
Craigleith Quarry
  and Drumsheugh development 218
  and National Monument 160
  and Register House 66
  and University portico 126
Cramond Road Trustees 271
Creech, William
  Creech's Land 52-3
  Creech's Levee 53
  on social eclipse of Old Town 226-7
  starts first circulating library 52
  town house in George Street 226
Crichton, Richard
  designs Bank of Scotland 161
  plan for Calton Bridge 142
  plan for University building 194
Cumberland Street
  details of Contract to build 209, 210
  feuings to builders 225

Darnaway Street 220, 223-4
Dean Bridge 271-2
Dean Street 214
Defoe, Daniel
  on High Street 52
  on the Union 22
Dickson's Feu 104
Donaldson's Hospital 281-2
Johnnie Dowie's Tavern 246
drainage 33
Drummond, George 3, 13, 15-17
Drummond Place 206, 209, 210
Drumsheugh
  and Articles and conditions of roup and
    sale 218-22
  architect for 216
  last area to be developed 217
  property of Earl of Moray 204-5
drunkenness 245-6
Dublin Street 208, 209
Duke Street 110, 205-6

Duncan Street 209, 210
Dundas, Henry (Lord Melville)
  and money for University 125, 130-1
  clubs of 248
  fall from political power 45
  life of 43, 299n51
Dundas, Sir Laurence
  house of: in New Town 84, 302n17;
    as excise office 158; as head office of
    Royal Bank 232
  life of 84
Dundas Street 209, 210, 212
Dundee 29, 50-1

Echo Bank 272
Edinburgh
  book making in 31, 42
  coach travel from 29
  effect of Union on 24
  occupations in 42
  population figures for 40-1
Edinburgh Academy 156, 158
Elder Street
  building of 110, 205
  feued to two builders 225
  Heriot Trust property 204-5
Elliot, Archibald
  and Calton Bridge 142, 147, 306n20
  designs governor's house (gaol) 159
  designs Waterloo Hotel 145
  plan for University building 194
Elliott, Sir Gilbert, *Proposals* 3
Elm Row 155
Exchange
  and Custom House 58
  architect for 53
  finance for building 58
  plans for 53
  proposal to build 8

Farington, J. 93, 95
Fettes, Sir William 229, 231
Fettes Row 210
Firth of Forth 22
Fleming, John, *Robert Adam and his*
    Circle 295n7
Mr Fletcher of Salton 6
Flodden Wall 297n1
food 243-4
Forbes, Sir William of Pitsligo
  and Waterloo Hotel 145
  life of 299-300
  member of Royal College of
    Physicians 49

Forbes, Sir William of Pitsligo (*contd*)
  on feuing on South side of Princes
    Street 86
  shareholder in St John's Church 192
Sir William Forbes and Co. (Bank)
  cash credit to Princes Street
    Proprietors 275
  loans for: Calton Bridge Scheme 139,
    140, 145; gaol 138; High School
    157; St George's Church 189;
    s and w approaches 182
  overdrafts to Commissioners of Calton
    Bridge Scheme 147
Forres Street 220, 224
Forsyth, John 224
Forth and Clyde Canal 30
Fortune's Tavern 230, 242, 247, 248,
    252, 311n13
Fountainbridge 273
Fowler, Adam and George 224
Frederick Street 92, 231
French Revolution 45
Friendly Insurance Office, The 24

Galashiels, woollen industry 34
Galt, *Annals of the Parish* 238
gaol
  Acts to build 135-6, 138
  allocation of cost 138
  architect for 135
  choosing site for 135
  difficulty of access to 138-9
  money borrowed from Sir William
    Forbes 138
gas lighting 38
Gentleman's Magazine
  on High Street 52
  on 'one family' houses 14
George iv Bridge, *see* King George iv
    Bridge
George Square
  building 68
  described by Chambers 301n43
  fashionable area 68-9, 229, 233
  inhabitants of 69, 229, 233
  outside Royalty 229
George Street
  Assembly Rooms 95
  building of 92
  general appearance 78, 93
  Physicians' Hall 84, 95
  St Andrew's Church site 83-4
  sewers 80-1, 270

Gillespie Graham
  development of Drumsheugh 216ff
  plan for Calton Bridge 142
  plan for Western New Town 216
  report on Calton Hill Scheme 149
Gillespie, James, *see* Gillespie Graham
Glasgow
  new building in 50
  population of 40, 266
  tobacco manufacture in 22
  trade 35, 266
  transport costs to East from 30
Glenfinlas Street 220
Gloucester Place 224
golf 255
governor's house 159
Grange, development of 273
Grant, James
  on Brown Square 68
  on Creech's Land 53
  on theatre in Shakespeare Square 250
Grassmarket
  industry in 269
  trading in 176
  western approach to 176
Great King Street
  and London Street as main axis 212
  building of 208
  details of contract for 209, 210
  first plan of 206
  objections by feuars to tannery in
    212-13
  slow development of 212
Great Stuart Street 224
Grindlay, John (and Grindlay's Trustees)
  guarantors for expenses of 1827 Bill
    188, 309n91
  owners of Orchardfield area 188
Guard House 304n5
Guard, Town 103, 239-40
Gwynn, John 78-9

Haldane, A. R. B., on lawyers 50
Hamilton, Thomas
  designs: Burns Monument 159; Dean
    Orphanage 293; George iv Bridge
    182, 184-7; High School 157, 158;
    Physicians' Hall 279-80
  life of 293, 296n15
  on Trotter's plan for Mound 172-3
  plan for buildings on Mound 162, 182
  plan for Mound and w approach 66-7
Hanover Street 81, 92, 210

Haymarket
  development of 273
  railway line 275, 277, 278
Heiton, J.
  on living conditions in Old Town 268
  on occupations in Old Town 268
  on poor 255
  on separation of Old and New Town
    256
Henderson, David
  later work on North Bridge, 62, 65
  plan for intended college 124
Henderson and Currer 224
Henderson's Feu 104
Hendrick, J. 26-7
Héré de Corny 77
Heriot, George 306n22
Heriot Row
  building of 208
  details of contract for 208, 210, 211
  elevations by Robert Reid 208
  feuars in 225
  poor access to 212
  sanitation in 270-1
Heriot's Gardens 111
Heriot's Hospital 281-2, 306n22
Heriot's Hospital Trust
  and Calton Hill Scheme 148, 155
  as landowners 204
  feuars for Shandwick Place area 215
  plan to develop North of Queen Street
    205-8, 211-12
  purchase houses in Lynedoch Place
    216
High Street
  access from, to north 13, 53
  and Mound schemes 167, 168-9
  cleanliness of 241
  life in 52-3
  lowering of 188
  new access roads to 167, 168
  opinions on 52
  proposal to demolish Luckenbooths in
    122-3
  site of road for South Bridge 112
Highlands
  clearance in 34, 41
  depopulation of 29, 30
  sheep-farming in 33-4
  Telford's survey of 29
Hillside Crescent 155, 156
Hogg, James, *Autobiography* 246-7
Holyrood House 1

Home, John 86
Horner, Francis 238, 239
housebuilding
  detailed regulations regarding 80-2
  development of, in outskirts 271-3
  slow progress in, after 1831 271
houses
  builders of: Brough, John 101; Butter,
    William 140; Butterworth, Edward
    100, 223, 224; Forsyth, John 224;
    Fowler, Adam and George 224;
    Henderson and Currer 224; Lorimer,
    Peter 144, 223; Pirnie, William 100;
    Reid, Alexander 101, 129; Reid,
    John 205, 225; Ritchie, James 223,
    225; Shennan and Walker 225;
    Sibbald, William 223; Smith, George
    223; Steedman, James and John 224;
    Tait, James 101-2; Wallace,
    William 225; Watson, Robert 224;
    Wilkie and Dobson 224; Wright,
    Robert 100; Young, John 101, 205,
    225
How Acres 104
Howe Street 208, 210, 212
Hume, David
  clubs 246
  feu 303n28
  objector to houses on s side of Princes
    Street 86
  residence 302n23
Hunter Blair, Sir James 82-3

India Place 214
India Street 208, 210
Infirmary 15, 24
Innes, Gilbert 149, 307n24
inns 241-2
Inverleith Row 313n19
iron industry
  Carron ironworks 35
  increase in output 36
  in eighteenth century 23
  uses of pig-iron 36

Jacobite Rebellion 24-6
Jamaica Street
  building of 208
  details of contract 209, 210
  living conditions in 270
James's Court 14, 24
Jeffrey, Francis 159

Kay, David 84
Kemp, George 279
King George IV Bridge
    and Hamilton 182, 187
    and George Smith 188
    building of 2
    size increased 186-7
    work on 182, 187
King's Bridge 2, 182
Kinnoul, Earl of 28

Labouchère's Report 265
labour
    for building Bank of Scotland 161
    for building North Bridge 64
    in cotton industry 41
    in mines 36
    statute 27
    wages for 37
Laing, Alexander 112
Lanarkshire 266
Lawn Market
    proposed road west 122
    purchase of houses by Town Council
        in 122
    use as road junction 167, 174
Learmonth, Lord Provost
    and estate of Dean 271-2
    Chairman of Glasgow-Edinburgh
        railway 276
    finances building of Dean Bridge 272
Leith, objections to South Bridge tax 112
Leith Battery 289
Leith Docks 30, 259-60
Leith Walk 152, 154
Leith Walk Toll 139
Leith Wynd 48
Leopold Place 155
Liberton's Wynd 13
lighting and cleansing 48, 304n1
lime, availability of 32
linen industry in 18th c. 23-4, 34
Littlejohn, H. D.
    on clerks, lawyers 299n49
    on density of population in Old Town
        267
    on New Town 270
    on sanitary conditions 269, 270
London
    compared with Edinburgh 4, 6
    described in *Proposals* of 1752 4, 6, 10
    Scottish families drift to 10
    squares built in 74, 75

London (*contd*)
    Wren's plan for 71
London Road 154, 156
London Street 209, 210, 212
Lorimer, Peter 144, 145, 223
Luckenbooths 52, 122-3, 300n4
Lynedoch Place 216

Mackenzie Place 214
Macpherson, D., on dress 38
Malcolm, A., on Bank of Scotland 161
Manor Place 216
Mansfield Place 210
manufactured goods 31
Mar, Earl of 13-14
markets
    cattle: at Crieff 33; at Dumfries 31, at
        Falkirk 33
    fish: at Cowgate 112; at Fishmarket
        Close, North Bridge 243
    flesh: near North Bridge 244
    flower 244
    fruit 6
    grain: at Haddington 31; at Dalkeith 243
    herb: in High Street 6
    vegetables: by Tron Kirk 244
Marline's Wynd 112
Mayfield, development of 272
Meadows
    and development south of 273
    as building ground for s approach
        179-80
    building forbidden on s approach 181
    parades and reviews in 238
Melville Street
    building of 271
    elevations by Robert Brown 215
    feuing of 215
    ground plan for 216
    Sir Francis Walker and 215
Milne, James 194, 216
Milne's Court 14, 24, 167
Milne's Square 14
Monkland Canal 30
Moray, Earl of
    and Charlotte Square 92-3
    development of Drumsheugh 216-23
    landowner 204-5
    own residence 310n19
Moray Place
    builders and feuars in 224
    conditions for building in 221-2
    Earl of Moray's house in 310n19

Moray Place (*contd*)
  retains social status 232
  style of 222
Morningside
  as a village 273
  development to Meadows and Jordan
    Burn 273
  East Morningside House 273
  Falcon Hall 273
  street geography of, mapped out 273
  The White House 273
Morrison, Robert 194
Mound, The
  access from High Street 167
  and Bank Street 174
  and New College 280-1
  Burn on 173-4
  Faculty of Advocates on 168
  Hamilton on 172-3
  Playfair's plan for 173
  Steps to 280
  Trotter's plan for 170-2
Multersey Hill 13, 60
Murdoch, William 21
Musical Society of Edinburgh
  and St Cecilia's Hall 248-9, 312n32
  inaugurated 24
  wound up 249
Mylne, Robert 248
Mylne, William
  life of 300n24
  plan for North Bridge 62

Nancy 75, 77-9
Nasmyth, Alexander 213
Nasmyth, James 21, 245, 254
National Gallery 283
National Monument 159-60
Nelson Monument 159
Nelson Street 209, 210
Newington, development of 272-3
New Town
  advertisement for plans 70-1
  and lawyers and country gentlemen
    49-50, 229-30
  builders in 100-2
  compared with Nancy 78
  compared with Richelieu 79
  costs of 103-5
  deterioration in 230-2
  feuing of 91-2
  general appearance of 77-9
  living conditions in 269-71

New Town (*contd*)
  movement north and west 237
  regulations regarding housebuilding in
    80-2
  sanitation in 104-5, 269-71
  shops in 243
  span of building period 186
Nicholson Square 229
Niddry's Wynd 112, 113
North Bridge
  and William Mylne 62-3
  building of 60-5
  collapse of 63
  costs of building 65
  labour for 64
  plans for 61-2
North Bridge Buildings 142-3
North British Hotel 279
North Loch
  drainage of 59
  proposals for gardens 13-14
  proposals to turn into canal 9
  shambles overlooking 6, 60
  suggested site for school 157-8
Northumberland Street 208, 209, 210, 212

Observatory, New 159
Observatory, Old 159
Old Town
  addresses of W.S.'s and others in 227-8
  Blanqui on 233
  living conditions in 255, 268-9
  occupations in 269
  separation from New Town 256
  social life of 226
Omond, G.W.T.
  on borough reform 46
  on Dundas 44
Orchardfield area 175, 188
Orphan Hospital 24
Osnaburgs, in Arbroath 34

Paper making 23
Paris 74-5
Parliamentary reform 43-6
Parliament Buildings
  conversion by Robert Reid 133-4
  W.S. library in 134-5
Parliament Square 24
Paterson, John
  and University building 129, 194
  proposer of new road to Calton Hill 139
  report on Calton Hill Scheme 149

Patte, Pierre 75, 77
peat 32, 33
Peebles Wynd 112
Perth
  bridge 27, 28
  ferry 27, 28
  new building in 50
  salmon fishing at 243
Peterhead 29
Physic Gardens 13
Physicians' Hall
  and Craig 84, 303n40
  and Thomas Hamilton 279
  building in George Street 95
  building in Queen Street 279
  costs of first building 95
  costs of second building 280
  earlier plans for 303n38
Pirnie, William 100
Pitt Street 208, 209, 210
Playfair, John 49, 238
Playfair, William
  and Calton Hill Scheme 152
  and Donaldson's Hospital 281-2
  and Free Church College and
    Assembly Hall 280-1
  and gateway and grounds of Heriot's
    306n22
  and Monument to Dugald Stewart 159
  and Mound 173-4
  and National Gallery 282-3
  and National Monument 160
  and New Observatory 155, 159
  and Princes Street railway line 278
  and Royal Institution 164-5
  and St Stephen's Church 191
  and Surgeons' Hall 279
  and University 127-8, 194-5, 197-200
  death 284
Pleasance, The 48
police system 48
poor relief 255-6
population
  decline in villages 41
  density increase in Old Town 266-7
  figures 299n41, n42, n43
  in Edinburgh 40-1
  in Glasgow 40
  in Scotland 36, 40
Porteous Riot 240
Post Office 65, 144
Prestonpans 16
prices of food 37

Princes Street
  Bill of Suspension on building 87-90
  deterioration of 230
  eastern approaches to 145
  feuing on south side 86-7, 90-1
  hotels in 230-1
  houses in 79, 93
  sanitation in 270
Princes Street Proprietors
  and proposed railway 276-8
  gardens: concealment of railway from
    276; finance of 276; lay out of 168-9
  membership of 275-6
  on North Loch 275
  on Royal Institution 164
prisoners in Tolbooth 122
Proposals of 1752
  consequences of 15
  origins of 3
  precedence for 12-14
  quoted 4-12
Public Buildings
  deficiency of 6
  effect of war on 133
  see also under: Assembly Hall;
    Assembly Rooms; Bridewell; Burns
    Monument; Calton Hill Scheme;
    Donaldson's Hospital; gaol;
    governor's house; National Gallery;
    National Monument; Nelson
    Monument; New Observatory;
    North Bridge; North British Hotel;
    Old Observatory; Parliament
    Buildings; Physicians' Hall;
    Register House; Royal High School;
    Royal Institution; St Andrew's
    Church; St John's Church; St
    Stephen's Church; Scott Monument;
    South Bridge; Surgeons' Hall;
    Theatre Royal; The University

quarries
  Bearford's Parks 60
  Culallo 163
  Craigleith 66, 126, 163, 164, 218
  Dalgety 163
  Maiden Craig 218
  Ravelstone 66
  Redhall 218
Queen Street 79, 92, 232, 270

Raeburn, Sir Henry
  and the world of art 21
  family home 214

Raeburn, Sir Henry (*contd*)
  knighted 204
  landowner 205, 213
  Stockbridge development 214-15, 271
Raeburn Place 214, 215
railway, railways
  Edinburgh and Dalkeith line 274
  Edinburgh Leith and New Haven
    Rail Co. 277-8
  Edinburgh to Glasgow proposals for
    275-8
Ramsay, Allan 52, 226
Ramsay, Bonar and Co. 139, 140, 182
Ramsay Gardens 281
Randolph Crescent 216, 222
Rasmussen, S. E., on growth of London
  74
Reform Bill 46
Register House
  architects of 66
  costs of 66, 67-8, 192
  further building 192
  Public Records 65
  site of 65-6
  stone for 66
Reid, Alexander, 101, 129
Reid, James 272
Reid, John 205
Reid, Robert
  and Bank of Scotland 161
  and Heriot Row 208-11
  and N of Queen Street plan 206-8
  and Parliament Buildings 133-4
  and Register House 192
  and St George's Church 189
  and Signet Library 134
  declines to submit plan for University
    building 194, 309n106
  reports on Calton Hill Scheme 149
Reid and Sibbald
  and New Town 206-11
  regulations for building 211-12
Rennie, John 21, 30
rents 42
Richelieu 79
Ritchie, James 223, 225
Robertson, G. 31, 32, 39
Robertson, Dr William, on commence-
  ment of University building 124
  on students 305n26
  reputation of 20
  sister of 242
Rose Street 82, 92, 270

Royal Bank
  founded 24
  lends money for Calton Bridge Scheme
    139, 140
  overdraft to Commissioners 147
  transactions over Royal Institution
    163
Royal Circus
  building of 208
  defective water supply to 212
  details of contract for 209, 210
  first plan 206
  gardens 221
  Playfair's elevations for 208
Royal Crescent 206, 210
Royal High School 157-8
Royal Institution 162, 163-5
Royal Terrace 155
Royalty
  defined 297n3
  extension of 9, 13, 59, 69, 70, 98, 104,
    122, 139, 210, 229, 304n1

St Andrew's Church
  and David Kay 84
  and William Pirnie 100
  money for building 83
  site in Craig's plan 83
  site of 83-4
  style of 85-6
St Andrew's Square
  as fashionable area 91, 228-9
  building of 81
  deterioration of 232
  feuing in 92
  general appearance of 77-8
St Andrew's Street 92
St Ann's Street 86, 91
St Bernard's Crescent 214-15
St Bernard's Well 213
St Cecilia's Hall 248-9, 312n32
St Colme Street 220
St Cuthbert's Church 192, 309n101
St David's Street 92
St George's Church
  Adam's plan for 189
  and Robert Reid 189
  money for building 189-90
  seat rents in 189
  style of 191
St Giles Church 176, 289, 308n68
St James's Square 98
St James's Street 270

Index

St John's Church
    and Princes Street Proprietors 191
    and William Burn 191
    and Sir William Forbes 192
    cost of building 192
    style of 191-2
St John's Street 228
St Mary's Chapel 189
St Stephen's Church 191
St Vincent Street 209, 210
Salisbury Crags 256
Salisbury Road 272
Scotland Street 209, 210, 277
Scots Magazine
    founded 24
    on High Street 123
    on zeal for improvements to High
      Street 26
Scott, Sir Walter
    and Parliamentary election 46
    and Princes Street Gardens 314n28
    clubs 247
    in Midlothian Yeomanry Cavalry 238
    subscriber to Edinburgh Academy 158
    subscriber to National Monument 159
Scott Monument 279
Scottish Register 289
sewers
    J. and W. Adam on 302n15
    in George Street 80-1
    in High Street 308n83
    in New Town 104, 270
    in Reid and Sibbald's New Town 210
    in s and w approach schemes 188
Shakespeare Square 94
shambles, overlooking North Loch 6
    60, 244
Shandwick Place 215
Shennon and Walker 225
Sibbald, William
    builder in Charlotte Square 223
    plans for n of Queen Street 206, 207
Silvermills 212-13
Smeaton, J. 28, 63
Smith, Adam 20, 52, 158, 246
Smith, George 188, 223
Smith, Sidney 246
Smollett 53
social life
    and shops in New Town 236, 243
    and taverns 236, 246, 312n29
    and the poor 255-6
    and the theatre 249-50

social life (*cont*)
    changing status of 230-3
    cleanliness in the Old Town 240
    concerts, dancing etc. 244, 248-9, 250-2
    departure of aristocracy from
      Edinburgh 237
    drunkenness 245-6
    effect of war on 226, 238
    ladies in 248
    meeting of 18th c. and 19th c. 236-7
    neighbourliness of Old Town 226,
      235-6, 311n29
    separation of 256
Somerville, R., on state of roads 26
Somerville, T. 17, 256
South approach to High Street
    Act of 1827 180-2
    by Bank Street to Bristo Port 174
    criticism of 177-80
    financing of 184-8
    great activity in 188
    plans for 174, 175
    proposed assessments for 176-7,
      181-2
South Bridge 2, 111, 112, 116
Southern districts 111, 304n1
South St Andrew's Street 91
South St David Street 91
South Sea Bubble 24
Spencer Street 209, 210
Stafford Street 215
Stark, J., on South Bridge 112
Stark, William 149-52, 296n13
Steedman, James and John 224
Steuart, Sir J., on transport 27, 30
Stevenson, Robert
    and Calton Bridge Scheme 139, 142,
      147
    and Edinburgh and Dalkeith line 274
    and Princes Street Gardens 275
    and road through Grassmarket 166
Stewart, David 205, 206-7
Stewart, Dugald 49, 159, 247
Stockbridge
    Cumberland Hill on 214
    inaccessibility of 271
stone, *see* quarries
Sun Life Office, Edinburgh branch of
    24
Surgeons' Hall 279

Tait, James 101-2
tannery 212-13

325

taverns
   doing business in 236
   drunkenness in 245-6
   meeting place of clubs in 246, 312n29
Taylor, Sir Robert 20, 295n4
taxation 83, 102-3
Telford, Thomas 21, 29-30, 271-2
textile industry 34, 35
Theatre Royal 94, 249-50
Thistle Street 82, 270
Tod's Trustees
   and Free Church College and Assembly
      Hall 280
   and Mound Schemes 173, 174
   and Royal Institution 164
Tolbooth 122
Topham
   on High Street 52, 239, 242
   on ladies 248
   on poor 255
   on social life 244
   on theatre 250
Town Council
   addresses of members 228
   and access roads to High Street 166-7,
      180-2
   and Exchange 58
   and gaol on Calton Hill 139
   and High Street Improvements 174,
      177, 180-2
   and Leith 59
   and Leith Docks 259-60
   and Mound 122
   and new school 156-8
   and New Town 70-1, 86-7, 90, 92-3,
      96, 110
   and North Bridge 60-1, 142
   and North of Queen Street 208
   and purchase of houses in Lawn-
      market 122, 160
   and Register House 66
   and St Andrew's Church 82-4
   and St George's Church 189
   and South Bridge 112
   and University 124-5, 128, 193
   and Waterloo Hotel 145
   city debt: in 1798, 258; in 1818, 258;
      in 1833, 262
   Cockburn on 48
   finances of 262, 263, 264-5
transport
   bridges 27-9
   cable-trams 314n25

transport (*cont*)
   canals 29, 30
   coaches 29
   costs in 18th c. 30, 37-8
   horse buses 274
   improvements in 30-3
   railways 274-8
   roads 26-7
   tram cars 274
Trinity, and railway line to Scotland
      Street 277-8
Tron, trades in 269
Tron Church 112, 118
Trotter, Alexander 170-2, 232
turnpikes 27

Union of 1707
   consequences of, in *Proposals* 8
   effects: on agriculture 23; on Edinburgh
      22, 24; on emigration 22-3; on
      Scotland 21-3; on woollen
      manufacture 23
University
   Adam's designs for 113
   and profits from s Bridge 111
   and s approach 304n11
   applies to government for money 130-1
   Commissioners appointed for 111
   contracts for 129
   dome added to 310n119
   foundation stone laid 128
   library 197, 199-200
   money for building 130, 200-2
   museum 197
   other architects plans for 194-5, 197
   Playfair's plans for 128, 198
   proposals for accommodation 124
   student population 123, 193, 305n26
   work on building 129-30, 193-4

Vitruvius 74

wages 37
Walker, Sir Francis 204, 205, 215-16
Walker Street 215
Waterloo Bridge 2; *see also* Calton Bridge
      Scheme
Waterloo Hotel 145, 242
Waterloo Place 144
water caddies 241
Water of Leith
   and Caledonian distillery 270, 272
   boundary of Raeburn property and 205

Water of Leith (*cont*)
  building along 273
  building up to 217
  diversion to North Loch proposed 14
water supply
  cost of, for city 304n54
  Edinburgh Joint Stock Water
    Supply 241
  in New Town 104, 212, 241
  in Old Town 241
  reservoir proposed 71, 74
George Watson's, foundation of 24
Webster, A., on population 299n41
Western approach to High Street 166-8,
  176-7, 180-1
West of Queensferry Street
  and Heriot's and Walker Trusts 205
  designs by Gillespie Graham for 216
  elevations by Robert Brown for 215
  feuing in 215-16
Whigs 45, 46, 49
Whitecroft or Halkerston's Croft 104

Wood, John 74
woollen manufacture 23, 34, 41
Wren, Sir Christopher 71, 74
Wright, Robert, architect 166
Wright, Robert, builder 100
Writers to the Signet
  addresses of 227-8
  commissions for library in Parliament
    Buildings 133, 134
  cost of library 134-5
  subscription to the University 128

York Place 92, 110, 205, 270
Young, John
  and Elder Street 205
  builds first house in New Town 302n26
  feuar of site of St Andrew's Church 84
  feuing by 91, 101
  house of 302n26
  member of Town Council 101
Youngson, A.J., on population 298n28